The Dynamics of International Competition

From Practice to Theory

Roland Calori, Tugrul Atamer
and Pancho Nunes
with contributors

SAGE Publications
London • Thousand Oaks • New Delhi

First published 2000

SAGE Publications Ltd
6 Bonhill Street
London EC2A 4PU

SAGE Publications Inc.
2455 Teller Road
Thousand Oaks, California 91320

SAGE Publications India Pvt Ltd
32, M-Block Market
Greater Kailash – I
New Delhi 110 048

British Library Cataloguing in Publication data

A catalogue record for this book is available from the British Library

ISBN 0 7619 6165 8
ISBN 0 7619 6166 6 (pbk)

Library of Congress catalog card number 99-76380

Typeset by Mayhew Typesetting, Rhayader, Powys
Printed and bound in Great Britain by Athenaeum Press, Gateshead

The Dynamics of International Competition

Sage Strategy Series

The objective of the *Sage Strategy Series* is to publish significant contributions to the field of management in general, and strategy in particular, with a special emphasis on young and rising authors. The books aim to make a scholarly and provocative contribution to the field of strategy, and will be of a high intellectual standard, containing new empirical or new theoretical contributions. We are especially interested in books that provide new insights into existing ideas as well as those that challenge conventional thinking by linking together levels of analysis which were traditionally distinct. We expect to receive some contributions from scholars in departments outside of strategy, such as accounting, where the theme is of relevance to strategy.

A special feature of the series is the active advisory board of strategy scholars from leading, international business schools in Europe, the USA and the Far East. They are endorsing the series in much the same way as the editorial board of leading journals such as the *Strategic Management Journal* endorses its articles. We believe that the contribution of the Sage brand name and that of an active and strong board will be a unique selling point for book buyers, and other academics.

Contents

List of Figures

List of Tables

Notes on Authors and Contributors

Authors

Roland Calori is Professor of Business Policy and Director of Research at the Ecole de Management Lyon (France) and has teaching experience in Japan (Waseda University) and in China (Zhongshan University). He is also an associate in the ORMIS consulting group. He has authored or co-authored a number of articles and books including *The Business of Europe: Managing Change* (1991) and *European Management Model, Beyond Diversity* (1994). He is deputy editor of *Organization Studies*.

Tugrul Atamer is Professor of Business Policy and Director of the Management and Strategy Unit at the Ecole de Management Lyon (France). He is also a visiting professor at the University of Southern Carolina and an associate in the ORMIS consulting group. He is the author or co-author of several articles and contributions in the domain of international strategic management. He coordinated (with Pancho Nunes) the study on which this book is based.

Pancho Nunes is Professor of Business Policy at the Ecole de Management Lyon (France). He first worked as an industry analyst (at Precepta) before joining the ranks of academia. His research and publications are focused on comparative management and industrial dynamics in international settings. He coordinated (with Tugrul Atamer) the study on which this book is based.

Contributors

Gianluca Colombo is Professor of Strategy and Associate Dean for International Projects at SDA Bocconi (Milan). He is also Associate Professor at the University of Pavia. He is doing research on the international development of family businesses and corporate governance.

Manuela de Carlo is Professor of Strategy at SDA Bocconi (Milan), and Professor of Business Policy at the IULM University of Milan. She is doing research on international strategic alliances.

Paul Emmanuelides is Professor of Strategy at SDA Bocconi (Milan). His research and consulting activities include the development of core competences and international mergers and acquisitions.

Peter Gustavsson is Associate Professor at the Department of Management and Economics, Linköping University (Sweden). He is involved in research projects on strategic change and internationalization, and also works as a consultant in several large international corporations.

Egbert Kahle is Professor of Business Management, Chair for Decision and Organization Theory at Lüneburg University (Germany). He has written several books on decision theory and is currently doing research on multi-criteria decision-making.

Sarah-Kathryn McDonald spent six years in a variety of policy and social research positions with the US Department of Commerce, the British General Election Study, and the Center for Urban Affairs and Policy Research at Northwestern University (USA). She served as a director of a UK and EU public affairs consultancy and returned to academic life in 1993 when she joined the Department of Management at Birkbeck College in the University of London.

Leif Melin is Professor of Management at Jönköping International Business School, Jönköping University (Sweden). His current research interests concern the ways of thinking and rhetoric of leaders, change and renewal processes in international firms, and networking principles of organizing. He is a member of the editorial board of *Strategic Management Journal* and *Organization*.

Martine Menguzzato-Boulard is Professor, Chair for Business Organization at the Faculty of Economic and Business Sciences, University of Valencia (Spain). She serves as a director of the Business Policy Department and doctoral programme. Her recent publications and research interests are in the management of international strategic alliances.

The late **Juan José Renau** was Professor and Chair for Economy of the Firm at the University of Valencia (Spain). He was Dean of the Faculty of Economics and Business Sciences and Chairman of the ACEDE (Spanish Economy and Management Scientific Association). He authored several books on strategic decision-making.

Acknowledgements

The authors and contributors would like to thank the other members of the MODEM research group for their important contribution to this study: Hans Heerkens (University of Twente, The Netherlands), Mikael Nilsson (Linköping University, Sweden), Peter Lawrence and Margaret Woods (Loughborough University, UK), and Jennie Piesse (University of London, UK) who participated in the interviews and discussions on which this book is based.

We are particularly grateful to the 122 executives who shared their knowledge with us, and to the European Commission (DG XII) who provided research funding.

Finally we are grateful to Valérie Puig and Valérie Queva who shared administrative tasks and to Elisabeth Epinat who worked on the preparation of the manuscript.

Foreword

How should we make sense of the world around us? What have others discovered that can help us? These questions confront managers and academics alike as both groups try to make sense of the same phenomena. In the field of strategy the questions typically revolve around asking how the firm works, how does it develop and grow, how competition is organized, and how does it shape and evolve over time. The Sage Strategy Series is committed to exploring these issues.

Despite the fact that the managers and academics are concerned with similar issues, they typically walk different paths. Insights from one field travel slowly to the other, but not so in this volume. Here is a genuine attempt to build a bridge, and the approach is unusual and creative. To the academic it builds new ways of arguing and shedding insight. To the manager it brings useable insights from other managers. To appreciate what it does differently, we remind the reader of our history.

Academics in the field of business typically try to build parsimonious models that seek to explain or make sense of the world they see. This is true whether it is Chandler's famous 1962 book on Strategy and Structure in diversified firms, or Michael Porter (1980) on how the forces of competition shape the destiny of the firm. These and other observations of strategy academics are based on observations from the field. Sometimes the data are first hand. They are built from watching managers at work and from reading documents (see for instance the work of Bower, 1970; Burgelman, 1994; and Weick, 1979). Sometimes they come from secondary data (as is the case of the insights of Hannan and Freeman (1984) on population ecology). More often there is a combination of data sources including, business histories, government statistics and newspaper stories (as we see in Hamel and Prahalad, 1994). Sometimes the theory building has been labelled as *grounded* to suggest the closeness to managerial observation (as is relevant to the observations of Mintzberg, 1994, on planning in organizations). At other times theory building is more akin to testing ideas already extant in another literature (for example in the case of agency theory). In almost all cases, academics link their work with data; and the result is held up as being useful and practical.

In contrast to academics, managers have a different sense of theory and model building. Relevance is high on the manager's agenda. The *Anglo-Saxon* manager in particular aspires to what is useful, and relies on ideas that are often very situational and very specific. There is a great emphasis on *what works*. This leads to less universalistic notions of theory to predictions that claim immediacy. As strategy researchers have pointed out, managers have strongly formed cognitive notions of their world (Bettis and Prahalad, 1995; Porac, Joc and Baden-Fuller, 1989). There are strengths and weaknesses here. Sometimes these theories work to the advantage of firms, in the form of highly developed positive routines (March, 1991), and sometimes to their detriment, when they degenerate into core rigidities (Leonard Barton, 1992).

The strengths and shortcomings of managerial practice provide a window of opportunity for academics. The strengths should allow academics to reinforce their findings, achieving a better middle ground for their work, often supplying richer and more situational theories. The weaknesses of managerial observation, which result in well-known traps, should allow academics the possibility of adding value.

Few writers have attempted to work on the gap between the manager and the academic. Most take one side or the other. This book is an exception, and holds out a challenge to academic ways of operating and to managers looking for very practical help. Unlike most works before, it takes a refreshing perspective. It uses the theories that managers hold in their heads as a basis for theory building. This approach is a distinct step from the traditional view that managerial theories are of little value, only their observations being of use. But the theories of managers typically need weaving and sorting, and here Calori and his colleagues have devised a recipe for building knowledge. Their method is similar to the ones employed in designing expert systems (see Spender, 1996). In the words of the American philosopher William James, they purify practitioners' knowledge and integrate contextual knowledge to form a collective theory.

The gap which Calori and his colleagues address is the fundamental question of the structural forces of competition in a sector. This old question is explored in a new way. Whereas there is a plethora of books that discuss this issue that are short on data and insight, here we have one that is rich and thoughtful. These authors choose as their canvas a large-scale enquiry into the strategic behaviour of more than one hundred firms that span four industries and eight European countries. They offer an account of the structural forces of competition and their recursive interplay. Whilst superficial accounts might label a sector as global or local, they show that most industries, and businesses within industries, are neither purely global, nor purely local, but very mixed. They show how managers hold diverse views about their environments, shaped by industry background, culture, constraints and successes.

The authors note that possibilities exist to bridge the managerial theory and the academic theory gap. Managers make frequent reference to established concepts of strategic and international management such as the Bartlett and Ghoshal global integration-local responsiveness dilemma. However, practising managers usually translate these ideas into something much more concrete. They typically focus on product-market segments within an industry, rather than on the industry per se. They pay explicit attention to issues such as geographic territories, and equal attention to technological and demand factors. Managers tend to view these structural forces in a dynamic interactive manner. They believe that the firm can sometimes transform its environment by acting as (in the authors' jargon) quasi-global players, or transnational restructurers, or world-wide technology leaders, or luxury niche players. They also believe they can challenge the status quo in other ways, for example by acquiring other firms to change the rules of the game.

Whilst a meso-level theory of internationalization is valuable, for researchers the real contribution of this book lies in showing how we can weave managerial conceptions with established ideas of academics, to build better theory. This is a new kind of richness, which blends the traditional parsimony with the world of theory in use. It attempts to avoid the dangers of blind spots and encompass the possibility of voluntarism.

What of the book's use to managers? We believe they will find the book useful and refreshing. They will hear the voices of other managers who have first hand experience in battling with international competition. These managers are drawn from four important industries: paint, cables, chocolate and sugar confectionery, and footwear. In this arena there is great variety. There are high tech and low tech situations, global and local segments, firms which are old and some which are new. The book documents aspects of well-known firms such as Alcatel, ICI, Hoechst, Nike, Mars and Ferrero, as well as insights from others less well known. It shows how variety exists within regions and within firms, and how managers see resolutions to the struggles they face. This is no abstract academic treatise, but a book filled with useful examples and insight.

Charles Baden-Fuller (London and Rotterdam)
Joerg Sydow (Berlin)
26 July 1999

Introduction

> After the discovery of America, Hernan Cortès took back a chocolate drink to Spain. In South America cocoa beans were used as a currency and also to prepare a drink based on cocoa, water, and pepper: it was a stimulant for the Indians. In Spain the cocoa drink was introduced into church celebrations, it had great success as it was supposed not to break the fast. It got to Central Europe in the eighteenth century and arrived in Switzerland. The Swiss had the idea to add milk, and that was it! Chocolate became famous . . . (Chief Executive Officer, Valor, Spain)

This book, and the study on which it is based, started with the assumption that executives responsible for international activities in their firms have something interesting to say about the dynamics of international competition. Reflection on their experience can enrich current economic and strategic management theories. Scholars would call such collective knowledge 'pre-theoretical praxis', or 'recipes', or 'cognitive maps'. We have tried to tap this knowledge, analyse it, structure it and return it to the wider community of managers concerned with international competition. The material on which this book is based takes the form of about 3,000 pages of transcripts of interviews with 122 executives in 117 companies. They told us stories about the international development of their industries and their firms; they shared their 'espoused theories' forged in action.

Theories

Economic theories first relate the international development of industries to the existence of comparative advantages based on production factors (Hecksher, 1919; Ohlin, 1933; Samuelson, 1948) or on the structure of demand (Linder, 1961). Trade (product flows) and direct investment (capital flows) are viewed as complementary, and barriers to international trade determine the substitution between product flows and capital flows (Mundell, 1957). More recent economic theories posit that firm-specific advantages (oligopolistic advantages) drive the international development of industries (Hymer, 1960; Vernon, 1966; Kindleberger, 1969; Caves, 1971). According to the internalization school, firms develop cross-border value-added activities because intermediate markets fail to operate efficiently (Rugman, 1979; Buckley and Casson, 1981; Teece, 1985). The 'eclectic' theory (Dunning, 1981) integrates the above perspectives and considers that the involvement of firms in foreign production is driven by ownership-specific advantages, localization advantages and internalization advantages. Finally some nations may exploit their competitive advantage in some industries and dominate international competition (Porter, 1990): this theory is at the frontier between economy and strategy.

Globalization became a hot topic in the 1980s and the work of business strategy scholars came to enrich understanding of the international dynamics of industries. In their frameworks the number of explanatory variables increased significantly. For instance Prahalad and Doz (1987) suggest that the importance of multinational customers, the presence of some competitors in several key markets, investment intensity, technology intensity, pressure for cost reduction, universal needs and access to raw materials drive global integration, and that differences in customer needs, differences in distribution, the need for substitutes and product adaptation, market structure (concentration vs. fragmentation) and host government demands drive local responsiveness. High global integration and low local responsiveness characterize 'global' industries; high local responsiveness and low global integration characterize 'multidomestic' industries, and between these extremes an industry is considered as 'mixed', not purely global and not purely multidomestic (Prahalad and Doz, 1987; see Appendix 1). The global integration and local responsiveness framework has been shared by many researchers in the strategic management literature (Bartlett et al., 1990), particularly those interested in organizational responses to industry transformation challenges (Bartlett, 1986; Bartlett and Ghoshal, 1989; Hedlund and Rolander, 1990; Ghoshal and Nohria, 1993). The origins of this framework can be found in Perlmutter (1969), who identified organizational and environmental factors driving 'geocentrism', and in Lawrence and Lorsch (1967) who discussed the integration–differentiation organizational dialectics in relation to environmental conditions. On the one hand the global–local dialectics simplifies the explanation of globalization by reducing it to two (a priori orthogonal) dimensions. On the other hand authors do not agree on the variables that load each dimension. Porter (1986) mentions a list of factors that increase international competition, but the list proposed by Prahalad and Doz (1987) only partially overlaps with Porter's. Bartlett and Ghoshal (1992) identify four factors driving global coordination, two factors driving worldwide innovation, and five factors driving local differentiation. Roth and Morrison (1990) consider 13 factors arranged into different categories, and Yip (1992) retains 25 drivers, arranged into different categories again.

Perspectives

The set of economic theories and the set of strategy theories are mutually compatible. Indeed strategic management borrowed many concepts from economy (see for instance Rumelt et al., 1991). However, there are some differences between the two disciplines. Porter (1991: 97) sees the traditional method of economics as 'model-building' which 'abstracts the complexity of competition to isolate a few key-variables whose interactions are examined in-depth'. The approach of strategic management is to build 'frameworks' instead of 'models'. A framework 'encompasses many variables and seeks to capture much of the complexity of actual competition. [. . .] In addition, all the interactions among the many variables in the frameworks cannot be rigorously drawn' (Porter, 1991: 98). To some extent frameworks are analogous to expert systems.

With the notable exceptions of theories of innovation and differentiation – Schumpeter (1934), Penrose (1959), Hymer (1960), Vernon (1966), Perroux (1973) – economic theories emphasize structural determinism. For instance Industry Organization economics (IO) presumes that 'above normal' profits are possible only as long as imperfections in the market exist: firm conduct is determined by market structure and eroded by market equilibrium forces. The field of strategy is grounded on the assumption that firms have options beyond those determined by the structure of the market in which they compete. Firms may create and sustain competitive advantages based on specific combinations of resources (the resource-based theory of the firm, Wernerfelt, 1984), hence the concept of 'strategic choice' (Child, 1972, 1997). The concept of 'strategic choice' recognizes both a pro-active and a reactive aspect in organizational decision-making *vis-à-vis* the environment: organizational agents are seen to enjoy a kind of 'bounded' autonomy, they can take initiatives yet the environment in which they are operating limits their scope for action (Child, 1997). Strategic management is a dialectical paradigm between choice and constraint: 'So, though environmental and internal forces act as constraints, strategy making often selects and later modifies the set of constraints' (Bourgeois, 1984: 593).

In this study we look for frameworks (more than models) that reconcile structural determinism and voluntaristic actions (Astley and Van de Ven, 1983; Hrebiniak and Joyce, 1985) *in order to explain the international dynamics of organizations and competitive systems.* We adopt a holistic and interactive perspective and, a priori, we accept the paradox of combining several competing theories (Child, 1997).

Internationalization is viewed as a process and the international dynamics of industries are driven by structural *and* competitive determinants (Birkinshaw et al., 1995). The structural forces perspective has its roots in industry organization economics (Porter, 1980), resource dependence theory: firms are competing for scarce resources needed to meet the demands of their environment (Pfeffer and Salancik, 1978), and contingency theory: firms' strategies should match the type of environment in which they compete (Lawrence and Lorsch, 1967). According to this perspective, structural forces shape the configuration of industries – 'global', 'mixed' or 'multidomestic' – and this has normative implications for business strategy content. The 'competitive action' perspective may focus on the collective strategies of businesses: population ecology says that firms have to adapt to environmental forces or fail (Hannan and Freeman, 1977), neo-institutional theory (Di Maggio and Powell, 1983; Oliver, 1991) says that a firm's (international) strategy is influenced by strategic norms in the industry (Knickerbocker, 1973): such norms result from a process of imitation of effective (international) strategies. Both population ecology and institutional theory are deterministic. The 'competitive action' perspective may also focus on first movers: the firms that create new norms (Schumpeter, 1934; Penrose, 1959; Vernon, 1966; Hamel and Prahalad, 1994). *Evolutionary theory* (Nelson and Winter, 1982) marries the concept of routines and the dynamics of Schumpeterian competition: firms compete primarily through a struggle to improve or innovate. But firms learn by doing; the capability of a firm is a function of its history, making it difficult to imitate other firms. *Strategic management frameworks that analyse interactions between structural forces and strategic forces serve as a broad theoretical basis of this study.*

In the 1980s the literature on international strategy was much concerned with the assessment of structural forces that determine 'global integration' and 'local responsiveness', and define types of industries: 'global', 'mixed', 'multidomestic' (Prahalad and Doz, 1987; Bartlett and Ghoshal, 1989; Hedlund and Rolander, 1990; Yip, 1992; Ghoshal and Nohria, 1993 among others). The general idea was that firms may exploit opportunities offered by structural forces and should match their international strategy with the type of environment in which they compete (Ghoshal and Nohria, 1993).

Several authors in the above list also conducted a number of case studies, some of which described innovative international strategies (see for instance Bartlett and Ghoshal, 1992). However, the shift of strategy frameworks and the recognition of strategic innovation as a central concept are more recent phenomena. Best-selling books such as *Rejuvenating the Mature Business* (Baden Fuller and Stopford, 1992) and *Competing for the Future* (Hamel and Prahalad, 1994) imposed the idea that some firms change the rules of the game in their industry, and that strategy is about doing things differently. These contributions are not focused on the renewal of strategic

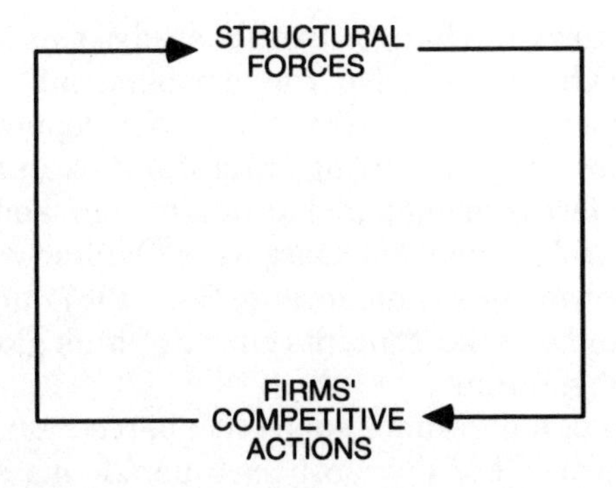

Figure I.1 *International competition, structural determinism and strategic voluntarism*

management models of *international* competition, but they provide direction for research:

> Managers are interested in how they can help an industry evolve in ways that are advantageous to them. Managing industry transformation is therefore an object of interest. [. . .] *Industry structure, increasingly, must be seen as a variable to be managed by firms and not accepted as a given.* (Prahalad and Hamel, 1994: 9, original emphasis)

Figure I.1 summarizes the broad theoretical standpoint that was proposed to the executives who shared their knowledge with us.

In spite of its simplicity this schema has major methodological implications. In a phase of theory building the adoption of an interactive process perspective (Van de Ven and Poole, 1988) requires the use of longitudinal case studies in the tradition of grounded theory (Van de Ven et al., 1989). Concerning the dynamics of organizational fields, theory building should rely on industry case studies (Melin, 1989).

The study and the book are based on a second broad theoretical framework: an industry is conceived as a 'field-of-force' (Melin, 1987). The field-of-force metaphor takes a holistic view of industry changes, and considers 'external forces' (also known as the macro-environment), 'strategic forces' (interactions between structural changes in the field of force and strategic actions of individual firms) and 'internal forces' (organizational characteristics which influence the firm's strategic choice). The field-of-force perspective is derived from 'interorganizational field' theory (Warren, 1967), 'power field' theory (Dahl, 1963), and Lewin's 'field-theory' (1951). Lewin's theory of social action defines a field as a 'totality of coexisting facts which are conceived of as mutually interdependent', and identifies two types of force in social fields: driving forces, which initiate locomotion and restraining forces which act as barriers to change. In this study, two initial questions were raised: which forces drive the development of international competition? Which forces restrain the development of international competition? In fact, during interviews executives often preferred to discuss 'forces driving global integration' and 'forces driving local responsiveness', as many of them were familiar with the strategy framework developed by Prahalad and Doz (1987) and Bartlett and Ghoshal (1989), and popular concepts such as 'think global, act local' or 'the transnational solution'.

The recognition of individuals' subjective perceptions of the world is related to field-theory: 'For the most part men do not act in the world as it is, but as they perceive it. It is in the subjective environment that all real possibilities for action are to be found' (Mey, 1972: 34–35). Indeed managers 'enact' their environment (Smircich and Stubbart, 1985), and powerful managers do shape the dynamics of their industry. This enactment process points to the fact that we must be interested in understanding their cognitive frameworks.

The collective knowledge of practitioners

Some scholars are primarily interested in the cognitive limits of managers (for instance Simon, 1957). According to this realistic perspective individuals should correct their cognitive biases in order to approach objective reality. Other scholars collect cognitive material so as to explain top management behaviour and decisions (see for instance Huff, 1990). As far as the dynamics of industries are concerned, Spender (1989) analysed 'industry recipes' shared by British managers in three sectors (dairy products, forklift rental and foundries), and Melander (1997) analysed the 'industrial wisdom' in the Swedish pulp and paper industry, in relation to strategic behaviour and the resulting stability or change at the industry level. According to this view, powerful executives 'enact' their environment (Weick, 1979): this means that actors respond to their own subjective definitions of the environment, and, following an idealistic interpretation, often make things happen as they wish.

In this book we recognize the bounded rationality of a single individual and the function of cognitive structures in decision making and behaviour. However, we adopt a third position and *consider executives' knowledge as pre-theoretical material that can be useful in theory development* (Tsoukas and Cummings, 1997); in other words we rely on a dialogue between scholars and practitioners in order to develop theories. In this process researchers provide a broad theoretical basis, and refine it inductively with the help of a diverse group of selected experts.

The American philosopher William James (1950) described such a scientific approach as a process of 'purification' which renders 'knowledge of acquaintance' into 'knowledge about'. While experience provides 'knowledge of acquaintance', 'knowledge about' is the result of the systematic thought that eliminates the subjective and contextual contingencies of experience and extracts the principles that lie behind 'knowledge of acquaintance' (Spender, 1996).

The stories that practitioners can tell about the dynamics of international competition in their industry have the quality of historical accounts that provide a synthetic view of a dynamic and complex phenomenon. Practitioners' knowledge is contextual in the terms used by Pepper (1942): it takes a pattern (a *gestalt*) as the object of study rather than a set of discrete facts, and it accepts change as an inherent feature of the world (Tsoukas, 1994):

> The richness of strategy making, therefore, can be brought out only through the narrative mode of exposition. Thus, in contextualist epistemology actors are given their voice in the researcher's narrative; they speak in their own words, and the researcher is merely the 'interpreter' between the community he/she describes and the audience to which he/she reports his/her findings. (Tsoukas, 1994: 776)

This book and the framework we aim to develop are based on the narratives of practitioners, hence the extensive use of citations. We define our role as that of 'interpreter-researchers', who organize a set of contextualist accounts, the collective knowledge of practitioners, into a consistent general framework.

The aim of this inductive process is to enrich existing theories, and produce a parsimonious and comprehensive framework. Parsimony is the ability to identify the key determinants of internationalization, in other words to select key factors among the many variables proposed by the literature. Comprehensiveness is the ability to capture the complexity and the diversity of internationalization scenarios: to account for the relativity of the globalization construct.

A framework formulated in the words of practitioners will speak to practitioners. It can also stimulate a theoretical debate among researchers interested in actionable knowledge.

The study

Executives responsible for international activities in their firms are considered to be 'experts' who can inform theoretical debate on the dynamics of international competition. The study on which this book is based can be viewed as a consultation with experts, in order to tap their individual and collective knowledge.

Such methods are often used in scenario planning (Wack, 1985), and for the design of expert systems. In his book on 'industry recipes' Spender pointed out the similarity between the analysis of managerial collective knowledge and expert system modelling:

> Some time after this research was complete I began to hear about expert systems. I saw that I had made a crude attempt to codify what might now be called the industry's strategic knowledge base. [. . .] The recipe is not a theory; it is actually a primitive knowledge-base for an as yet unspecified expert system. Like most practical expert systems, the recipe is advisory rather than prescriptive. (Spender, 1989: 9)

Consultation with experts-practitioners is also used to map issues that research should address (see for instance the Delphi study on international business and trade by Czinkota and Ronkainen, 1997).

The present study focuses on historical accounts and predictions made by executives in four industries, about the dynamics of international competition. It adopts a cognitive model of industry analysis (Lenz and Engledow, 1986) and employs methods that are similar to the ones used by Spender (1989) and Melander (1997).

A total of 122 managers in charge of the international strategies of their firm were interviewed, in four 'mixed' industries: chocolate and sugar confectionery, insulated cables and wires, footwear, and paint. The 117 firms in the sample are listed in Appendix 2, by industry and by country. Appendix 3 gives the positions of the executives who participated in the study: all of them had significant experience of international business and industry and all were responsible for the international strategy of their firm. The interviews were unstructured and relied on five broad themes (see Appendix 4), they lasted between one and two and a half hours and were tape-recorded. The chapters of this book are based on the transcripts and the content analysis of these interviews.[1] Transcripts of unstructured interviews were analysed so as to surface concepts and links between concepts. Content analysis was conducted in the way described by Calori et al. (1994); this is summarized in Appendix 5. Similar methods are also used for case study research (Eisenhardt, 1989; Miles and Huberman, 1984).

Global industries have attracted several researchers (Roth and Morrison, 1990), particularly because they offer opportunities to characterize an extreme configuration and to contrast it with the opposite extreme (multidomestic industries). In the same way economists focused on extremes when they formulated the theory of monopoly and the theory of perfect competition. However, some economists, such as Chamberlin (1933), were more interested in the 'grey area' between monopoly and perfect competition, and they came up with theories of imperfect competition, thus laying the ground for the concept of differentiation. In the present research the empirical study focuses on the grey area of 'mixed' industries (not purely global, not purely multidomestic according to Prahalad and Doz, 1987) in order to capture complex and diverse sets of forces, conflicting effects and a variety of strategies. The focus on four industries is a compromise between depth and variety: it provides the opportunity to rely on a sufficient number of experts in each industry and to compare industries in order to identify commonalities and specificities.

The four industries were selected as belonging to the middle area in the global integration and local responsiveness map presented by Prahalad and Doz (1987). Two ratios were considered in this selection: the ratio of imports to national consumption and the ratio of exports to national production had to be higher than 10 per cent and lower than 50 per cent in the main countries and geographic zones in the study (Laurencin, 1988). Appendix 6 gives details on the selection and the characteristics of industries. Among industries (at the three-digit SIC code level) chocolate and sugar confectionery, footwear, paint, and insulated cables and wires fulfilled the above criteria. Cost constraints limited the geographical scope of interviews to experts based in Europe. This created a bias: managers probably were influenced by the zone of the world they knew best, although questions concerned the dynamics of the industry *worldwide*. However, managers from companies originating from several European countries were represented (Belgium, France, Germany, Italy, the Netherlands, Spain, Sweden, the United Kingdom), as well as managers in charge of European strategy in European divisions of US multinationals (in the four mixed industries, we did not find any Japanese multinational significantly involved in Europe). Appendix 7 explains how the selection of firms was made within each industry. The exclusion of service industries certainly limits the conclusions of the study and the scope of this book.[2] However, the four industries represent a diverse set of activities: confectionery and footwear are mainly consumer product industries, paint includes consumer and industrial products, and cables is mainly a business to business activity.

These four industries are researched less than 'flamboyant' globalizing or high-tech sectors such as electronics, telecommunications, airlines, car manufacturing or biotechnologies. Many associate footwear, cables, paint and chocolate with mature industries populated by uncreative firms, yet they contain some of the world's strategic innovators, such as Nike, Alcatel, ICI, Akzo Nobel, Mars and Nestlé, and there is high technological intensity in several of these businesses, for instance in car finishes and in submarine cables. So the sample is limited but it is not biased in terms of technological and strategic maturity.

Introduction to the findings

Managers confirmed the initial broad theoretical perspective. The dynamics of international competition are best described as the ongoing interaction of structural forces and competitive actions. The combination of managers' cognitive maps produced a holistic framework for understanding complex configurations of forces and diverse scenarios of international competition. Table I.1 summarizes the key findings.

The majority of managers adopted the global integration/local responsiveness dialectical framework at least at some point in the discussion. Many of them made a distinction between a driving force and a restraining force. For instance cross-national differences in customers' behaviour drive local responsiveness whereas high tariff barriers restrain international development. The majority of managers had problems with attributes such as 'global' or 'local', which they considered as simplistic or to which they attached different meanings.

Figure I.2 maps the field of force. It includes 18 forces clustered into four main categories.

- structural forces driving global integration and/or international development;
- structural forces driving local responsiveness and/or restraining international development;
- competitive actions driving global integration and/or international development;
- competitive actions driving local responsiveness and/or restraining international development.

This represents the executives' aggregated map of the dynamics of international competition.[3] It will be refined and discussed in Chapters 3, 4 and 5.

Content analysis of interviews also surfaced a number of details and nuances which are crucial in understanding international competition and often 'make the difference' in business life. In order to express these practical details and nuances and to preserve the original meaning, the text includes extensive citations.

The first two chapters show that, within an industry, the dynamics of international competition are heterogeneous, and provide frameworks to analyse and understand the variety of product-market segments, and the variety of geographic competitive territories (regions). Mainstream models of international competition are very vague about the appropriate level of analysis and tend to focus on extreme configurations (global or local) whereas managers point out the need to focus on product-market segments and explain the formation of regional competitive territories.

Table I.1 *Summary of the findings*

- *High product-market variety*
  - Each industry is composed of a set of global, local and mixed product-market segments.
  - Each product-market segment is characterized by a specific set of competitive forces that require a specific international strategy.
  - Product-market segments generally do not correspond to SIC codes, hence the necessity to rely on expert knowledge to segment the industry.
  - High scope variety within an industry offers high strategic freedom to firms, opportunities for dual strategies, and a variety of product portfolio strategies.

- *Regional competitive territories separated by fracture lines*
  - The bulk of international competition is organized into regional competitive territories separated by fracture lines.
  - Division into regions is specific to each industry and to each product-market segment within each industry.
  - Six structural forces delineate the fracture lines that separate competitive territories, firms exploit the potential determined by these forces, and some innovative leaders modify the map and create new boundaries.

- *Structural forces driving local responsiveness and global integration*
  - Seven structural forces drive local responsiveness and/or restrain international development.
  - Necessary proximity, protectionism and diversity influence dispersion and local responsiveness.
  - Coordination ('the action to bring into proper relation ... the adjustment of various parts so as to have harmonious action') is the way to manage diversity.
  - Seven structural forces drive global integration and/or international development.
  - Some determinants have been widely recognized in the literature: technological intensity, economies of scale, comparative advantages. Practitioners also emphasize the major influence of demand factors (powerful international customers, emerging high-growth markets).
  - Marketing intensity has a dual effect on the dynamics of international competition.

- *Competitive actions, firms' strategies*
  - Relocation strategies, international mergers-acquisitions-alliances, and innovative strategies drive global integration.
  - The presence and defensive strategies of strong local players restrain the international development of industries.
  - Innovative international strategies create new structural forces and change the rules of the game.
  - International strategies are defined with the following dimensions: geographic scope, segment scope, foreign investment policy, standardization (vs. differentiation), international integration of value chain activities, competitive advantages, and internationalization process.
  - Based on these dimensions eight types of international strategy are empirically derived: quasi-global players, transnational restructurers, worldwide technology specialists, global luxury niche players, continental leaders, opportunistic international challengers, geographic niche players, and country-centred players.

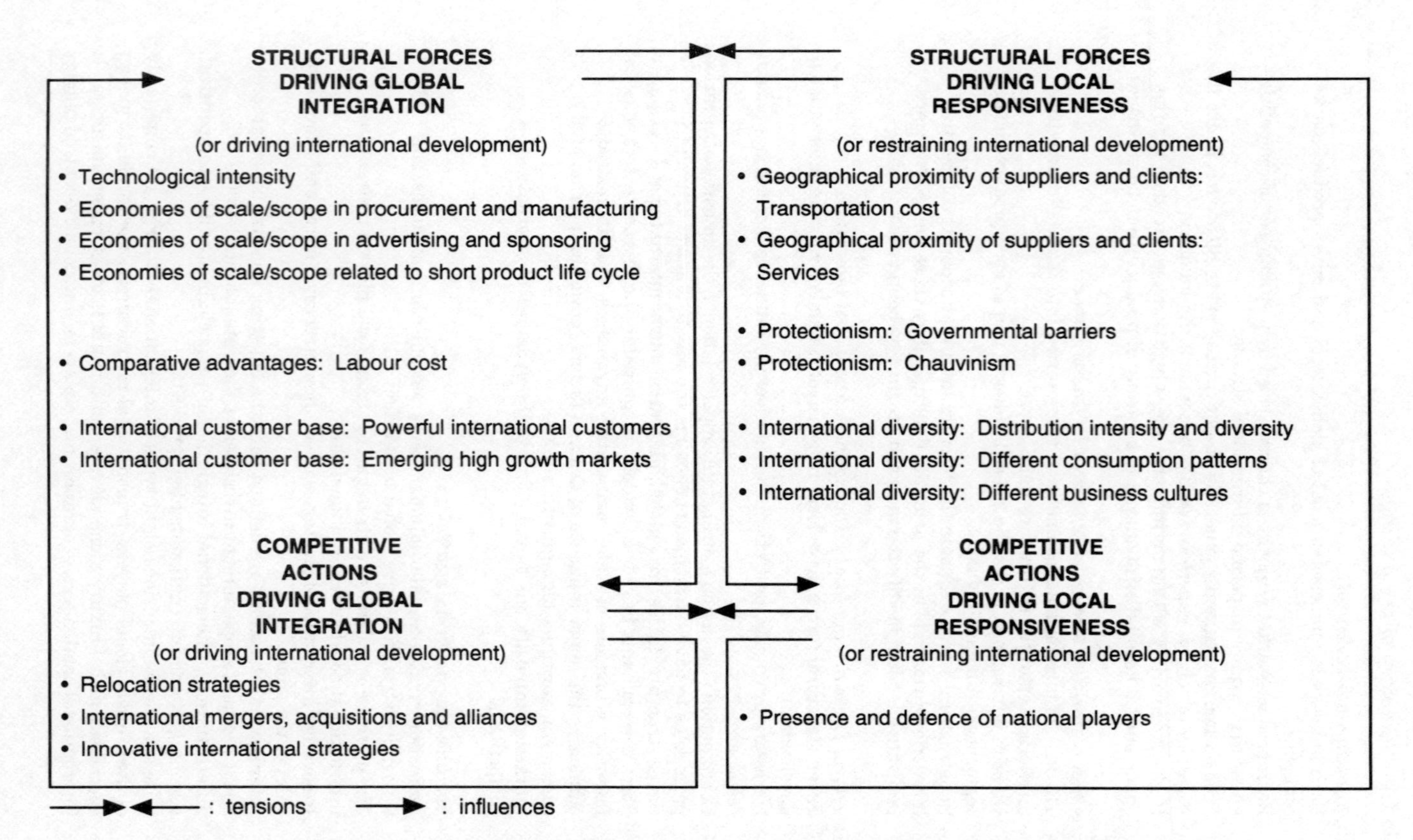

Figure I.2 *Structural forces and competitive actions driving global integration and local responsiveness*

Chapter 1 shows that each industry is composed of a set of 'global', 'local', and 'mixed' product-market segments, each characterized by a specific set of competitive forces that require a specific international strategy. Confronted with *scope variety*, firms may adopt dual strategies; alternatively some firms are driven to focus their business portfolio on particular segments. In brief, variety has major strategic implications. The chapter gives a framework to analyse variety and elicits three scenarios of international development.

Chapter 2 shows that simple categorization of market scopes – 'local', or 'regional' or 'global' – is misleading. The bulk of international competition is organized into *regions* (sets of countries, geographic zones, competitive territories) separated by fracture lines. The division into regions is *specific* to each industry (and to each product-market segment within each industry). The chapter gives examples of geographic competitive territories in three industries, and most importantly it elicits the set of forces that shape regions and fracture lines. The resulting theoretical model can easily be turned into a practical grid to assess and predict the formation of competitive territories. There are major implications for strategy formulation. The mapping of competitive territories is useful to assess the risks of each strategic position or move and the necessary resources and skills. The chapter also explains how firms' international strategies shape the evolution of regions.

Chapters 3, 4 and 5 discuss the integrative framework presented in Figure I.2: the interaction of structural forces and competitive actions.

Chapter 3 reviews the structural forces that drive local responsiveness or restrain international development: geographic proximity of suppliers and clients (transportation cost, services), protectionism (governmental barriers, chauvinism), and international diversity (distribution intensity and diversity, different consumption patterns, different business cultures). It provides the first sub-set of elements for assessing and predicting internationalization. The organizational consequences of local responsiveness are discussed, particularly acquisition strategies, and the concept and practice of *coordination* as the best way to manage diversity.

Chapter 4 reviews the structural forces that drive global integration and international development: technological intensity, economies of scale and scope (procurement, manufacturing, advertising and sponsoring, short product life cycle), comparative advantages (mainly labour costs), and the international customer base (powerful international customers, emerging high growth markets). It provides the second subset of elements for understanding the international dynamics of industries, and reveals some strategies that exploit global opportunities. As compared to mainstream models, the dual effect of marketing intensity and the influence of demand factors are pointed out.

Chapter 5 reviews the competitive actions that transform the international configuration of industries. The defensive strategies of strong national players in some key countries restrain international development. Offensive international strategies that drive global integration are discussed: relocation strategies (particularly in the footwear industry), mergers-acquisitions-alliances, and innovative international strategies. The chapter presents several cases of innovative international strategies, among others Alcatel Cables, Bata, Nike, Fila, Mars, Nestlé, Ferrero, Godiva, ICI, Akzo-Nobel, and reveals six types of strategic innovator across borders. Practical and theoretical conclusions are drawn on the interaction of structural forces and competitive actions.

Chapter 6 provides a typology of international strategies derived from the empirical study. It builds on existing theories but offers an original selection of concepts and an integrative framework to design international strategies: geographic scope, segment scope, foreign investment policy, standardization (vs. differentiation), international integration of value chain activities, competitive advantages, and the process of internationalization. Eight types of international strategy are revealed: quasi-global players, transnational restructurers, worldwide technology specialists, global luxury niche players, continental leaders, opportunistic international challengers, geographic niche players, and country-centred players. Each type is exemplified by several cases. This framework should be useful to practitioners who design international strategies and to the academic audience in search of a synthesis.

The concluding section offers a practical method for analysing the dynamics of international competition and formulating an international strategy. The theoretical characteristics of the framework are discussed in relation to the respective roles of practitioners and researchers in the development of collective knowledge.

Notes

1 Data obtained via the interviews is supplemented in some cases by various published sources (mentioned in the text and summarized in the list of references). The mention of a particular firm in this book should not be taken to indicate that the organization named was surveyed during the course of this research.

2 The discussion in Chapter 3 ('proximity: services', p. 71) gives some indication of the specificities of many service activities which drive service firms to be locally responsive: the simultaneity of production and consumption, the necessary co-location of suppliers and clients, and the high human capital intensity. Clearly in many service activities the proximity factor will

be crucial. Probably the impact of 'different business cultures' (cf. Figure I.2, p. 12) will be significant given the high level of human added value. Otherwise we suggest that the framework constructed in this study fits service activities as well as industrial and customer goods.

A few services offer a unique and interesting paradox: transportation (airlines, road haulage, railways, shipping), telecommunications, travel agencies, international banking, etc. These activities support international flows of products, money, data and people. As such they contribute to the global integration of firms and industries. But these activities have not yet reached a global scope. Many international companies involved in transport, telecom or banking (etc.) do set up hubs and networks of branches in all continents, but the core of their activity often remains in their home territory.

3 In this book we are not interested in the differences between managers' cognitive maps within an industry, although significant differences were found (probably due to different societal, organizational and individual effects). We are interested in the differences between industries and between product-market segments. Such differences will be elicited and discussed throughout the book. However our main objective is to surface commonalities and complementarities in the knowledge-base, so as to produce a general framework for analysing international competition.

The book does not report the four original industry case studies (i.e. the full picture of each industry one after the other). We take one step further towards theory development and take a multi industry perspective: the chapters present the conceptual blocks of the framework. The presentation of each element relies on fragments of the original material from one, two, three or four industries (depending on the level of specificity/commonality). So each chapter provides a kaleidoscopic view of the four industries.

The reader who would like a complete view of the dynamics of one of these industries can select the subsections and citations that explicitly refer to the industry (most of the subsections are industry-specific, and the industry origins of the other citations are mentioned). Indeed, taking an industry lens can be an alternative way to read the whole book.

1

Geographic Scope: Exploring Product-Market Variety

Roland Calori, Gianluca Colombo, Peter Gustavsson and Pancho Nunes

A mixed industry, defined at the three-digit level, includes several subsets of activities. For instance the paint industry is composed of car finishes, marine paint, can coating, decorative paint, varnishes, etc. As far as the international dynamics of a business is concerned, managers make clear distinctions between activities in a given industry. Moreover, they suggest a segmentation of their industry which seldom corresponds to the subdivisions adopted in codifications at the four-digit level (or beyond). As a consequence it is relevant first to define the industry at the three-digit level (e.g. paint, cables and wires, chocolate and sugar confectionery, footwear) and then rely on the segmentation most commonly adopted by managers. Within a given 'mixed industry' some segments have a global scope (or tend to globalize), some have a local geographic scope (multidomestic), and some are in between (mixed segments). The coexistence of global, multidomestic and mixed segments appears to be a fundamental characteristic of mixed industries. For instance in chocolate and sugar confectionery:

> 'Chocolate bars', such as Mars, is the most international segment, with an international standard taste, originally Anglo-Saxon but now accepted worldwide. When you come to plain chocolate *tablettes*, business is much more local because there are taste differences between regions; as a consequence there is no truly global player in this activity. . . . And the same applies very much to the praline business, but there in the very upmarket segment, the luxury type of things in fancy packaging, they sell all around the world. Actually a few well-known brands, such as Godiva, sell all around the world. . . . Other upmarket products are completely local, with very small companies where the plant is the back office of the shop. It is either completely international or completely local.[1]

Confronted with such a variety of geographic scope, firms adopt dual strategies: global strategies in some industry segments and multidomestic strategies in local segments. Alternatively some firms are driven to focus their business portfolio on particular segments: either on global activities or on multidomestic activities. In turn, such strategies strengthen the global, or multidomestic or mixed structure of each segment, thus maintaining a variety of geographic scopes. Firms' competitive actions will be analysed in Chapters 5 and 6. At this stage, comparisons between segments in a given industry reveal the main structural forces that drive international development. For instance, within the paint industry, comparing global segments such as car finishes, merchant marine paint, industrial anti-corrosive paint, with multidomestic segments such as decorative paint for professionals, points out two forces: technological intensity, and the international scope of powerful customers.

There are several global market segments in the four industries we studied: in the cable and wire industry, submarine cables, special applications, high voltage cables; in the chocolate industry, countlines (chocolate bars and candies such as Mars, M&Ms, etc.), chewing gum and some luxury brands; in the footwear industry, sport-leisure footwear and luxury shoes. There are also several multidomestic market segments in the four industries: low and medium voltage power cables, sugar confectionery (except chewing gum), safety footwear, etc. Several segments are considered as mixed: consumer paint in retail chains (particularly wood treatment products), car wiring, enamelled wires, branded upmarket chocolate (*tablettes*, boxes), and medium-range street shoes (see Figure 1.1).

In this chapter we review the structural forces that characterize global, multidomestic and mixed activities and, based on comparisons between the three categories, we elicit three configurations of forces driving international development.

Global activities

In global activities forces driving global integration are high and forces driving local responsiveness are low. In such businesses a worldwide presence in most of the key countries is a major source of competitive advantage and, generally, a necessary condition for long-term survival.

Global activities within the paint industry

The market for car finishes represents 6 per cent of the total paint industry. Automotive finishes is a technology-intensive business as

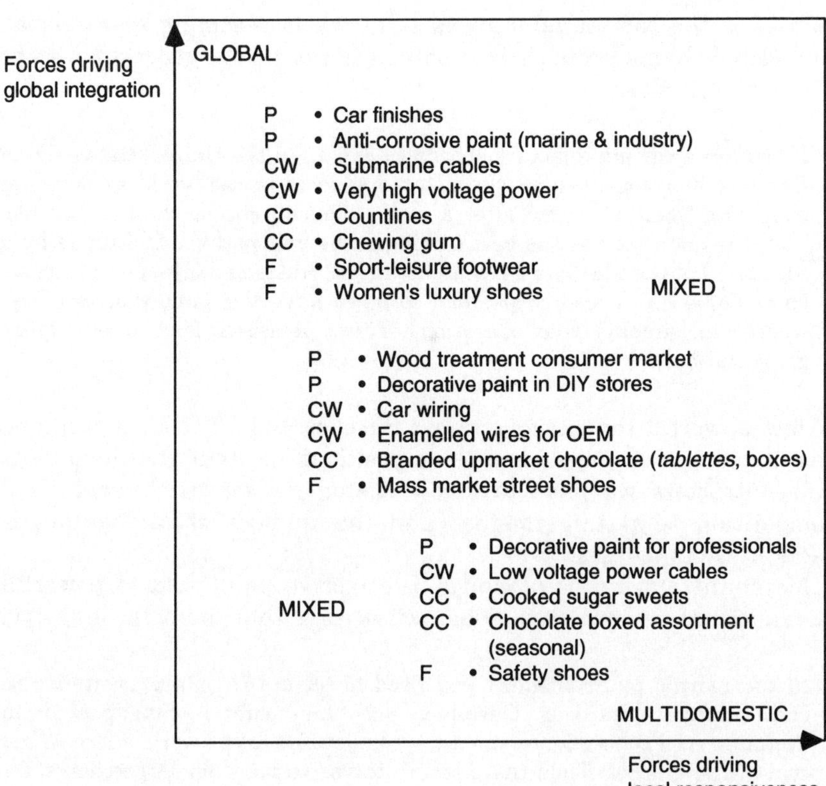

Figure 1.1 *Product-market segments and geographic scope*

compared to decorative paint. Research and development is a key factor of success in order to meet the sophisticated demands of car manufacturers: improve application processes, meet total quality requirements, reduce cost and come out with environmentally friendly products.

> Automotive finishes is a high technology business, it looks like a good deal for the supplier. But because there are only a few very big customers, they are cruel as hell. You do a really good job and then they just say 'next year we want prices 15 per cent down', and they will get it 5 per cent cheaper in the end. . . . Car manufacturers are pushing for a situation where there are only a small number of suppliers. . . . It is just a question of who is the strongest.

Moreover the car manufacturing industry is becoming more global, and global clients press their suppliers to extend the geographic scope of their activities.

> If you are a car manufacturer based in Japan, in the United States and in Europe, then you have all the paint producers in the world as potential suppliers. Then of course after a while you will choose the one you like best, the one that has the best technique: he was perhaps in Europe from the start but then he gets a free ticket to the States and also a free ticket to enter Japan. You also choose one so as to have the same system everywhere and simplify your operations. These pressures lead to very quick globalization.

A few powerful industrial groups, Hoechst and PPG among others, responded and strengthened their positions in other continents: 'As sub-contractors we have to follow customers' moves. International competition is getting tougher and the number of competitors is reduced by takeovers.'

Merchant marine paint and anti-corrosive paint sold to powerful clients are also considered global activities within the paint industry.

> In the marine paint business you need to have a sales representative in each important harbour. Customers may buy paint in Singapore or in Vietnam. As a consequence about ten competitors in the world share 90 per cent of the market. Then there is anti-corrosive paint for large clients, for instance in the oil industry or for nuclear plants. In this activity you have to be certified by the client (ELF, Electricité de France, or SNCF. . .). There is a particular form of dialogue with such clients. It is a small world: in Vietnam we meet some Russians whom we saw in Bakou, in Bakou we meet the same people that we met in Caracas. It is a world market with global competition.

Again the high negotiating power of clients and their international scope appear to drive the international development of suppliers.

Global activities within the cable industry

Submarine cables are used for high voltage power connections between countries and for telecommunications. In this business managers agree that the competition is worldwide. A small number of suppliers were involved: Alcatel, ATT and Pirelli together hold about two-thirds of the world market. The supply of submarine cables is part of complex long term projects that include cables, electronics, terminal equipments (etc.) and take several years to complete (about ten years for high voltage connections and two years for telecommunications). Technological intensity is high, particularly in high voltage connections and for firms who provide the full range of equipment and services. Most projects involve customers from different countries.

> Imagine a connection that goes from Japan and South Korea in two lines which meet in the Russian harbour of Nakhodka, goes through all of Siberia to Moscow, divides itself to go south down to the Black Sea and to go north up to the Baltic Sea, then through the Black Sea to Southern Europe, and through the Baltic Sea to Northern Europe. There are many nations involved; that is therefore a global task – one can only take over with global capacities and international consortia.

Indeed the whole business of high voltage cables (above 100 kilovolts) is global.

> In high voltage there are very few manufacturers, all of which are international. On the other hand, in low voltage cables the industry is national. The sales turnover of the whole cable industry is about 50 billion US $, and cross-border trade is about 20 per cent on average. In the high voltage industry we export 80 per cent of our production, whereas in low voltage we only export 20 per cent.

Technological intensity is considered as the main force explaining the international scope of the high voltage cables market.

> Cables up to medium voltage, which form the skeleton of a power distribution network, can be manufactured by practically anyone. High voltage are much harder to manufacture. There are very few companies in the world capable of making and supplying very high voltage cables. When you need high voltage cables and when there is no local supplier, of course you turn to foreign suppliers.

Finally, managers consider that the market is also global for special applications which require very specific competences: cables for mines, oil rigs and off-shore platforms, cables for the chemical industry which must resist corrosion, umbilicals that transport a variety of conductors (for oxygen, fresh water, etc.), cables for aeronautic and aerospace industries, cables for elevators that must be flexible and resistant to intense friction. For such specific products there are a few worldwide specialists:

> The geographic scope of competition depends on how global is the customer base and what level of standardization has been achieved. . . . When it is more high tech it is more global because there are not so many players who can compete.

Global activities within the chocolate and sugar confectionery industry

In the chocolate and sugar confectionery industry a few products and brands have become global.

> Clearly, certain products you see everywhere, again and again. Chocolate mints for instance . . . a gift box of mints is always compared to After Eight which is the trail-blazing brand. There are other megabrands where again comparisons are made, like Mars, M&Ms. . . . There are certain products that you will see everywhere you go.

These brands belong to three segments of the chocolate and sugar confectionery industry: countlines, chewing gums and luxury products.

> The most international segment is the countlines. These products are truly global, the brands like Mars, Snickers, Kit-Kat, etc. are sold in all the continents and known worldwide like Coca-Cola or McDonald's. They are for the young people but also for the people who were young 20 years ago. Advertising of these products is now part of the food cultural heritage of the world.

The countline market is relatively new: it was invented and has grown fast during the last 20 years: 'In countline, image is the key success factor. There is a lot of media investment, worldwide sponsorship; you must have a critical size to be profitable.' The competitive actions of a few innovative companies created the global rules of the game, and now advertising-sponsoring intensity has become a major structural force in this segment.

There were two global players in the chewing gum business: Wrigley, the world leader, and Warner Lambert (also involved in the pharmaceutical industry), followed by the Kraft group and Stimorol (a Danish company).

> Unlike sweets, chewing gum is a profitable market. For instance Wrigley gets about 20 per cent of operating profits. Chewing gum is an image product for which advertising is the key to international development. Since it is not a very capital-intensive activity it attracts local competitors who segment the market (Perfetti in Italy, Lotte in Japan, General de Confiteria in Spain . . .). However, international players keep on growing and rely on their marketing power.

Large retail chains have captured between 40 and 60 per cent of food distribution in most developed countries. From the manufacturer's perspective, size, international scope and massive advertising balance the growing negotiation power of clients: 'You have got to be the number one or the number two in your business, otherwise the negotiation with mass food retailers is not balanced, and you lose out.' Moreover, food retail chains are now quickly expanding abroad, particularly in Europe; manufacturers follow distributors wherever they go.

There used to be thousands of very small businesses dedicated to small-scale production of exclusive confectionery. A few of them succeeded developing an international venture. For instance Godiva (from Belgium) became a global brand known for its superb chocolates. The American Campbell group (soup, biscuits) took over Godiva and provided the resources for the globalization of the brand.

Global activities within the footwear industry

Nowadays sport shoes are used for leisure. Managers see this evolution as a long term trend towards a new lifestyle all over the world. Consumers from all continents have the same expectations.

> Today sport-leisure footwear has become global – the same brands and more or less the same products are sold in every market from the USA to Europe and Asia. Generally the US market sets the trend, it reaches Northern Europe immediately, and the rest of the world within one year.

A few global players dominated this market: Nike, Reebok, Adidas.

> Their international growth and their strength rely on marketing, enormous advertising, promotional and sponsoring budgets. Very large production runs so that they can lower the cost. Moreover manufacturing is subcontracted to the Philippines, in China or in Vietnam where labour is cheap. The whole thing is just marketing prowess. Price is rather high, indeed consumers pay for the marketing.

The relocation of manufacturing to Asia is a source of comparative advantage. As long as production runs are planned well in advance, geographical distance and transportation costs (by boat) do not constrain globalization. Product design and downstream activities are coordinated globally. Indeed the international dynamics of sport-leisure footwear was driven by the competitive actions of some major players who heightened marketing intensity.

> The strong are getting stronger and the weak are going nowhere. For instance, Nike have grown and gone from strength to strength. Reebok have gone from strength to strength. The bigger companies have really stamped their authority on world sales within the sports industry.

The growing power of large retail chains also stimulated the concentration and the international development of the sport-leisure footwear industry.

> Small retailers from the backwoods of Creuse [a French region] were not playing with imports. In the past the fragmented structure of the distribution network protected local manufacturers from imports. As soon as distribution became concentrated, the bargaining power of specialized and mass distribution superstores reinforced international trade.

The case of women's luxury shoes is different. Luxury shoes represent about 1 per cent of the total footwear market: they are priced above US $200 a pair. Upmarket fashion footwear is the domain of world-renowned brands such as Charles Jourdan, Clergerie, Stéphane Kélian, Rossetti and Pollini. Exports, mainly from France and Italy, are directed toward the richer countries: the United States, Japan and Northern Europe.

> There is a golden rule in our niche: it is that you should not hope to sell a lot in one country but rather sell few in many countries. We need a large territory to live. . . . So we export a lot to the United States, a little in Canada, we sell to Australia and New Zealand, and we sell a lot to South East Asia: that is growing a lot right now. We sell to Korea – they have some beautiful sales outlets called 'Chin Sigi' – we sell to Singapore, to Hong Kong and a little to Japan. Definitely our business is not limited to Europe but it is nevertheless limited to developed and developing countries.

Know-how, creative design, brand image and international scope are the key factors of success in this business. International fashion shows set the trend and relate suppliers and retailers within a tight network.

> We sell the same product lines in all countries. Fashion at the top is the same everywhere. Magazines such as *Marie-Claire* or *Elle* are now sold throughout Europe, in North America and in South Asia. We sell to a social class that travels a lot, so the product line is the same worldwide.

The elitist international clientele is reached through exclusive boutiques located in international cities.

> For me America is not a country, it is five cities: New York, Los Angeles, San Francisco, Chicago and Miami. The rest is a desert to me. While it is true that I have a customer in Charleston, I basically work in large cities, because I create fashion and I go to the large cities where fashion is important.

In this business, manufacturing cannot be relocated too far away. It is both a problem of speed and a problem of communication between the designer and the manufacturer during the production process.

Multidomestic activities

In multidomestic activities forces driving local responsiveness are high and forces driving global integration are low. In such businesses, international scope does not provide any significant competitive advantage *vis-à-vis* national players.

Multidomestic activities within the paint industry

Decorative paint for consumers and professional painters is considered as local business. First this is because technological intensity (research and development, manufacturing) is relatively low, as compared to car finishes for instance.

> The technology and the investment for manufacturing decorative paint are quite low. You might even do it in your garage or in a rented warehouse. It is the same with varnishes, very easy to do: you buy a couple of basic products, a mixer and you become a translucent varnish manufacturer. As a result, in Spain there are many varnish manufacturers, they act at a very local level within the province.

Since the 1980s, particularly in North America and in Northern Europe, technological intensity has increased due to various regulations pushing firms to develop and produce environmentally friendly products, for instance water-based paints as opposed to solvent-based. However, this new technological barrier has not upset the positions of the strongest national players.

There are millions of occasional handymen and thousands of professional painters in a country like France; they have to be reached through a complicated distribution network.

> The key to success is distribution, not manufacturing. Now everyone knows how to manufacture paint in terms of quality and level of production costs. But not everyone knows how to sell. The ones who will win will be the ones with a state-of-the-art distribution network.

Access to distribution appears to be a barrier to international competition; at least, international competitors do not enjoy a significant competitive advantage when local players control distribution. This is particularly true for professional painters who buy their products from a network of wholesalers and are considered the most conservative, local-minded clients:

> The paint worker is very conservative. He has his favourite tints, his preferred wholesaler, he is accustomed to a certain type of paint, a particular brand. You can put something else in the paint container, he will be happy as long as it is the same brand.

Moreover, different countries have different traditions:

> You have to adjust yourself if you want to be successful locally. [. . .] In decorative paints there are two large competitors in Europe, and a number of regional ones, and then there are some very local ones. We compete with ICI in Europe. But in England it is the British division of our company that competes with ICI's British division; in Sweden we compete with Alcro Beckers. The competitors vary from one country to the other. Behind, you sometimes find the same owner, but the companies are still local.

In summary, local clients, local distribution systems and relatively low technological intensity preserve local competitors and require local responsiveness from international companies.

Multidomestic activities within the cable industry

Low and medium voltage power and telecommunication cables are multidomestic activities. First this is because low technological barriers leave room for many competitors worldwide. For instance new local businesses are being launched in developing countries (particularly in Asia). Moreover, given the relatively low added value of these products, transportation costs limit long distance international trade.

> You cannot export 1 kilovolt power cables to India, it is just copper with a bit of PVC around it. That does not work. You have to manufacture locally and sell locally.

Moreover, for years, local norms and national protectionism hindered international development and pushed firms to be locally responsive.

> Seven years ago the cable industry for power and telecommunication was very local, almost closed markets, cartels, local clients, local orders and deliveries. Three years ago competition became more international within Europe particularly in telecoms. Foreign competitors such as Alcatel, Pirelli, BICC now also produce according to German norms, and gain market share in Germany. Today Brussels urges European coordination; however, different standards still exist.

The combination of low technological intensity, low added value and local clients in protected national markets shaped the multidomestic character of this segment of the cable industry.

Multidomestic activities within the chocolate and sugar confectionery industry

Except for chewing gum and a few specific brands (for instance Chupa Chups, TicTac) sugar confectionery is viewed as a multidomestic business.

> Sugar confectionery is run in a completely different manner than what we call chocolate confectionery. First of all competitors are not the same. Sugar confectionery producers, in the vast majority of cases, are small enterprises of a national character, or even local within a country, who produce specialities or rather inexpensive products and who have no desire to become international. There are some exceptions of course, in the chewing gum business for example, but, in general, these are products that are manufactured for very specific tastes and preferences in a certain number of countries, or products with low added value that cannot be transported long distances.

Most sugar confectionery products are relatively standardized with a low added value.

> Sugar confectionery is a fragmented business with many local competitors. This is because it is not a technology-driven business. In a technology-driven business you need scale in order to build efficient plants and you need scope, you need to explore market opportunities. In sugar confectionery you can afford to be competitive and develop a profitable business on a very limited scale.
>
> Cooked sugar candies are very simple products. I would not try it myself in my kitchen, but apparently it is very simple. Actually, in every country we find competition for the very simple candies. The only products where international business can develop are the ones that require a bit more technology, greater specificity in the production lines that allow firms to have a more competitive price: for instance chocolate-covered caramel, jelly candies with a citric or sour taste.

Some managers point out that the segmentation between sugar confectionery and chocolate is blurring. Are 'M&Ms' sweets or are they chocolate? Mars launched small Mars bars in the form of candy, individually wrapped and sold in bags. They suggest that, in this industry, the segmentation between global and local products is driven by advertising intensity. A few competitors rely on heavy brand advertising in order to globalize their brands. As a consequence international brands can be found both in chocolate and sugar confectionery. Ferrero relied on marketing for its TicTac sweets; Chupa Chups sold its lollipops in 125 countries. On the other hand a significant share of the chocolate industry is still multidomestic – local specialities small-scale production of premium chocolates, unbranded chocolate box assortments – for which advertising intensity is very low.

Multidomestic activities in the footwear industry

Within this industry the only activity considered multidomestic is safety footwear.

> In safety footwear the competition is local. For instance in France, French companies compete with each other. Bacou is becoming the leader; there is Jalatte which was the leader for a long time, there is Parade that belongs to ERAM, and a few other brands. We started to do business in Germany, but we had to work hard for several years to get over the barrier of German technical norms. Norms are important in safety shoes.

In this business close supplier–client relationships preserve national champions from foreign intrusion. When there are exports, they are mostly to the old colonies. Some manufacturers also import shoe uppers from low labour cost countries, but in general safety footwear remains a local activity.

Mixed activities

Between extreme global and local positions, some activities are viewed as 'mixed'. Forces driving global integration *and* forces driving local responsiveness are moderate but not insignificant. In such businesses international competitors coexist with local competitors. The geographic scope of international firms often is limited to a few countries or to a continent, and the world market is divided into regions separated by fracture lines.

Mixed activities within the paint industry

Decorative paint sold in DIY ('do it yourself') retail chains (such as Castorama in France) tends to become a 'mixed' activity. This is partly because the occasional handyman is less conservative than the professional painter.

> The consumer market is more European. As a consumer you do not paint often enough to have any special preference in what you want. If you enter into a shop and want to buy paint, you do not ask for 5 litres of Becker's white, you tell them that you want white paint that does not smell bad and dries quickly. You will not leave the shop and say 'They did not have Becker's so I will go somewhere else.' So the key success factor in consumer paint is to be present with the right kind of product where the consumer is.

When DIY superstores expand their activities into new countries, their suppliers follow them. Also, at the end of the 1980s, leading manufacturers started to spend more and more on advertising (including TV). They had to reach a critical size to amortize advertising expenses and respond to the increasing negotiation power of retail chains. They achieved that through mergers and acquisitions, first within a country and later on across borders. However, these forces driving global integration still are balanced by forces driving local responsiveness: cross-border differences in customers' tastes, relatively high transport costs (as compared to the product's added value).

Wood treatment products ('lasures') sold in DIY superstores are considered a mixed activity. Technology is more sophisticated and added value is higher than in regular decorative paints. Leaders spend a lot on advertising when they enter a foreign market: this is a way to raise barriers against new entrants.

> In wood treatment, the relevant market is European, and competitors tend to be European with European strategies. The leader, the Danish company Dyrup with its brands Bondex and Xylophene, is also present in other geographic zones. But in Europe there are practically no extracontinental brands. These products were invented by the Danish; actually another major competitor, Gori, is also Danish. Then there is Xyladécor that belonged to Solvay-Bayer (and now belongs to a British DIY retail chain), and other more local competitors, such as V33 in France, Southern Europe and England.

Mixed activities within the cable industry

Competition in automotive cables and wires is regional; the European zone is separated from the American zone. This activity is labour intensive and manufacturing can be relocated in cheap labour countries, but not too far from the manufacturer.

> There will be an increase in demand for cables and wires for cars. The number of wires per car is increasing as we get more functions. In this business most competitors also assemble the cables into bunches. These operations are generally located close to a car manufacturer or in low-cost countries. . . . Our production today has moved to Estonia, to Portugal and more recently to North Africa.

Clients are international and comparative advantages drive international development, yet relatively low technological intensity and high transportation costs limit the geographic scope of this business.

Enamelled wires for cars and electric appliances are also viewed as a mixed activity, with regional boundaries.

> Take the case of enamelled wires, this is a simple product (copper wire covered with enamel or insulated with special paper and used to make coils for machinery, cars and electrical appliances): here the market is continental. The current market leader is Invex, a firm that manufactures wire partly in Italy and partly in Spain and sells it all over Europe: the same product to the same category of customers who make cars, machines, domestic appliances.
>
> As far as enamelled wires are concerned, industrial clients formulate their own specifications on top of general specifications. Spain and Italy enjoy competitive advantages. Given the devaluation of the peseta and the lira, Italy and Spain are the two countries which export the most. Competition is taking place within geographic areas, for instance within Europe, because transportation costs limit the geographic scope for exportation. Americans do not usually come to Europe. We have exported to Canada and to South America, but that is unusual.

Mixed activities within the chocolate and sugar confectionery industry

In branded upmarket chocolate, *tablettes* and boxed assortments, international businesses (brands) coexist with local businesses (brands), and international competition is regional: significant within a continent and marginal between continents.

> I would have more of a European message about *tablettes*. The market is both international and local. There are some groups like Jacobs Suchard who have a truly European status with their brand Milka, in Western and Eastern Europe. And a number of national producers play a very important role in this market, particularly in Germany. There are also some of them in France and in Italy.

Advertising intensity is driving global integration, while differences in customers' tastes are driving local responsiveness.

> Let us start with chocolate *tablettes*. There are three distinct tastes in the Western world for chocolate. In Britain taste is represented by Cadbury, in America it is represented by Hershey, and on the continent it is represented by Suchard and Lindt. And the three types of chocolate have completely different tastes. [. . .] Some companies have lost millions trying to sell one type of chocolate in other markets. Cadbury failed on the continent and in America. Suchard lost millions in trying to sell their

> chocolate in the UK. Americans have never tried to sell Hershey chocolate in Europe but if they did I think they would come an absolute cropper.

Consumer tastes also differ across continental Europe, and such differences leave room for local manufacturers. A few competitors achieved regional (or global expansion) with quality products (sometimes developed to satisfy a variety of tastes) and with massive advertising.

> Even if you go to America and look for boxed mints you are likely to see After Eight, and there might be one or two disgusting local cheap mint bars of chocolate. Similarly in Germany After Eight is by far the brand leader. There are a couple of minor brands in Germany with funny names but they are not good enough to expand internationally. There is also greater international competition at the top end: products like Guillian Chocolate Seashells, Lindt boxed chocolates.
>
> What I am saying is relevant to Europe. You always have different tastes in different parts of Europe. Therefore there are local businesses. But besides there are some companies like Ferrero who try to make products like 'Mon Chéri' more international, exactly the same product and they are successful. Some products and brands can become Euroglobal, but many others remain local.

Mixed activities within the footwear industry

Medium range 'street' footwear (or 'classic') is considered a mixed market segment.

> Stuck between two categories, luxury and low range, the medium range products follow the trend without ever setting the trend itself; the manufacturing of these products has not been totally relocated. Since the manufacturing has not been completely relocated, the price is too high for developing countries. Thus the middle market segment is not so international.

In this activity international competitors coexist with local businesses.

> André is an international player in Europe, with a French base and also sales in Switzerland and in Germany. There are very few truly international players. The biggest one in footwear is Bata: they sell shoes in 104 countries, but there are not many others as far as the mass market is concerned.

On the one hand upstream activities (manufacturing) are partly relocated (comparative advantages driving global integration); on the other hand downstream activities (distribution) are still national or limited to a few countries where retailers extend their territory.

Advertising intensity is relatively low, as compared to sport-leisure footwear, and brand image is not so decisive, as compared to luxury shoes. Managers also point out slight cross-national differences in customers' expectations.

> The sport and leisure footwear brands – Nike, Reebok, Adidas, Timberland – are the truly international businesses. On the other hand in mid-market fashion shoes, there are different national characteristics: Germany is comfort, Italy is elegance, UK is street, France is more classic fashion. So what you can sell in one country you cannot necessarily sell in the other, although some brands cross those boundaries successfully.

A summary example: the cables and wires industry

In the cables and wires industry a specific set of structural forces shapes the geographic scope of product-market segments. Local responsiveness is mainly driven by national norms and regulations. The size of the market relative to the critical size of production units, and the need for customized local services, explain the local scope of several product-market segments. International development and global integration are mainly driven by technological intensity and high product added value relative to transportation cost. The international scope of customers also explains the global development of some product-market segments.

Each product-market segment is characterized by a specific set of parameters (forces) and a particular position on the global–local map (see Figure 1.2).

From the most 'global' segment, submarine cables, to the most 'local' segment, low voltage power cables, this mapping shows the high variety of international scenarios within a given industry. Such variety creates high complexity for firms that compete in a mixed industry. This type of analysis is useful for practitioners responsible for the international strategy of their company, particularly when the firm has a broad portfolio of businesses.

Competitive forces underlying geographic scope

Comparison between global, multidomestic and mixed activities across the four industries studied reveals a set of competitive forces that drive or hinder international development.

Each sub-set of activities within a given industry is characterized by a particular set of forces. For instance in the paint industry, car

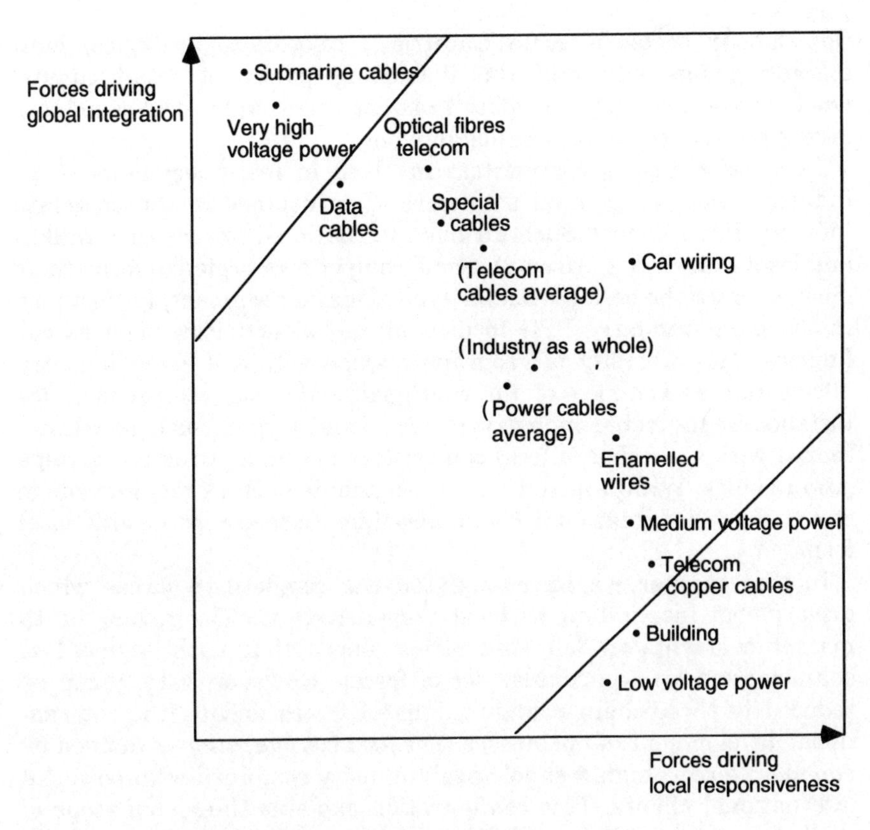

Figure 1.2 *Cables and wires: mapping product-market segments with the global–local framework*

finishes (global) is characterized by high technological intensity and powerful international customers, whereas decorative paint for professionals (multidomestic) is characterized by relatively low technological intensity, local customers, high barriers to access local distribution networks, and different traditions across countries. In the cable and wires industry, the global scope of submarine cables is driven by high technological intensity and international clients whereas the multidomestic scope of low power and telecom cables is driven by low technological intensity, high transportation cost, low product added value, national protectionism and the defensive strategies of local players. In the chocolate and sugar confectionery industry, the global scope of the countline business is driven by innovative international strategies, high advertising intensity and powerful clients (retail chains) whereas the local scope of cooked sugar sweets is driven by low technological intensity, low added value and low advertising intensity. In the footwear industry, the global scope of sport-leisure footwear is driven by comparative advantages (low labour costs in some countries), relocation strategies, high marketing intensity and the increasing power of retail chains, whereas the local scope of safety footwear is driven by local customers giving preference to national champions.

As a consequence, competitors involved in many segments of an industry often adopt dual strategies. For instance in the chocolate industry Kraft Jacobs Suchard has international brands (e.g. Milka) and local brands (e.g. Krema). Some competitors prefer to focus their business portfolio on a particular type of market segment, for instance in the paint industry PPG focuses on global activities such as car finishes. The diversity of geographic scope within a given industry allows the coexistence of international and local competitors, for instance in the cable industry international groups such as Alcatel coexist with a number of local competitors manufacturing low voltage power cables. Within mixed market segments such as medium range street shoes international companies like Bata compete with local firms.

In this chapter we have analysed the competitive forces which drive global integration or local responsiveness. The review of 19 market segments in four industries shows that each segment is characterized by a particular set of forces. However, variety can be reduced to three main configurations of forces driving the international development of businesses. *The first configuration* is defined by two main forces: high technological intensity combined with powerful international clients. This configuration explains the global scope of the following activities: car finishes, anti-corrosive paint for merchant marine and large industrial clients (the oil industry, nuclear power plants . . .), submarine cables and cables for special applications. *The second configuration* is defined by two main forces: advertising/sponsoring intensity which creates opportunities for economies of scale and scope and increasing negotiation power of retail chains. This configuration explains the global scope of the following activities: chocolate countlines, chewing gum, sport-leisure footwear. *The third configuration* characterizes luxury products: high added value, brand image, global-minded consumers, and fashion. This configuration explains the global scope of businesses such as women's luxury shoes and a few brands of luxury chocolate gifts.

In each of these configurations global strategies, based on technological innovation or universal brand image, interact with structural forces.

This typology does not pretend to be exhaustive as it is based on a limited number of industries defined at the three-digit level and a limited number of market segments (19). However, it suggests a variety of configurations and questions simple parsimonious theories explaining the international development of firms. It reveals that the influence of customers is significant in the three configurations: their international scope (in configuration 1), their negotiation power (in configuration 2) or their international lifestyle (in configuration 3). It also confirms that technological intensity (and high added value) is a major factor influencing globalization (in line with Kobrin, 1991). On the other hand it questions the view that marketing intensity drives local responsiveness (contrary to Kobrin, 1991). Distribution/sales intensity does preserve local players from foreign intrusion, but advertising/sponsoring intensity has an inverse influence. It drives globalization when a few competitors achieve economies of scope with their worldwide offensive communication strategies. In this case competitive actions drive international development and shape new structural forces. Finally, between global and local, mixed activities (such as enamelled wires, wood treatment products, medium range street shoes and chocolate *tablettes*) appear to be characterized by a *regional geographic scope*. The world is divided into several international regions, there is intense rivalry within a region (for instance Europe) but competition between regions is marginal. The next chapter analyses the factors that underlie the regional character of mixed industries.

From practice to theory: a summary

Defining different product-market segments characterized by different sets of competitive forces and regional configurations is a crucial task in international business. Industries defined at the level of three-digit SIC codes are composed of several activities with different geographical scopes and competitive rules. The relevant sub-sets of activities cannot be defined a priori by using standard codifications (for instance four, five or six-digit SIC codes). The identification of product-market segments requires some experience and knowledge of the industry. Different experts have different views concerning the segmentation of their industry, then a synthesis is needed, it can be done by the researcher or through a debate among experts. As far as quantitative research is concerned, the structure of databases and comparisons across time and space motivate the use of standard definitions of units of analysis. However, the biases that exist when using four-digit SIC definitions should be corrected: quantitative studies should be based on finer-grained categories, further clustered by a panel of experts. For instance in the paint industry (defined at the three-digit SIC code level), the 30 experts who participated in the study distinguished nine product-market segments, each one characterized by a specific configuration of forces and geographic scope: car finishes (global), car refinishes (global), can coating (global), anti-corrosive paint for industry and marine (global), industrial paint (local, mixed or global depending on the geographic scope of clients), coil coating (mixed), wood-treatment products (mixed), decorative paint sold in DIY stores (multidomestic becoming mixed), decorative paint for professionals (multidomestic).

Such differences are a source of complexity for practitioners and scholars. *Variety* should be recognized: it creates constraints but it also increases firms' strategic freedom. Depending on the specific resources of their firms, managers may use this segmentation when making product portfolio decisions. For instance, for a small or medium-sized business it could be wise to focus on one mixed segment or on a few multidomestic segments. A large firm may be tempted to select global segments and implement an aggressive global strategy in these activities. Large firms which are involved in both global and multidomestic activities should separate them into different divisions (in the case of the paint industry there are very weak synergies between the four global segments and the two multidomestic segments).

Probably the coexistence of several activities with different rules is particularly marked in 'mixed' industries, on which our empirical study focused. We suggest that it is a fundamental characteristic of such industries. However, we also suggest that there is some level of heterogeneity within global industries and within multidomestic industries. Indeed recognizing this heterogeneity can be a source of competitive advantage for international companies. The manager who recognizes a mixed product-market segment within a global industry may find an opportunity for a differentiation strategy. The manager who sees a mixed product-market segment within a multidomestic industry may find an opportunity to be the first mover across borders. In any case practitioners can draw a straightforward lesson from this finding: international strategies should be formulated at the product-market segment level, for the rules of international competition are specific to each segment.

Beyond diversity, we identified three main configurations of structural forces that drive the international development of businesses:

- high technological intensity, combined with powerful international clients;
- advertising/sponsoring intensity which creates opportunities for economies of scale/scope, combined with the increasing negotiation power of distributors;
- luxury products (high added value, brand image, global minded consumers, and fashion).

The first configuration produces the most dramatic globalization scenarios.

Global strategies based on technological innovation (in the first configuration) and global strategies based on universal brand image (in the second and third configurations) interact with structural forces.

Further studies could usefully adopt such a configurational approach. Technological intensity appears to be the main driver of internationalization (in line with existing theories), but the influence of customers – their international scope, their negotiation power or their international lifestyle – also appears to be a significant force in the globalization of businesses (these factors tend to be undervalued in existing theories).

Analysis of 'mixed' segments reveals the existence of regional (several countries) competitive territories and the relevance of a regional approach to competition.

Note

1 Two types of ellipsis are used in quotes: '. . .' denotes that the interviewee was silent for a few seconds, whereas '[. . .]' denotes that the author has cut out pieces of text.

Bibliography

Key concepts – 'global', 'mixed', 'local', and forces driving global integration and local responsiveness – are defined by Prahalad and Doz (1987), and in the strategic management literature based on the 'Global Integration – Local Responsiveness' framework (see the Introduction, p. 8).

The aggregation bias associated with four-digit SIC codes, and most standard classifications, has been discussed by Schmalensee (1989) and Scherer and Ross (1990) among others. Lubatkin et al. (forthcoming) suggest reducing this bias by turning to specialized knowledge databases where these exist (for instance they use the database of Selling Area Market Inc. in the United States for the food manufacturing industry).

Concerning product-market segment variety in relation to the dynamics of international competition, Atamer (1991) studied a number of internationalization scenarios in six industries in Europe, and provided empirical evidence of the heterogeneity of product-market segments as far as international competition is concerned.

2

Regions: between Global and Local

Roland Calori, Sarah-Kathryn McDonald and Pancho Nunes

The geographic scope of competition varies between two extremes: local (nationwide) and global (worldwide). Yet very few activities (industries or product-market segments) are characterized by a purely local or a purely global competitive scene. Some activities tend toward the local extreme: a rule of thumb is that when two ratios – the sum of imports to total consumption and the sum of exports and foreign direct investments to total production – are lower than 10 per cent, competition is local. Conversely when the two ratios are greater than 50 per cent, competition is described as global. Between these limits it is expected that trade flows and foreign investment flows will be significant enough to stimulate international strategies but low enough to allow selective international strategies. Moreover, trade and investment flows are not evenly distributed around the globe; international competition often takes place within geographic areas. These (industry-specific) geographic areas, or regions, are sets of countries within which products, knowledge and financial flows are significant, or, put another way, they are competitive territories. Between such regions trade and investment flows are relatively low (with ratios lower than 50 per cent). Consider the example of international flows in the car industry. In the mid-1990s, across the three regions of the Triad, North America, Europe and the developed countries of Asia (mainly Japan), intercontinental flows were close to 30 per cent. Together US and Japanese car manufacturers had a 37 per cent market share in Europe (trade and investments), together Japanese and European car manufacturers had a 30 per cent market share in North America, and together US and European car manufacturers had a 10 per cent market share in the developed countries of Asia. Clearly the car industry was not yet purely global; there was a high level of intra-regional flows (above 50 per cent) but a much lower level of intercontinental flows. Indeed quasi-regional competitors could survive (at least for some time).

The identification of regions as competitive arenas is not simple. Managers in our study approach this task from three different perspectives. Some of them define geographic scope according to the international development of production (manufacturing). This is particularly the case in the footwear industry (see Chapter 1), where in some segments (for instance sport-leisure) manufacturing is located in foreign developing countries. Cross-border trade and investment flows may be high and international firms may have a significant share, but the targeted market generally is regional. Others define geographic scope according to the homogeneity of markets across borders. For instance in decorative paint, Northern European consumers have relatively homogeneous consumption behaviours and distribution channels are similar; hence Northern Europe is viewed as a competitive territory (regardless of the actual market shares of competitors). Both views can be accepted, but both are partial. A third (more comprehensive) perspective considers that competitive territories are defined by the positions of competitors across borders. When one or several competitors have significant shares in several key markets, the set of key markets is considered the competitive territory: a region. The identification of such regions is subjective (thus variable) as the meaning of terms like 'significant', 'several' and 'key' are matters of judgement for the managers themselves. Actually the three criteria that define geographic scope (international production, the homogeneity of markets, and the international positions of competitors) are related. For instance in sport-leisure footwear, young consumers want the same product and the same image worldwide; key players manufacture their products in low labour cost countries, sell them around the globe and dominate key markets. Other examples of the interplay among these three approaches to describing the geographical scope of the studied industries are provided below.

Not included in this analysis are product-market segments which were viewed as global (for instance car finishes, can coating, anticorrosive paint for marine and industry, submarine cables, cables for special applications, sport-leisure footwear, women's luxury shoes, countlines and chewing gum), or product-market segments which were viewed as local (decorative paint for professionals, low voltage power cables, safety shoes, cooked sugar sweets and chocolate boxed assortments). Their regional outlines are too attenuated to draw useful conclusions. The remaining product-market segments on which our arguments are based represent, on average, about two-thirds of the turnover of the four industries studied.

Based on the managers' cognitive maps of regions, the chapter begins by describing the competitive territories which characterize the cable industry, the chocolate and sugar confectionery industry, and the paint industry.[1] The comparison shows that each industry is characterized by a specific geographic segmentation that cannot be defined a priori. We then examine the structural forces and competitive actions that shape regional competitive territories. This analysis shows that the combination of several forces creates 'fracture lines' between regions, and that each industry is characterized by a specific configuration of forces. These fracture lines are not static; regional boundaries move, or vanish with changes in the set of forces.

Maps of competitive territories

When executives described competition as taking place within regions, we asked them to discuss the characteristics of each region compared to the other one(s) and the factors that determined the fracture lines between competitive territories. The resulting (mental) maps were all unique, yet they possessed enough common elements to construct composite pictures of international activity in each of the three industries: cables, chocolate, and paint. Table 2.1 summarizes the aggregated maps of regional competitive territories in the three industries. For each industry the aggregation has been done by superposition of individual answers; regional limits cited by most experts in an industry define a fracture line. Depending on the level of agreement among experts fracture lines separate regions (high level of agreement) or sub-regions (medium level of agreement).

Regions in the cables and wires industry

In the cables and wires industry, managers agree that competition is focused on several competitive territories around the world. Interestingly, while their individual maps differ (there are no two identical maps provided by the 19 respondents who discussed geographic segmentation), there are no fundamental incompatibilities among them. For instance one manager identified four competitive territories: (1) North America, Western Europe, developed countries in Asia (including Japan), (2) Eastern Europe, (3) South America, the Middle East and Africa, (4) China and the rest of Asia. Another respondent identified two geographic areas: (1) Europe, North America, Japan, (2) South America, Asia, Africa. Yet another manager observed,

> We could divide countries into three groups. First there are the sophisticated demand and high income countries: Europe, North America and Japan. In these rich countries demand for services is traditionally strong. They represent important markets in terms of volume and technological level. Second there are the intermediate countries, for instance South America and developing countries in the Far East, where technology is no longer elementary, but it is not advanced either. In some of these places,

Table 2.1 *Regional competitive territories in three industries*

Regions in the cables & wires industry	Regions in the chocolate & confectionery industry	Regions in the paint industry
The Triad (Western Europe, North America, Japan) – Western Europe – North America – Japan	Western Europe – The United Kingdom – Northern Europe – Southern Europe	Europe – Northern Europe – Southern Europe – Eastern Europe
	Eastern Europe	North America
Eastern Europe, South America and the rest of Asia – Eastern Europe – South America – The rest of Asia	North America	South America
	The 'rich' countries of Asia	'Developed countries of Asia'
Underdeveloped countries	'The rest of the world'	'Less developed countries'

however, there are big strides forward, sometimes going straight from analogue to digital technologies. Finally the bottom level includes continents like Africa or countries like Bangladesh which currently have no resources for development.

Collectively the individual managers' mental maps identify three regions, with different levels of economic development, in which competition is centred.

The first region, which includes Western Europe, North America and Japan, is characterized by large but low-growth markets, overcapacity and high technology. All major international competitors originate from this region. This competitive territory can be further divided into three sub-regions that correspond to the three continents. The level of intercontinental competition is moderate (American companies have strong positions in North America, Japanese companies have strong positions in Japan, European companies have strong positions in Europe and in North America). Moreover each continent is bounded by specific technical standards and norms and characterized by some specific competitive forces. North America is characterized by sophisticated demand for telecommunications, low prices, low margins and powerful distributors. Japan is characterized by powerful national players who dominate the large domestic market. Europe is characterized by recent deregulation and slow harmonization of norms, public utilities, and large-scale restructuring headed by powerful manufacturers.

Europe includes several countries; each country had a national preference – I am speaking of the past. Thus national industries flourished in each protected national market. The large clients, the power utilities and telephone companies represented more than 50 per cent of our customer base; they were giving a preference to national manufacturers. Now the European Union encourages the mutual recognition of norms, standardization and harmonization of products. The trend is towards a single market and industrial concentration, which has already begun. The small cable makers are having a hard time resisting the big ones with production capacities and economies of scale. Factories are and will be closed to reduce overcapacity. Supply will concentrate around powerful competitors. Just look at the list: in Europe there is Alcatel, BICC, Pirelli, Siemens. . . . Now Nokia is growing, ABB, in England Delta has growth ambitions, and a number of small German cable makers are strong enough to survive.

In the USA cable makers were quite profitable in the past. Then competition increased and their services got poorer. They did not know how to give their clients the right response to what they were asking for. So between the client and the cable maker came people we call 'master distributors' who established their policy only on service . [. . .] In order to offer these services while maintaining competitive prices to clients, they forced American cable makers to lower their prices and their profitability, which means that over the last 20 years American cable makers have been in difficulty. A few managed to make it, but the majority went under. On the other hand the master distributors have been doing very, very well. So this has brought a restructuring of the industry; nobody wanted to establish new units, and the foreign companies who wanted to settle in the USA bought these cable making units. And today, in the USA, the leading cable makers are Alcatel Cable, Pirelli, BICC – the three Europeans who were comfortably established in their national markets and had the financial resources to go and take over and restructure the American industry. [. . .] Now they all have trouble in the US; they do not make a profit.

In the telecom market, the US cable industry is far more competitive than we are: their average prices are half of those paid in Europe. [. . .] The fact that Americans are seriously thinking of constructing information superhighways is an indication of a latent demand for services. [. . .] The seven regional Bell operating companies were set up quite a long time ago and made to compete with one another in telephone and other services; there the market is more advanced and the communication services also cost much less than in Europe.

Japan is a very protected market; you cannot go there. It is really impossible to sell anything from Europe to Japan. [. . .] Japanese stay in Japan very much.

The major competitors from the Triad also target markets in the other regions.

The second region which the managers collectively identify includes Eastern Europe, South America and the rest of Asia (except Japan). It is characterized by growing demand and needs for new infrastructures, low labour costs, and competition between national companies (in low technology products) and international players from the Triad. This competitive territory is further divided into three sub-regions that correspond to the three areas: Eastern Europe, South America and Asia.

Eastern Europe is characterized by the presence of local businesses, particularly in low added value products; growth potential is modest (compared to Asia) due to limited financial resources for the development and renewal of infrastructures.

> Before the collapse of the communist empire, trade flows between Eastern and Western Europe were not significant. State industries from the East exported low-tech, low added value cables, particularly to Germany to get foreign currency. Nowadays a lot of Eastern companies have been taken over by or are managed through joint ventures with Western firms. [. . .] They still have competitive labour costs, but labour costs are not so significant.
>
> Eastern Europeans manufacture a lot of enamelled wires, but the quality of their products and services is poor. Now their governments no longer help them, many firms have closed down. [. . .] There is a market in Russia, but the quality is very low.

South America is characterized by high growth potential, but limited resources to finance investments in infrastructure. The local industry is weak, still protected from foreign imports, but gradually opening up.

> South American countries have great potential but lack the wherewithal to make the investment they need. The level of investment is so low, particularly in Brazil, that the growth of local businesses is limited. [. . .] In Argentina since the telephone company has been privatized and divided into two businesses, there have been more international bids but local suppliers are allowed to charge prices that are 10 per cent higher than foreigners'.

Indeed international players are attracted by the third sub-region: *Asia*. Asia (except Japan) is characterized by a large potential market, high growth, large-scale turnkey projects, high foreign investment from international players (mainly the Europeans), joint ventures, and the development of local businesses.

> It is not like we sit here and participate in the growth of Asian markets through our European base. Instead we must be there locally. So we have a number of joint ventures on their way with companies in Asia and we make money locally by being there. On the other hand the synergies between these units and our European units are not significant.
>
> Certain areas are growing at an incredible pace and if I need a communication network I cannot wait for my local industry to be equipped

> to provide it. I do my best for my local industry, but my choice will fall on a supplier who offers me a complete package, a system, not just the cable; I also need fast access to the funds needed to set up the whole business. In the Far East and South East Asia the availability of financing can be a key deciding factor when choosing between a local supplier and an international supplier.

The Korean cable industry is now strong enough to compete in Malaysia and in China. China and India are being equipped with a cable industry.

> China will soon be able to meet its high growth domestic demand with its local cable manufacturing industry. In the far future it may even become a new international competitor.

The third region groups together underdeveloped countries, mainly in Africa. In this area demand is very low, local industry is very weak and the lack of financial resources constrains future growth. As one of the managers put it in an abrupt statement: 'Markets like black Africa are practically non-existent.'

This map of competitive territories in the cable industry is somewhat simplistic; for instance in Asia the rules of competition differ between countries such as Korea, China and Indonesia. International players have to adapt their strategies to each region, sub-region, and key market. Moreover, regional boundaries are moving:

> I have been in the company for the last seven years. Seven years ago, the cable industry was local. As far as power and telecom utilities were concerned, national markets were protected and cartels controlled competition. [. . .] In the last three years international competition has emerged at least within Europe. The foreign key players can produce according to our domestic norms and they penetrate vigorously into the main markets in Europe.

International cable makers adapt their organization to the segmentation of competitive territories:

> Our geographic organization may change. Three separated business areas – Southern Europe, France, Germany – may become one: Europe. Just as the USA and Canada were merged into a single area: America. East Asia is already an area and not a group of nations. We are going towards vertical product lines further divided into broad geographical areas: Europe, the Americas, Middle East, East Asia. We are changing our style from extreme decentralization at the country subsidiary level (which met the demand of national utilities) to decentralization at the level of business lines and regional coordination.

Clearly, when powerful international leaders adopt regional organization they reinforce the formation of regional blocks. In other words, competitive territories (regions) shape and are shaped by competitive actions.

Regions in the chocolate and sugar confectionery industry

Managers' maps are idiosyncratic and biased by the particular situations of their firms. Nevertheless it is possible to construct a 'combined' map, in which five main regions are delineated: North America, Western Europe, Eastern Europe, 'rich' Asian countries, and the rest of the world.

> There is Western Europe, it is the primary market in the world for the chocolate industry; then there is North America (the United States and Canada) and you really need to single out these markets. After that there is the Asian market, and last the former Eastern bloc countries of which Russia is the principal market. [. . .] What differentiates them first of all is the per capita consumption. [. . .] In Europe we have a per capita consumption of 6 kilograms per year on average. Here consumers are very demanding when it comes to quality and you buy chocolate to eat it yourself. In Asia per capita consumption is lower and you buy chocolate to give as a gift. North Americans consume local chocolate products, especially in the United States with one dominant firm who produces a quality that is not adapted to European tastes.
>
> Eastern Europe and Russia is an important region, high consumption. In Russia the per capita consumption is at the same level as in Western Europe, that is to say around 6 kilograms a year. The climate is right and as the standard of living increases the market for quality products will increase. This is a very attractive market for Western European companies and of course the global companies like Mars. And they are already there or on the way with their own production facilities in Poland, Russia and the Baltic states. If you talk about where the market is today, of course, you have the USA. A few European companies sell on the American market, but American companies, particularly Hershey, have a strong position in their home market. Hershey is a very big firm but they are almost non-existent here in Europe. Then the new countries in South East Asia are very interesting too. The problem with them is the climate: heat and humidity impose air-conditioning throughout the whole chain of production and delivery. In countries such as Malaysia, Singapore and Indonesia the per capita consumption is below 1 kilogram, but the market is growing as the standard of living rises. In this zone the Japanese market is somewhat different: higher consumption but strong local competitors.

A closer look at the respective positions of key competitors shows that there were six main international companies: Nestlé, Mars, Kraft Jacobs Suchard, Ferrero, Cadbury and Lindt. Then there were a number of local players, some of them quite big: Hershey in the USA, Lote in Japan, Alpia in Germany.

> Nestlé and Mars are truly worldwide players, KJS is strong in Europe and also in South America, Ferrero is particularly strong in Europe but their products sell around the world, Cadbury has its strength in the Commonwealth countries, Lindt is a little bit locally oriented: based in Switzerland and doing really good business in France, in Spain and in Italy.

Western Europe is a mature market that grows with the increase of population and with the weak increase of per capita consumption in Southern Europe. In general Europeans consume a lot of chocolate *tablettes* (plain chocolate bars for the Anglo-Saxons) as compared to the Americans and the Japanese, and a lot of traditional products. Confronted with international competition (e.g. from Mars, Philip Morris-KJS from the US, Nestlé, Ferrero from within Europe) and the growing power of retail chains, the European chocolate and sugar confectionery industry has gone through intense restructuring, involving mergers, acquisitions, exits, and rationalization of production capacities. Beyond these common features, the European region is heterogeneous, particularly in terms of consumption patterns.

> You need to know that the French prefer a chocolate that is more cocoa-flavoured, that the North Europeans prefer a milder chocolate with more cocoa butter, more milk-flavoured even honey-flavoured for the Swiss. In England Cadbury products do not really meet continental Europe's criteria: their chocolate has a very weak percentage of cocoa – 20 per cent on average – and this represents about 80 per cent of the national consumption of milk chocolate in Great Britain. Scandinavian countries could also be considered as a particular market with strong local brands and chocolate with a caramel taste. [. . .] France falls into a category with a per capita consumption of 6 kilograms, in Great Britain it is about 8 kilograms, Switzerland is about 10 kilograms per capita, and consumption is even higher in Scandinavia.

According to the managers, Western Europe can be usefully divided into three main sub-regions: the United Kingdom, Northern Europe and Southern Europe. Southern Europe is characterized by lower levels of consumption, not much 'chocolate heritage', the purchase of chocolate more as a gift than a snack, more fragmented distribution than in the North, and a particular taste (with for instance, as far as sugar confectionery is concerned, no special interest in sugar-free products). Meanwhile, Northern Europe is characterized by higher levels of consumption, increased purchase of chocolate as a snack, concentrated distribution, and a different taste for sugar confectionery (with, for instance, interest in sugar-free products). Finally, the United Kingdom is characterized by a special formula for chocolate products (as described above), countlines represent a high share of the market, and the distribution system is split largely between confectionery-tobacco-news agents (CTN) and powerful retail chains.

Eastern Europe is characterized by specific consumption patterns, and by the confrontation of local manufacturers with increasing competition from international players, as the following comments illustrate:

> The annual chocolate consumption per capita is lower than in Northern Europe, whereas the consumption of sugar confectionery is significant and that is primarily due to economic reasons. Furthermore the chocolate consumed in Eastern Europe is clearly of an inferior quality.
>
> Chocolate is replaced by chocolate cookies or all kinds of inferior substitutes. For instance they [manufacturers] replace the cocoa butter and the cocoa paste with a bit of dry cocoa powder and mostly vegetable fat. This is the least expensive formula and it goes with the low level of purchasing power. This being said, our experience in Russia reveals that they prefer dark chocolate with very little milk and a strong cocoa flavour. I believe that, if they had a higher level of purchasing power they would shift toward a product with a higher degree of cocoa.

The third of the five regions in the chocolate and sugar confectionery industry, *North America*, is characterized by specific consumption patterns, and by the presence of two strong US companies, Hershey and Mars, who dominate the market and leave little room for small local firms or for European companies to set up. The per capita consumption is high (comparable to the highest scores in Northern Europe), and chocolate and sugar confectionery belongs to the huge snack market. Europeans agree both that North American chocolate has a very particular taste (and formula), and that setting up a distribution network there is a daunting challenge.

The fourth of the five regions, comprised of *'rich' countries in Asia*, is characterized by a low level of per capita consumption due to climate and the lack of a 'chocolate tradition' (with the exception of Japan which was influenced by Americans after World War II). Chocolate is thought of primarily as a gift, eating chocolate is a Western habit that people like to emulate, and packaging is paramount. Sugar confectionery is consumed in moderation.

> If I am a nice boy and I do my homework, I get a piece of candy from my mother (whereas in Europe you buy these huge bags of candies which you eat yourself or share with your friends). But in Asia it is more pick'n'mix where the mother buys a bag of candies and shares it so that the kids do not get the whole bag. It is a reward . . . and people are health conscious.

Local competitors are strong, in part because they are well equipped to deal with complex local distribution networks.

> Local producers are engaged in a ferocious battle and they constantly innovate, particularly in terms of packaging and flavour. Chocolates have different flavours: orange, mint, banana, kiwi, all sorts of exotic fruits. The leading competitors, Lote, Gluko, Meidi, are trying their best to differentiate their products.

The rest of the world is considered insignificant or unattractive because of very low consumption, resulting from factors such as low purchasing power, the hot climate, and the absence of a chocolate tradition. South America is sometimes viewed as an exception, especially Brazil where consumption is growing, but the taste and chocolate formula preferred by consumers are specific, which only leaves room for a few global brands (chocolate bars, chewing gums, luxury products).

Managers perceive signs of a slow convergence of consumption patterns across regions. For instance in Europe the level of consumption in the South is growing. This trend is creating opportunities for more global strategies in the industry.

> Homogenization in Europe will get stronger and stronger. There are some countries in Central Europe who within the timespan of ten to twenty years should, barring any serious accidents, adopt the consumption habits of Western Europe. Regarding Russia, it remains quite uncertain, but all in all we should end up with a European region that is more homogeneous and more significant. Regarding the other regions of the world, I do not know.
>
> It is a worldwide tendency; consumers will adopt global brands. Coke and Mars have shown the way. . . . Satellite television will communicate our messages.

Regions in the paint industry

In the paint industry managers identify five broad competitive territories. The first three regions, Europe, North America, and the developed countries of Asia, include the rich countries of the Triad. The other two, South America, and the rest of the world, include countries which are still fighting for development. As described by one manager:

> There is Europe, not just the EU, [but] the large Europe which includes the Czech Republic, the Slovak Republic, Hungary, Poland, the Baltic states. . . . Then there is the American zone which is the USA plus Canada, plus Mexico. I do not know the South American zone very well. And then there is another zone which is Asia, Japan and the 'tigers'.

Looking at the rationale behind their 'mental maps', we find that some managers define regions according to consumption patterns (e.g. consumption per capita, product quality, culture), and many define regions according to the geographic scope and positions of the main competitors. With respect to the latter a few leading companies had intercontinental activities (ICI, Akzo Nobel, PPG), but they were not yet implementing pure global strategies in the business of decorative paint.

> Capital is controlled by the multinational, but paint is produced and sold locally, often with local or regional brands. This is because they have to match product and market specificities.

The international positions of key players confirm the regional division of the industry. ICI was strong in Europe and gained a significant share of the US decorative paint market after several acquisitions in North America. Akzo Nobel had their strengths in Europe. PPG and Hoechst had an intercontinental position but they were mainly involved in global segments such as car finishes. Then there were very significant competitors with regional strengths, for instance Alcro Beckers and Becker Ind. (of Sweden), Total (of France) in Europe; Nippon Paint and Kansaï Paint dominated the Japanese market, while Sherwin Williams, Dupont and Benjamin Moore had their strengths in North America.

The strength of some local players in their home market restrains the opportunities for global development.

> It is difficult to get into the USA market at the moment and I do not see the US companies getting into the European market of varnishes. [. . .] We do not go there because things are already well set up.
>
> The concentration of producers mainly takes place within zones. There is some concentration within the Asian region; the Japanese take over a lot of companies. There is concentration within the American zone. Clearly there is concentration within Europe. These big masses are formed within regions: the Europeans within Europe, the Japanese and the Koreans in Asia, and the Americans within North America.

On average, *Europe* is a mature market dominated by European competitors. A few strong groups emerged after a number of mergers and acquisitions: Akzo Nobel, ICI, Total, Alcro Beckers (with their main area of activity decorative paint). Several companies were among the world leaders in businesses such as car finishes and refinishes, industrial coating and coil coating: Hoechst, BASF, Becker competing with the American PPG. Spanish and Italian firms were among the world leaders in varnishes. The European region is also characterized by the importance of lasures (wood treatment coatings).

> [in lasures] There are practically no extracontinental brands in Europe. Lasures were invented by the Danish company Dyrup, with its Bondex

> brand. The main market for lasures is Northern Europe, but the Eastern European countries represent an attractive market; there the culture is the same, they like wood a lot and they do not like to paint it (like the Americans). [. . .] On the other hand the consumption of lasures is still low in Latin Europe.

Overall consumption patterns lead the managers to subdivide the European region into three areas: Northern, Southern, and Eastern Europe.

In Northern Europe the market is characterized by high consumption per capita, high quality, greater use of water-based paints (which reduce environmental pollution), and a highly concentrated industry. In Southern Europe the market is characterized by less use of water-based paints than in the North, relatively high consumption of varnishes, more do-it-yourself than in the North, and a lower level of industry concentration. As one manager said:

> The use of water-based paints is a recent development; they replaced solvent-based paints that pollute the environment. The market share of good acrylic water-based paint varies from one country to another. In France it is around 50 per cent for acrylics and 50 per cent for solvent-based paints. In England and in all the Scandinavian countries the market has been turned upside-down: more than 90 per cent water-based. This was mainly for ecological reasons. [. . .] On the other hand Latin countries are still loyal to oil-based paints in the solvent stage and the breakthrough of water-based paints is still weak . . . in Spain, Portugal, Italy, Greece. . . very limited.

Other differences between the two sub-regions relate to climate and culture:

> In Northern Europe lasures protect wood from humidity and funguses. [. . .] In Southern Europe the sunshine dries the material out with high levels of ultraviolet rays. Altogether that means different requirements depending on the region.
>
> [In the North one pays] more attention to things looking nice and well-kept. That is the 'Lutheran belt' that you can spot in Germany, the Netherlands, Switzerland, Austria and the Nordic countries, where you pay a lot of attention to things looking good. Therefore customers ask more of many materials [. . .] not only paint.

The third sub-region, Eastern Europe, is characterized by lower levels of per capita consumption, lower quality and local competition. However there are signs that Central Europe and Baltic states will catch up with Western European consumption patterns in the long term.

The second of the five major regions which managers described, *North America*, is also a mature market with strong local competitors and a high level of per capita consumption. This region (like Northern Europe) is very oriented towards acrylic water based paints as there, too, concern for environmentally friendly products has been strong for many years (with the state of California in particular known for its environment-protection concerns and constraints). Given their geographic proximity it is perhaps not surprising that several US companies have significant activities in South America, often in the form of licensing agreements. Nevertheless, the two regions differ in important ways.

The *South American* region has a low level of per capita consumption and a low level of quality. Local producers have marginal exports to Europe and the US (particularly varnishes) and two countries seem to emerge as attractive targets: Chile and Argentina (Mexico is seen as part of the North American zone in terms of competition and as part of the South American zone in terms of consumption patterns).

The fourth of the five major regions, *'developed Asia'* is divided into three sub-regions. The first one, Japan, is a mature market characterized by strong local competitors such as Kansaï Paint and Nippon Paint which are backed up by a powerful chemical industry and have a broad range of products. Thailand is typical of the second region with its growing markets and medium-sized businesses. Korea is typical of the third sub-region, falling somewhere in between the other two. The unity of the Asian competitive territory is based on the international positions of Japanese firms, achieved through takeovers and licensing agreements.

The rest of the world includes a number of 'less developed countries' (some of which can be called underdeveloped). Consumption and quality levels are very low. According to one manager this is the terrain for local and international 'opportunists', generally small and medium-sized businesses who take risks in these countries, which do not attract the big players.

There are some signs of convergence among the sub-regions, particularly within the 'large Europe', between the North, the South and the East: the general trend is favourable to water-based paints and higher quality. There are some signs that intercontinental consolidation may take place among the three zones of the Triad in the future. While this has already happened in certain product-market segments (such as car finishes or can coating), it will be harder to achieve in the bulk of the market (decorative paint). Perhaps the most important factor in determining the speed and extent of convergence in that sector will be the intercontinental ambitions of the top companies, and the competitive actions that top managers will decide to take.

Forces creating fracture lines

Fracture lines that delineate regions are created by the combination of several forces. Two forces underlie the formation of competitive territories: the distribution of knowledge and know-how across the world, and logistics. Two economic forces further shape division into regions: barriers to trade and foreign direct investment (e.g. tariffs, regulations and the existence of trade blocs) and the level of economic development. Two sociological forces complement these structural determinants: different customers' preferences and political-economical-cultural influences. The combination of these six structural forces determines firms' international strategies and the geographic scope and organization of their activities. In turn, the geographic scope and organization of international firms contribute to the shaping of competitive territories (regions) and drive changes in the configuration of structural forces (see Figure 2.1).

The distribution of knowledge and know-how

The concentration of knowledge and know-how in a single location in the world (in other words, technological monopoly by one nation or region) creates the conditions for the development of export flows and foreign investments originating from this location. In a monopoly there is a single international competitive territory composed of the entire set of nations who can afford to purchase the goods. An attenuated form of monopoly is known as a nation's competitive advantage (Porter, 1990). The case of high voltage power cables (considered a global activity and an exception in the cable industry) illustrates the point:

> In high voltage, competition comes close to global. There are a few countries that have a strong home industry: Sweden has got one, the Italians are capable, the French are capable. If you target one of these markets, you get retaliation the next day, so there is a bit of a terror balance within Western Europe. Outside these home markets all other markets are accessible: Asia (except Japan which has a strong home industry), Australia, Africa, and several states in the Eastern bloc. The Americans are not particularly skilled at this: the modern high voltage cable technology installed in the USA is owned by European companies, the major part is imported.

Conversely, a precondition for the emergence of several competitive territories separated by fracture lines is that knowledge and know-how are distributed in several locations. Each of these locations then becomes a potential pole around which a region may be formed. In many industries this is what happened in the second half of the twentieth century. Just after World War II the USA dominated the

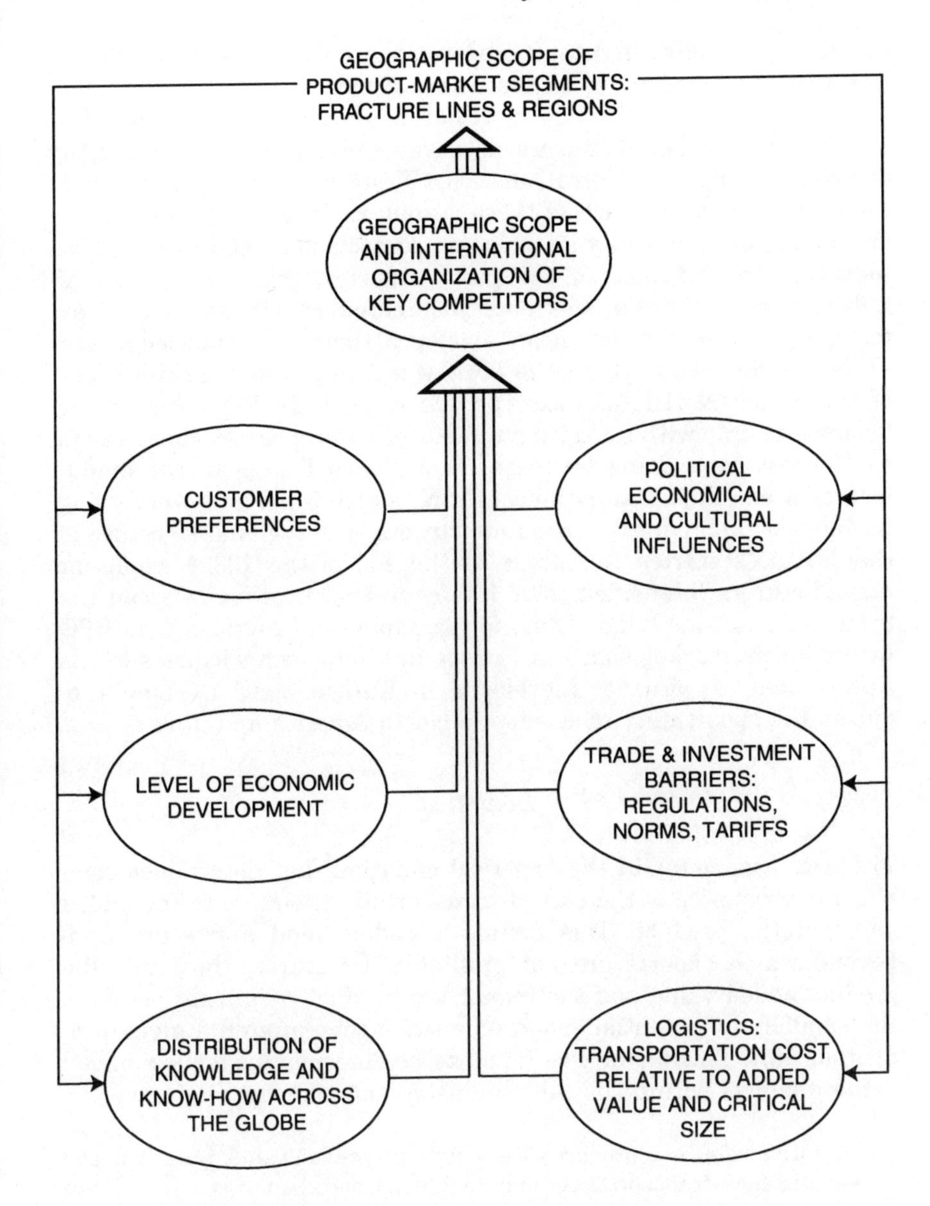

Figure 2.1 *Configurations of forces creating fracture lines and regions*

world economy (except the socialist bloc) in many industries. Then Europe rebuilt its strengths in many sectors (e.g. chemicals, automotive, electromechanics) and caught up with new technologies: nuclear power, electronics, aerospace, biotechnologies. Finally Japan caught up with its occidental counterparts and developed its own knowledge bases. In the 1980s, in most industries, there were strong knowledge bases in the three zones of the Triad: North America, Europe and Japan (Thurow, 1993). Such a distribution of knowledge explains why, in many industries, managers delineate three main regions among developed economies: North America, (Western) Europe, and the rich countries of Asia. In each of these, strong regional competitors have developed; we found this in cables, in confectionery and in the paint industry. For instance in the paint industry, the business of car finishes and refinishes was once dominated by US and European technology, then the Japanese developed their own knowledge and skills and, for several years, the world was divided into the three zones of the Triad. North American producers such as PPG were doing business mainly with US car manufacturers, European producers such as Hoechst were doing business mainly with European car manufacturers and Japanese producers such as Nippon Paint were doing business with Japanese car manufacturers. The regional structure of this business started to change at the end of the 1980s when car manufacturers intensified their intercontinental moves between the three zones of the Triad. Thus, for example the American firm PPG increased its market share in Europe and new technologies such as water-based car finishes (developed in Europe) gave German producers the opportunity to develop in North America and in Asia.

Logistics

The first parameter in the logistical equation that determines competitive territories is the cost of transportation relative to the added value of the product. This defines a radius (and a fracture line) beyond which exports are not profitable. Of course, the lower the product added value and the higher the product weight (or volume), the smaller the potential geographic trade zone around a given production unit. This factor was found to be determinant for low added value products within the cable industry and the paint industry.

> Decorative paint is a product with a quite low added value: it cannot take long distance transportation and high transportation costs. [. . .] For instance it is very unlikely that American paint will be found in Italy . . . except maybe for some products with high technological content.
>
> Traditional cables are very heavy. First cable manufacturers have to get raw material delivered to them, copper, and steel wire, and plastic. Then the product has to be delivered to customers. Transportation costs are rather high, and you have to think twice before concentrating manufacturing in a single central plant.

Two other parameters have to be considered in the logistical equation: (1) the critical size of a manufacturing unit (i.e. the size that allows economies of scale), in relation to (2) the size of the market. When the ratio (1)/(2) is low, manufacturing tends to be geographically dispersed in order to reduce transportation costs (and delivery times); when the ratio is high, a compromise must be found between manufacturing economies and transportation cost: as a consequence the dispersion of manufacturing tends to be reduced. As a rule of thumb, we found that the logistical equation for traditional cables and decorative paint gives a radius of between 1,000 and 2,000 kilometres around a manufacturing unit. This is enough to include several countries within a region like Europe. Beyond this scope, an inter-regional competitor will not enjoy a cost advantage as compared to a regional competitor located in the place of consumption. Admittedly this is a very simplified view of international manufacturing and logistics, and as the case of the footwear industry (see Chapter 5, p. 104) illustrates, the unit cost of manpower and delivery times may also be included in the equation. Moreover, beyond the regional scope defined by production and transportation costs, international players do engage in foreign direct investments which are a significant part of international competition. Finally it should be noted that, while our focus has been on goods-producing businesses, the logistical factor has similar implications in service activities, with communication costs in the place of transportation costs. In service industries, the challenge is to organize a network with a centre, nodes and local branches where most front office activities take place.

Trade and investment barriers

Fracture lines between competitive territories are sometimes created by barriers to international trade and foreign direct investments. Customs duties are frequently cited as barriers to international trade, although, when a market is attractive enough, tariff barriers may stimulate foreign direct investment. Different norms (notably product standards) and regulations across countries may also raise barriers, as we saw in the cable industry and, to a lesser degree, in the paint industry.

> Different [geographic] zones result from different regulations, different standards that hinder the use of some products and manufacturing practices. For instance you do not use the same heating systems in Brazil, in the USA and in France.
>
> Trade barriers were the main reason why we did little business on the German market. [. . .] In five years' time we may well be successfully competing with Alcatel, Siemens and other local manufacturers in supplying cables to German customers. [. . .] A recent European directive

> opens invitations to bid to foreign suppliers. It is a question of regulatory procedures and standards. When standardization puts foreign and local producers on the same level, the competitive situation clearly changes.

Indeed, harmonization of norms within the European Union contributes to the development of a new Europe-wide competitive territory in the cable industry.

> In the energy sector and in telecoms, privatization and deregulation will open up domestic markets to international competition. And here by international I mean within the geographic area. [. . .] The main structural change has been the creation of large geographic trading areas like the European Union or NAFTA.

In the paint industry we found that such trade zones seem to stimulate regional trade and shape a new map of competitive territories, which roughly correspond to the three regions of the Triad.

> In North America there are the ASDM requirements, in Europe there are the SAM requirements. A certain standard is being established. However, within a zone, the common denominator is still vague enough to allow each country to define specific requirements. [. . .] I attended an international senior management programme. . . . There in principle everything was 'global' . . . but in practice it will be very difficult to globalize the paint industry.
>
> The new regulations about environmentally friendly products and so on will help harmonization in Europe. Thanks to the EU the products will gradually become more similar whether they are from the North or from the South.

International harmonization is a slow process that starts at the regional level. Before globalization can be achieved, international players have to comply with local and/or regional requirements that often hinder inter-regional trade. The creation of regional trading blocs – the European Union, NAFTA, Mercosur and APEC – seems to achieve its goal of regional consolidation.

The level of economic development

The level of economic development shapes the competitive territories identified by managers in the industries studied: cables, paint, and chocolate and sugar confectionery. Speaking about the cable industry:

> In power cables (including enamelled wires) or in telecommunication (including data cables) demand and competition are directly linked to electrical power consumption, or to the level of telephone equipment and

to the development stage of information industries. Furthermore, electrical consumption per capita is correlated to the Gross National Product per capita. The level of development of phone services is also correlated to the GNP per capita. So it is not at all surprising that our markets are in industrialized countries.

In the chocolate and sugar confectionery industry climate combines with the standard of living to determine consumption patterns. For instance there are significant differences between 'rich' Asian countries (such as Japan) and developing countries.

> When it comes to developing countries of Asia, the climate, hot and humid, and the low income drive demand towards basic product categories. This reflects the standard of living. On the other hand when the climatic conditions are good and the standard of living is high you find a different competitive environment.

The main difference between Western and Eastern Europe is purchasing power: the Russians and the Ukrainians would love to turn to Western quality confectionery products but the mass of consumers cannot afford these yet. Thus the map of the confectionery industry is predicted to change as higher standards of living obtain in developing countries.

> In East Asia the market will grow with the growth of per capita GNP. This is also true for China. In these countries we are working from scratch. Can you imagine what will happen when the per capita consumption goes from below 1 kilogram up to 2 kilograms!

Paint consumption is also related to GNP, and the differences in consumption levels between rich and poor countries determine the type of competition.

> I think there are two broad zones. First the so-called developed countries where big international paint companies meet; there they pretty much run things. On the other hand there are all the countries that are not considered as developed; these markets are open doors for all opportunists. There, small and medium-sized businesses run their own risks. . . . Sometimes they succeed, sometimes they fail, and sometimes they have very nice surprises.

Political, economic and cultural influences

Political, economic and cultural influences sometimes correspond to administered trade blocs, but not necessarily. An example of one such influence is the preference given to national suppliers, a factor which was described as potentially important in the cable industry.

> [In Germany] There are strong ties between customers and local manufacturers. [. . .] Why should customers start buying cables abroad.
> It is the same all over the world; countries obviously favour suppliers who work in their area and speak the same language. [. . .] Now we are becoming Europeans, so one day there should be a European market. . . . But it will take time. . . . Moreover we do not speak the same language! [laughter]

Political, economic and cultural influences are often 'inherited', for example as part of the legacy of old colonial empires. Such influences were observed to have an impact on some players in the paint and confectionery industries:

> Regions depend on historical influence. France has traditionally been in Africa [. . .] in the former colonial territories: French-speaking Africa, Indochina. . . . That is where we do good business. We have never been interested in Nigeria for instance, which is under British influence, although it is in the middle of a French-speaking region.
> Cadbury is very English, they are strong in the Far East and in the old English colonies. [. . .] And the taste there is the Cadbury's taste.

Competitive territories are also delineated by cultural proximity. Decision-makers tend to direct the early stages of international expansion towards countries with similar cultures; for instance from Sweden to other Scandinavian countries and to Finland, from there to the other countries around the Baltic Sea.

Generally speaking, geographical proximity and the combination of political, economic and cultural influences reinforce the regional segmentation of industries, as the following observations about the paint industry illustrate:

> In South America and in Mexico the vast majority of paint manufacturers work under a licensing agreement with an American company. French-speaking Africa works with French licensing agreements and French assistance. English-speaking Africa is under English influence. And in Asia, obviously, you find a lot of people who are working under a Japanese licensing agreement. They do not especially like the Japanese but in this region Japan is the most advanced in terms of technology.

To some extent customers' preferences are also rooted in history.

Customer preferences

In the chocolate industry each region is characterized by specific tastes and consumers' preferences:

> It is impossible to sell the American, Hershey-type chocolate in Europe, because of its flavour, its intrinsic quality. The reverse is also true as far as the mass market is concerned. Of course there are exceptions, for instance Mars bars came to Europe and Godiva chocolates found a market in the USA. But the bulk of the market is dedicated to specific regional taste.
>
> There are three distinct tastes internationally in the Western world. In Britain it is represented by Cadbury, in America it is represented by Hershey, and on the continent it is represented by Suchard and Lindt. And the three types of chocolate have completely different tastes. Those result partly from the fact that the beans come from different parts of the world. The British have always bought their beans from Ghana, because it used to be a British colony. On the continent they used to buy their beans from the Ivory Coast. So that in itself gives a different flavour, and so does the processing method. . . . For instance Cadburys developed the milk crumb method. [. . .] Some companies have lost millions trying to sell one type of chocolate in other markets. [. . .] Once you are hooked on a particular chocolate taste you just do not change. [. . .] KitKat made on the continent is made from a different chocolate than KitKat made in the UK. There is a recognition by Rowntree, now part of the Nestlé group, that, since KitKat is 70 per cent chocolate and 30 per cent biscuit, they had to adapt the chocolate in order to succeed, even in the countline market.

When one considers differences in consumers' tastes, broad regions are not homogeneous (see Chapter 3). For instance within continental Europe there is a Scandinavian taste, a German-Swiss taste, a French-Belgium taste, etc. However, fracture lines are even deeper between continents. This is because of different traditions and because strong local chocolate manufacturers have imposed their taste, generation after generation. The existence of such chocolate traditions is perpetuated, in part, by the fact that it is very expensive to establish a brand in the chocolate industry:

> A strong brand is an asset and we cannot change the market. If you put Milka in the place of Côte d'Or in Belgium it will not sell.

Regional preferences are also significant in decorative paint, where they affect choices of colours, the use made of particular products, the emphasis placed upon environmental protection, and the availability of environmentally friendly products.

> In Asia they like the pastels, very few bright tints [are offered, whereas] in Africa bright colours, bright reds and blues are preferred. In Asia they

> import the paint base and they add pigments. They are not yet familiar with rollers, they apply the paint with a brush, or whatever, these thingumajigs made of raffia. It is difficult to change these habits. [. . .] Here in Europe we still use brushes; in the US it is all rollers. You have to make adaptations if you want to sell your products across borders.

There is not yet any global brand in decorative paint, and international competitors hesitate to kill the local brands when they take over foreign firms. Thus they cannot fully exploit economies of scale in manufacturing and in marketing. They manage a portfolio of diverse products and brands, some of which have the potential to become regional or global.

Overall there is some evidence of convergence in customers' preferences across borders, but it is very slow to obtain, and seems better described as the *coexistence* of national products and global products in the same market, than as the homogenization of customer preferences and products.

> There is a breaking down of barriers between nations as people travel more and become more cosmopolitan. The barriers between Cadbury in the UK, continental chocolates, and Hershey chocolate in America will, at the margin, break down. But it is not going to be a fundamental breakdown. We are not all going to suddenly develop a taste for Suchard chocolate in this country [the UK] overnight; it will be gradual, in the same way as 30 years ago you would never have believed there would be a Tandoori in most high streets. And even today Indian food is still only a very small fraction of what we eat, but there is absolutely nothing wrong with being a small fraction and I think we might see a similar trend in chocolate.

International scope and organization of major players

In the industries of cables, confectionery and paint, a few leading competitors exploit structural forces or change them and shape competitive territories.

In the *cable industry* European leaders (Alcatel, BICC, Pirelli) took over a number of American firms and restructured the American cable industry. In Europe Alcatel took over foreign businesses (in Germany, Spain, etc.) and contributed to the formation of a European region before the advent of privatization and harmonization, when they rationalized manufacturing and logistics across borders, in order to achieve synergies.

In the *chocolate industry* regions or sub-regions are dominated by strong regional players who tend to maintain fracture lines: for instance Hershey and Mars in North America, Fazer in the Nordic countries, Japanese firms in Japan. They dissuade foreigners from penetrating their markets.

> To go into the US chocolate market would be a mistake. [. . .] It would automatically fail because starting from scratch or from a very low position, fighting two companies each of whom has 40 per cent share is a nigh on impossible task in a well developed market.
>
> Brands have a big impact. [. . .] Scandinavian companies have strong positions in [their home] countries because [they] have brand leadership. [. . .] It is hard for example for American and British companies to break into [their] markets.
>
> We are growing where there is no effective local production, for instance in the Eastern European countries. We sell to Singapore, Taiwan, Hong Kong, South Korea but consumption is limited. We do not go to South America, it is kind of like a wildlife reserve for the North Americans. They also buy a lot of cocoa beans from them for their own production; it is perhaps for this reason as well.

The most effective way to break into other regions dominated by regional brands is via takeovers. This is how Philip Morris-Kraft managed to become one of the European leaders when it took over Jacobs-Suchard, and how Nestlé expanded in Anglo-Saxon countries and in the countline business when it took over Rowntree in the UK. Such strategies remove regional boundaries although they do not necessarily upset the map of competitive territories.

> Take the three main actors, Jacobs Suchard, Nestlé and Mars: these are worldwide groups, but they compete in a rather different manner on the continental level. [. . .] That is linked to the history of each company and to geographical footholds that have been reinforced through acquisitions. Companies give a priority to one continent over another, then they develop themselves in this business area. So it is a question of setting up in a geographic zone that is critical rather than a question of global product range.

Moreover, international leaders tend to have dual brand strategies that preserve some regional brands alongside a few more 'global' products.

> Here in Spain Cadbury bought Hueso, Jacobs Suchard bought El Almendro. [. . .] Generally they keep these brands in their portfolio but they also introduce their international umbrella brand.
>
> We have a certain number of global brands; the advantage is the economical and technological synergies, the transfer of know-how from one continent to another. It is normal *both* to favour the habits of a given continent and to offer regional products, and then have a certain number of products that can cross all the continents. We have both.

In 1995 four companies covered almost 40 per cent of the world chocolate production; it is expected that they will cover 49 per cent of world production in the year 2000.

> Mars and Ferrero are the most global in their approach; both are focused on countlines, which they turned into a global segment. Nestlé is stronger in chocolate *tablettes*; they are particularly strong in Europe but they also have significant positions in other continents. Kraft Jacobs Suchard is more regional; they started in Europe with very different products from one country to another. [. . .] Anyway, now they all push for the development of their umbrella brands across borders.

When international leaders expand the geographic scope of their international activities and develop their umbrella brands, they effectively form new regions and merge competitive territories. For instance the three sub-regions in the European chocolate industry will probably form a single broad territory in the future.

> In Eastern Europe, including Russia, the restructuring is going strong. All the international groups are going to these countries, either buying companies or building plants. [. . .] You could say that these countries are going to become like any Western countries in the future, at least as far as competition is concerned: all the big international players are [already] there.

Similarly, in the *paint industry* successive mergers and acquisitions turned the multidomestic structure of the European industry into a Europe-wide region. The consolidation process was led by three groups: Akzo Nobel, ICI and Total. Other major competitors followed this trend and also achieved regional integration.

In the wood-treatment product segment (lasures), the Danish firm Dyrup progressively created a European business. Local competitors, such as V33 in France, followed this trend and expanded across borders. The industrial coating segment was characterized by the same evolution.

> [The first business area] covers Denmark, Sweden, Norway and Finland, plus some export to the East. Then we have England: that covers England, Germany, Switzerland, Austria and also Hungary. The canvassing in Eastern Europe is shared between Germany and us. The French Area business manager has got France, Belgium and Spain. So we cover all of Western Europe and we have a foothold in the East.

Clearly international players define and redefine the scope of competitive territories. Simultaneously they often adopt a regional or sub-regional organization that fits with existing regions and fracture lines.

> Europe is our base. [. . .] The European region is then divided into two business areas. One that we call North and one that we call South. Then we have a country-based organization.

When international leaders change their organizations in order to exploit synergies and increase the share of international brands, for instance by creating Europe-wide or worldwide business lines, they certainly contribute to the redefinition of fracture lines and to drawing new maps of competitive territories.

To sum up, the analysis suggests that the regional dynamics of competition result from a combination of structural forces and competitive actions. Product-market segments which do not lie at the extremes of the global–local framework are regional in nature as a result of the interplay of seven forces which define the fracture lines that delineate competitive territories. Regional segmentations appear to be industry-specific. Each industry is also characterized by a specific *configuration* of forces shaping competitive territories. More precisely, some forces are common to cables, paint and confectionery (e.g. the distribution of knowledge in the three zones of the Triad, the level of economic development, cultural influences, competitive actions) while other forces are specific to some industries, (e.g. logistics, trade and investment barriers, and customers' preferences). Logistics shape competitive territories in cables and paint, trade and investment barriers shape competitive territories in cables (and to a lesser degree in decorative paint), and customers' preferences shape competitive territories in the chocolate and sugar confectionery industry (and to a lesser degree in the paint industry).

The next chapter further explores the structural forces that drive local or regional responsiveness.

From practice to theory: a summary

On the one hand the global–local dialectics has highlighted conflicts between forces; on the other hand it has concentrated attention on the extremes (pure global and pure local) and blurred the fact that, in many industries, the bulk of competition is organized by regions separated by fracture lines. Each region is characterized by a specific set of demand factors and/or a specific set of supply factors. Regions are generally composed of a set of countries that share similar competitive characteristics and international companies tend to organize their operations by regions or at least to adapt their market strategies to each region. When global business lines are set up, regional coordination and differentiation are attenuated but still exist. So the recognition of regional competition has very practical consequences for international businesses, not only when distinguishing familiar from unfamiliar territory when venturing abroad, but also when organizing international operations.

Regions can hardly be defined a priori, and their identification requires some experience and knowledge of the industry. For instance one needs some experience to find out that in the decorative paint industry Northern Europe and Southern Europe are two different regions that require different strategies. As far as chocolate *tablettes* are concerned Europe should be divided into three regions: North continental, South continental and the United Kingdom (together with a few Commonwealth countries). As far as car finishes are concerned Europe is a single region, not so different from North America and Japan. *Each industry or product-market segment is characterized by a specific configuration of regions.*

It is important for both researchers and practitioners to identify the forces which underly the formation of regions and delineate fracture lines. The empirical study suggests that the effects of six structural forces may combine to shape regions: their interactions were summarized in Figure 2.1 (p. 53). The availability of know-how in diverse geographical locations and logistical opportunities (and constraints) are considered as basic conditions. The level of economic development and growth, the structure of trade barriers (or the existence of free-trade zones), differences in customers' preferences, and cultural influences further deepen fracture lines. These structural forces create opportunities and constraints for firms to deploy their international strategies. In turn, firms' strategies (the seventh force) the perimeter of their international operations and their international organization delineate regions and bring about changes in the map and in the set of structural forces. A careful assessment of the above seven factors is particularly useful when one takes a dynamic perspective and tries to anticipate the evolution of competitive territories. Future regional market strategies and the future organization of international operations depend on them.

The regional structure of competition is particularly marked in 'mixed' industries, on which our empirical study was focused. We suggest that it is a fundamental characteristic of such industries. However, we also suggest that there are attenuated forms of regional competition within 'global' industries and within 'local' (or multidomestic) industries. In other words, there are no *pure* global industries and no *pure* multidomestic industries. Indeed recognizing a level of regional competition can be a source of competitive advantage for international companies. After correcting strategic presbyopia one sees regions in a 'global' industry and opportunities to differentiate from global competitors. After correcting strategic myopia one sees regions in a 'multidomestic' industry and opportunities to exploit economies of scope across countries.

Note

1. Analysis of regional competitive territories in the footwear industry (mass market street shoes) is not included in this chapter, because it is complicated by the split between manufacturing and the rest of value chain activities. There are two different maps of the footwear industry: the map of manufacturing activities and the map of marketing activities.

Bibliography

The literature on international strategy does not emphasize the regional character of international competition. There are some exceptions, particularly contributions on the regional structure of multinational corporations (MNCs): Sabel ('Flexible specialization and the re-emergence of regional economies', 1989), Morrison et al. ('Globalization versus regionalization: Which way for the multinational?', 1991), Aoki and Tachiki ('Overseas Japanese business operations: The emerging role of regional headquarters', 1992), Daniels ('Bridging national and global marketing strategies through regional operations', 1997). Reasons given for preferring regional over global organization are economic (limits to economies of scale), geopolitical (regional political boundaries), strategic (cross-regional differences of markets and employees), as well as organizational (the need to protect subsidiary initiatives). Recognition of the regional dimension of business does not necessarily imply the growth of regional headquarters; cost-cutting and communication technologies make management by (regional) council possible (Egelhoff and Gates, 1994). Regional structures are sometimes seen as a transitional form, from decentralized to network-based MNCs (Malnight, 1996).

Research in international business could learn a lot from economic geographers and international political economists (Dunning, 1998). In their introduction to the symposium organized by the *Journal of International Business Studies* in 1997, Guisinger and Brewer (1998: 3) suggest that the traditional economic debate, North–South/East–West, is evolving towards the analysis of 'multiple and overlapping international regions'. Other contributors emphasize the effect of the distribution of technological knowledge (Ostry, 1998, after Anand and Kogut, 1997, and Porter, 1990), the influence of public policies (Rugman and Verbeke, 1998), and the effect of economic development (Wells, 1998), on the scope and intensity of international competition.

Makhija, Kim and Williamson (1997) provide a measure of industry globalization (using a national industry approach) that can be adapted and adopted for the delineation of international competitive territories.

3

Structural Forces Driving Local Responsiveness

Roland Calori, Manuela De Carlo, Egbert Kahle, Leif Melin and Juan José Renau

The international dynamics of industries is best described as a field of force. On the one hand structural forces, for instance technological intensity or cross-national differences in customers' behaviour, create a potential for competitive actions. On the other hand competitive actions, for instance mergers and acquisitions or global advertising strategies, shape a new set of structural forces. Interactions between structural forces and competitive actions are the core of the international dynamics of industries. The strategy literature (Bartlett, 1986; Prahalad and Doz, 1987; Bartlett and Ghoshal, 1989, among others) considers two categories of force: forces that drive global integration and forces that drive local responsiveness. The two sets are combined in an open dialectical movement. In our study, the majority of managers adopted the global integration/local responsiveness framework at some point in the discussion; however, many of them made further distinctions. For instance they made a difference between 'forces that drive local responsiveness' and 'forces that restrain international development'.

Cross-national differences in customers' behaviour require product adaptations and specific local marketing: they create a need for 'local responsiveness', whereas high transportation costs (relative to the added value of the product), high tariff barriers or quotas limiting imports 'restrain the international development' of an industry.

A firm may not respond in the same way to the two categories of structural determinant. For instance, when a foreign market is attractive enough, foreign direct investment in manufacturing may resolve problems such as transportation costs or tariff barriers, whereas the need to adapt products and marketing to local demand may require learning and development efforts, not necessarily a dispersion of manufacturing activities. This chapter analyses the structural forces that drive local responsiveness or restrain international expansion (see Figure I.2, p. 12; the other categories of forces will be reviewed in Chapters 4 and 5).

Managers identify three categories of structural forces that drive firms to be locally responsive or hinder international development:

- the need for geographical proximity of suppliers and clients;
- barriers to international trade and/or to foreign direct investment;
- cross-national differences (in distribution systems, consumption patterns or work behaviour).

The need for geographical proximity depends on transportation cost relative to the added value of the product: high transportation cost restrains international *trade*. It forces firms to set up local production units in order to be competitive. In this case international competitors do not enjoy any significant advantage over national players: firms have to be located close to consumption areas and reach a critical size. Transportation cost is an impediment to international trade when products have a low added value, a heavy weight (relatively to added value), or a large volume (relatively to added value). For instance mass market beer, cement, and plastic packaging fall into these categories. When competitors want to expand their international scope, they may take over local production units that are close to customers. So transportation cost is not an impediment to foreign direct investment when a given market is attractive enough to set up local operations that can reach a critical size.

Geographical proximity of suppliers and clients is a success factor when services are an important part of the business. This is particularly true when cycle times have to be reduced: just-in-time delivery or quick after-sales services, when the added value of services is not high enough to pay for quick transportation, and when services require face-to-face interaction (as opposed to electronic communication). In these situations, international competitors have to set up local units to deliver services, and they do not enjoy a significant competitive advantage over national players of a similar local size.

Barriers to international development or protectionism take several forms. First, national governments and/or regional authorities that organize trade blocs may raise barriers to international trade: tariff barriers, quotas limiting imports, policies fixing the amount of local content in foreign transplants, and various industrial policies that control mergers and acquisitions or define industrial priorities. Barriers to trade are sometimes combined with governmental policies for attracting foreign direct investment, especially when the local market is attractive (for instance in China or in India). Thus it is important to distinguish trade flows from investment flows when analysing the international development of industries. Second, local protectionism may take the form of preference given to national businesses and products. There are signs of chauvinism in consumer behaviour: for instance German consumers have the reputation of preferring German beer and German cars (cynics may argue that they are not the only ones). In public procurement, national competitors may be preferred to foreigners: the French public sector is known for such a bias. Third, protectionism is often hidden behind specific local regulations and norms that limit the entry of foreign products which do not comply with these norms. The diversity of technical norms limits the potential for standardization and scale economies, therefore it is a barrier to international trade flows. However, production under foreign norms may develop when a foreign market is attractive enough.

Differences in customers' behaviour and distribution channels across countries drive firms to be locally responsive.

High international diversity in customers' behaviour may require particular products or product adaptations, packaging adaptations and different pricing strategies. Such variety limits the potential of scale/scope economies, and international players do not enjoy any competitive advantage over national players who tailor their products to local demand. For instance in the pork processing industry, French *boudin noir*, German *Bratwürst*, Spanish *chorizo*, Finnish *makkara* and Scottish *haggis* coexist within the European Union. Small quantities of these products cross borders to please a small upmarket segment of international gourmets. Some products such as Italian *salami* have reached international status, but the mass market still looks like a mosaic of diverse national consumption patterns.

When distribution and sales represent a significant percentage of the product added value (high marketing intensity), foreign competitors who enter a market have to set up local distribution in order to compete with national players. When local distribution channels are tied to local manufacturers, foreigners may have difficulty in accessing the market. This is the case in the brewing industry where wholesalers and retailers are often tied to brewers. As it can be very costly to create a new distribution channel from scratch, new entrants may prefer to take over local firms. When the structure of distribution is very different from one country to another, international competitors have to learn new rules in every new country: diversity drives local responsiveness. When combined, distribution and sales intensity and diversity protect local competitors from foreign intrusion. However, when the market is attractive enough it may not protect them from takeovers.

Finally there are international differences in the way businesses are managed, different work-related values and management styles across borders. International firms may find it difficult to adapt

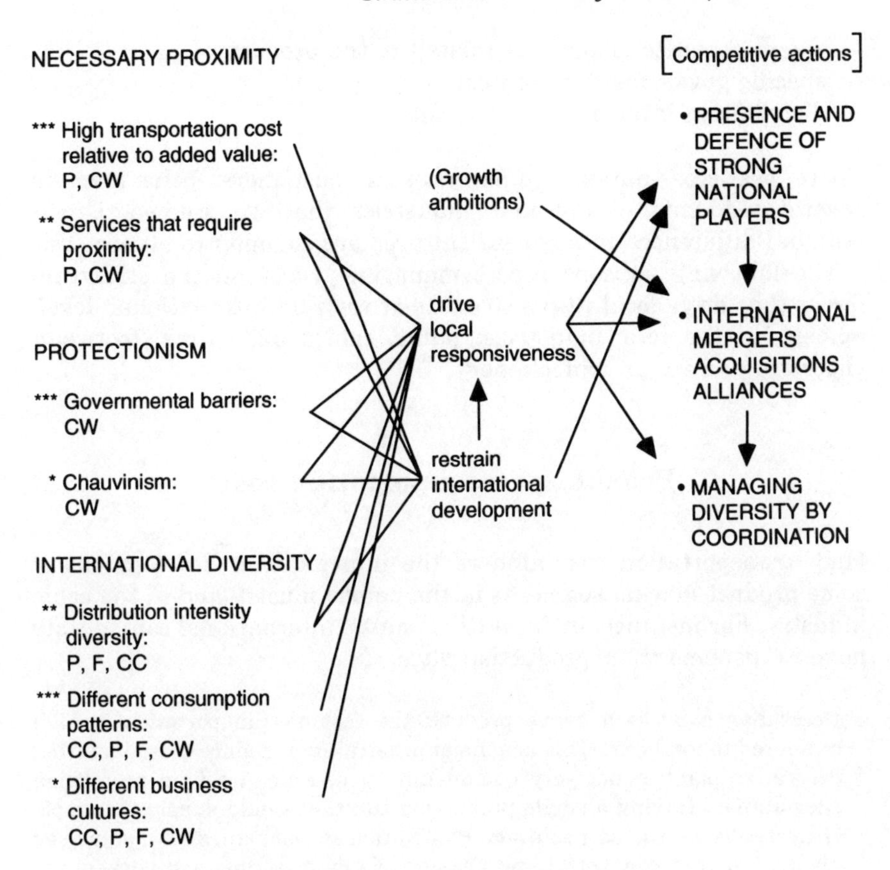

Figure 3.1 *Structural forces driving local responsiveness and/or restraining international development*

their management practices to 'cold' countries (those with a radically different business culture) and limit their expansion to 'warm' countries (similar to the home country business culture). Thus differences in business cultures may restrain international development or force firms to adapt their management style to local practices.

Figure 3.1 summarizes the combination of structural forces that may drive local responsiveness or restrain international development. Most of these forces are specific to certain industries, or product-market segments; they depend on four parameters which are inherent in the product:

– the added value of the product;

- the importance of services related to the product;
- specific governmental policies;
- distribution intensity and diversity.

There are cross-national differences in customers' behaviour, in several segments of the four industries that we studied. Cross-national differences in business cultures are common to all sectors.

The following sections report managers' views on the structural forces that drive local responsiveness or restrain international development in the four industries: paint, cables and wires, footwear, chocolate and sugar confectionery.

Proximity: transportation cost

High transportation cost hinders the international development of some product-market segments in the paint industry and in the cable industry. For instance, in decorative paints, international competitors have to disperse their production sites:

> Decorative paint is a heavy product; the cost of transportation is high compared to total cost. This is a major constraint, and since manufacturing decorative paint is not very capital intensive, we can set up production sites abroad. Having a single production site that would supply the whole of Europe is not the best solution. Pan-European companies have dispersed plants, but they concentrate purchasing of raw materials and packaging.

International competitors do not benefit from economies of scope in manufacturing when factories can only deliver within a limited geographical area; the scope depends on the weight and the added value of the product. Manufacturing units are competitive when they reach a (minimum) critical size within a given geographical area.

> In our decorative business the picture is mostly regional, because it tends to be specific to markets and the added value is not great enough to justify moving it a long way, whereas for high concentration colours, our basics, we make them in the UK and sell them in Outer Mongolia – it can travel as far as that.

Building wires and low voltage power cables 'do not travel very well': they are too heavy and too simple to be transported far away.

> Building wires are standardized products for which the cost of manufacturing is a key success factor. Since those are metal cables, essentially copper, they are heavy and transportation cost becomes a barrier to globalization. The market will rather be regional – for instance European.

> Moreover there are local norms that sometimes limit production to local markets.
>
> Cable is heavy. It will not get lighter. Copper will always be heavy. So we try to produce cables where electricity is produced and consumed. There, everyone knows how to produce copper cables, and local factories are set up. For instance today, China and India are getting equipped with a cable industry, they have no reason to buy their cable elsewhere.

These examples reveal several parameters which determine the logistical forces that may restrain international development. Logistical barriers limit the amount of international trade (import–export) and explain the dispersion of manufacturing units within international firms. Local players can compete as long as their manufacturing units have reached a critical size and their domestic market is attractive enough.

Proximity: services

When short delivery times are a source of competitive advantage, suppliers try to locate themselves close to customers. This is particularly important in business-to-business activities such as car finishes, varnishes for furnitures, and cables. Moreover geographical proximity helps in developing services around the product: product adaptations, quick after-sales services, technical support, etc.

Car manufacturers want to share risks with their suppliers of car finishes: they want just-in-time delivery systems and joint development of new products. Consequently suppliers have to disperse some elements of their value chain in the different geographical locations where their customers are based. However, in the case of car finishes other forces driving global integration are so strong that local competitors cannot survive.

> Varnishes for furnitures require compliance with detailed specifications defined by the customer. We do not work with catalogues. The specifications often have to be modified; adaptation is very complex. Moreover there is an increasing need to produce in small quantities, orders come just in time. As far as logistics is concerned it is impossible to resolve this equation when the supplier is based thousands of kilometres away. Then you have to start production abroad. Finally you need to be close to customers for transferring the technology, in order to produce good quality consistently.

The relationship between a supplier and a client can be seen as a long term investment; there may be significant switching costs that protect local suppliers from foreign intrusions.

> The customer is extremely conservative. There are strong ties between customers and local manufacturers. I will not say a single manufacturer, but Germany has about ten capable and qualified manufacturers of cables. They have good relations with their customers. Why should customers start buying cables from Sweden? They want close access to expertise, help, and quick deliveries.

International suppliers adopt dispersed configurations in order to manage relationships with customers and deliver good service. In this case international players do not enjoy a significant advantage over local players. However, there is an exception: when the customer is an international firm, international suppliers will be preferred, as they can provide a consistent level of quality across borders.

Protectionism

Protectionism is significant in the cable industry, concerning medium to high voltage power cables and telecommunication cables. This is because several customers are public utilities still in a monopoly position in some countries.

> Concerning high voltage cables, until now there have been national preferences in buying behaviour. Clients used to buy national products. The EDF (Electricité de France, French utility) buys French cables that can hardly be exported, except in certain regions where the EDF has an adviser role. But in general these products remain within the national territory. It is the same in most countries.

Public utilities prefer national players.

> We sell power cables to Deutsche Telecom. The only reason we are able to sell it is because they want to buy from a German supplier; otherwise we are not so competitive on these products.
>
> Japan is a very protected market, you cannot go in there, it is impossible to sell anything from Europe to Japan. The local protection comes from the government, the industry and all the lobbying. It is also impossible to sell cables in France, or in Germany.

Protectionism is supposed to preserve local jobs and national independence in sectors considered strategic: energy, communication, defence and so on. In this context, cable manufacturers with international ambitions had to take over local players. This was the strategy of Alcatel, for instance. Since 1996 government intervention has been reduced and deregulation has been taking place within the European Union. Some power utilities and telecom carriers have started to implement international strategies. Protectionism is decreasing but some managers believe that it will take a long time to upset the comfortable status quo among European countries.

Tariff barriers still limit international development across trade blocs, particularly toward developing countries that are trying to preserve their emerging industries. This was the case 20 years ago when the Spanish market was protected by high customs duties in the four industries in this study. For instance in the cable industry high tariff barriers maintained high prices and profits for local manufacturers of enamelled wires. These manufacturers were progressively confronted with foreign competition until customs duties were abolished. Nowadays the Spanish enamelled wires industry is strong enough to export to France and Germany.

National norms raise barriers to international trade in the cable industry.

> Specifications and norms made the market quite local. There is a driving force in the cable industry to minimize international competition; there is no real wish to change the specifications.

There is some risk involved with products like power cables, so security systems and norms had to be developed. It was tempting for domestic cable manufacturers to influence normalization so as to keep foreign competitors out of the country.

> The different standards differentiate between five zones: Europe, the Middle East, the Far East, North America, and South America. If you want to export to the USA you will have to conform with 'UL' standards. UL is the American equivalent of 'UTE' in France: it is the agency that certifies cabling. You will have 'CSA' for Canada, 'VDE' for continental Europe, 'BS' [British Standard] for England. Central Europe is dominated by German standards, and in Asia you will find a mix of UL, CSA and VDE. These differences can be seen as protectionistic, they do hinder standardization at the manufacturing level. [. . .] Nowadays the general trend is towards European standards.

Harmonization is slowly gaining ground within Europe:

> Nothing much happened on 1 January 1993, but there is slow harmonization anyway. Harmonization was first enforced by the electrical appliances industry. It came from international customers; now for instance harmonization is achieved for rubber cables. Today one has few synergies as a manufacturer of low voltage wire in several countries. Standardization moves slowly, but it is coming. In the far future we will of course get international norms and an internationalization of the market.

The creation of the European Union encouraged standardization. The companies who once supported different specifications are coming to accept international standards defined by the International Electrotechnical Committee. Indeed competitors who have extended their activities worldwide (Alcatel, Pirelli, etc.) want to get rid of the barriers. As a consequence there will be more concentration: small cable manufacturers will have a hard time competing with the big ones, who will enjoy scale and scope economies.

Distribution intensity and diversity

Distribution and sales typically are local activities. When distribution costs represent a high percentage of total cost, international competitors are no better placed than local players. This is the case in decorative paint.

> The key to success is distribution, it is not manufacturing. [. . .] Large paint manufacturers will have to acquire distribution networks in order to improve their positions. In Germany manufacturers convey orders to distributors who take care of delivery. German distributors are more like depots. In France distributors have a broader commercial role and a greater impact. In Italy distribution is fragmented. Future Pan-European paint manufacturers will have to handle this diversity and organize an effective distribution system.

Access to distribution channels is also a key success factor in fashion businesses such as footwear.

> We live in a very fast market, driven by fashion. Retailers and consumers want their shoes within a few days, so you need to be close to the distribution network.
>
> Women's footwear goes with the fashion. Fashion gives an opportunity to manufacturers who can serve the market quicker because they are better placed. When you are in the market, or close to it, you can react to demands very quickly, in four to five weeks.

In the footwear industry local manufacturers often rely upon a franchised retail network. For instance the French manufacturer Eram sold through franchises and wholly owned retail shops, both in France and in foreign markets (Belgium and Germany). As far as 'street shoes' are concerned, access to distribution channels is a barrier to foreign competition. This is not true for the low end of the market that can be accessed through discounters and for branded sport-leisure footwear that is sold in retail chains.

Japan is noted as a market difficult to enter because of its complicated distribution system:

> When we started to do business in Japan, ten years ago, we realized that the distribution system was a nightmare. Our French shoes would be sold to an importer, who would sell to a wholesaler, who would sell to a semi-wholesaler, who would sell to a shopkeeper. We would never make it to the consumer. So we tried hard to bypass the system and work directly with a few large department stores. We succeeded because our products are exclusive and because we agreed to provide local services: merchandising, price tagging, taking-back unsold articles, etc.
>
> In the end entry barriers are measured by the time it takes to penetrate a foreign market. It takes us about five years on average, but in Japan it took eight years. (Chocolate and sugar confectionery)

The diversity of distribution systems further complicates the task of international competitors. For instance in France non-specialized discount hypermarkets coexist with specialized footwear discounters and with specialized retail chains of smaller stores. For each channel there are different product lines, different brands, different pricing and different people. High international diversity preserves local competitors. There can be dramatic differences between two neighbouring countries such as France and Italy: both are Latin countries at similar stages of economic development but they have completely different distribution systems: 'France is in the post-supermarket era whereas Italy is in a pre-supermarket era.'

International diversity of distribution systems drives local responsiveness in the footwear industry and in the chocolate industry.

> Italy has a specific distribution structure for footwear, with specific opportunities and constraints. In Italy you will find a luxury shop in every small town. When you manufacture upmarket products like ours you need to be present in more than 300 sales outlets through Italy, whereas in Germany you can cover the whole market with less than 90 sales points.
>
> Distribution issues are quite different from country to country. In France large retail chains such as Carrefour and Promodes dominate distribution; in Italy distribution goes through small retailers; in Germany, in Belgium and in Holland you find medium-sized retailers and hard-discounters; in Spain there were only small retail stores until the recent development of French superstores. (Chocolate and sugar confectionery)

Even the most global manufacturers have to set up local distribution units and learn new rules of the game every time they cross a border. In the chocolate industry, a global player like Mars has commercial subsidiaries in many countries (usually called 'Masterfood') and they have to adapt their distribution strategy to the particular system in each country.

To some extent the diversity of distribution systems is related to the diversity of consumption patterns, a major force driving local responsiveness in mixed industries.

Diverse consumption patterns

Customers' preference and behaviour differ from one country to another in many segments of the four industries in this study.

In the *cable industry*, in the late 1990s there were still differences in standards between the three zones of the Triad, even with relatively new products such as mobile phones. Differences between countries may stem from different climates and environmental conditions. For instance, the Scandinavian market requires PVC cables that withstand a temperature down to minus 50 degrees Celsius.

> Regions differ from one another in the type of installation required. In the Middle East for instance (big cities surrounded by deserts) power is used within a small area and it is transported mainly by high voltage cables. In Africa you find high voltage power lines and for telecommunications radio links and satellites are preferred to cables. In the USA there is a mix, in Europe cables predominate over radio links due to frequency saturation. As multi-media systems develop and broadband ISDN [Integrated System Digital Network] becomes more widespread, more and more fibre optic cables will be needed.

The level of technological development may also vary dramatically across countries (even across industrialized countries). Therefore competitive rules turn out to be radically different.

> The US cable industry is far more competitive than we are: their average prices are normally half of those paid in Europe. Also the Americans are constructing information superhighways. Information superhighways make it possible for everyone to receive the whole world of multi-media in their homes: cable television, data transmission pictures on videotelephones. The majority of American homes are equipped with personal computers connected to a variety of databases. For the Americans cable television is a reality. We are far from that in Italy and in other European countries. [. . .] Telephone services cost much less in the US than in Europe. The Americans decided long ago to work on a large scale and here is the result: when you pay ten for a cable in Italy, you pay three for it in America.

Germans believe that German customers are the most sophisticated and stimulate manufacturers' high quality strategies.

> The Americans do not look for sophisticated products. If you drive through America, you see wires nailed in the walls everywhere. You will never see that in Germany: we aim at superior quality whereas the Americans are more sensitive to price.

With enamelled wires, the Americans (and the Japanese) use average enamel quality with layered insulation whereas 'the Germans prefer better enamel quality, higher thermic resistance and chemical resistance to solvents'. It sounds as if the German technical bias is still strong.

In the *paint industry*, particularly in decorative paint, different climatic conditions also shape diverse customers' preferences.

> In Northern Europe people are much more interested in lasures than in varnishes. Varnishes come off in layers when they deteriorate and to renovate a house you have to sand the walls entirely. On the other hand lasures protect the wood from funguses in humid countries, they deteriorate slowly and when you renovate the wall you just put another layer on.

Climatic conditions relate to types of housing and cultural backgrounds.

> In Nordic countries we have a lot of wooden houses, while in the South they more often use plaster or bricks. That means different requirements for the colours and types of paint. The climate as well – in Southern Europe sunshine and ultraviolet rays dry paint very quickly. That means different requirements compared to the Nordic countries.

The Nordics, the Anglo-Saxons and the French prefer matt varnishes with open pores, whereas in Germany, in the South of Europe, in South East Asia and in Latin America people prefer shiny varnishes with closed pores. Northern Europeans prefer water-based paints that protect the environment, whereas Southern Europeans are still happy with solvent-based products.

Professional painters have many habits:

> In France and in Holland painters want the paint to be well laid out, very smooth. For that you need a lacquer that dries slowly. In Spain they do not care about small imperfections, they want something that dries quickly. So if you come to Spain with products that were made for France, you will be wiped out of the market.

Different traditions often coexist within a country. For instance in Spain houses in the Basque country are painted white with red and green shutters, whereas in Ibiza white limestone and blue shutters are the norm.

Confronted with such international diversity in consumption patterns, international decorative paint manufacturers have to adapt their product range to each market. Only a few products become common denominators across borders. Diversity protects local manufacturers who can reach quality standards and local critical size and the ones who focus on local specialities (such as limestone).

In the other segments of the paint industry (car finishes, car refinishes, marine paint, industrial paint, coil coating, can coating, etc.) there is no such diversity. However, as for enamelled wires, German manufacturers point out a slight bias that characterizes American customers:

> I see differences concerning demands by the American motor industry in contrast to demands by the Japanese car manufacturers and the Europeans. They use somewhat different technologies. Roughly speaking the American motor industry does not ask for first class quality finishes. To some extent there has been some convergence during the last five years, but there are still some regional differences.

In the *footwear industry* everywhere in the world consumers want the same pair of Nike, Reebok, Adidas or Timberland shoes: these are perfectly global products. Also, when women buy luxury shoes they buy worldwide fashion. For the rest of the footwear industry there are slightly different consumption patterns across borders. The main difference is between North America and Europe. American consumers care about comfort above all: for instance the main American brands (priced above average) provide shoes in three widths (narrow, average and wide). European customers may have narrow, average or wide feet, but they have little choice when they buy their European shoes. But Europeans are more sensitive to fashion.

> In the USA manufacturers keep their models indefinitely, there is no fashion effect, because people 'don't give a damn' about their look and go around in jeans, with training shoes on their feet. They do not worry about fashion or renewal at all. Well, there is obviously a very Europeanized class of people who dress in Italian suits, who go to Europe, who are familiar with European products. And what you see in the stores in New York are the renowned European brands, which represent 'le chic', the absolute reference. But the bulk of US standard consumption deals with products which are not exportable.

Climatic conditions also determine consumption patterns. In Scandinavia people prefer shoes with rubber soles, whereas rubber soles are inadequate in the Middle East. Some managers point out significant differences within Europe. In Northern Europe consumers' behaviour is more utilitarian. In the South people care about fashion, stylish products, their 'look'. As the Italians say: they care about *bella figura*.

Differences start with children's footwear. German and Northern European consumers are interested in the quality–price ratio, they notice details and make sure the product does not contain chemicals that could be dangerous for the child's health, whereas in Italy what is important is the designer label.

Even when it does make sense to think about the global nature of some product-market segments it does not necessarily follow that a firm will employ a standard, uniform marketing mix in constructing their total product offer. In the case of sports shoes, consumers worldwide may be seeking the same 'core' solutions and benefits (e.g. comfort, style, status) when they contemplate purchasing a pair of cross-trainers. However, the anatomical differences in people across the globe mean that the products actually offered in the marketplace are likely to contain differences which, while they may be subtle or imperceptible to the consumer, are important to the manufacturer. For example managers report that, migration notwithstanding, groups of people with similar physiological characteristics still cluster within various nations or regions; morphology encourages managers to think in terms of selling to national or regional market segments.

> People have different feet in different continents: American feet are narrower and longer than European feet, which are shorter and wider. [. . .] That is to say, you absolutely cannot sell a shoe in the USA or in Japan that was manufactured on a German or European last [. . .] you have to make another last.

Geography is also important with respect to the development of promotional programmes. The languages spoken, the entertainments pursued, and the types of individuals likely to make good product spokespersons differ in significant ways. The global segments of the footwear industry also require adjustments to tactical aspects of the promotional programme.

In the *chocolate and sugar confectionery industry* consumers' tastes and behaviour are very different from one country to another.

First the average consumption per capita varies greatly from one country to another. It is very high in the UK as compared to Italy. Italians consume about 2 kilograms of chocolate a year as compared to an average of 7 kilograms per capita in Europe. Clearly chocolate consumption is much higher in countries with a cold climate than in countries with a hot climate like Australia and Asia. A hot climate combined with a low level of economic development predicts very low consumption.

American taste is very different from European taste.

American chocolate is a very special thing, and we Europeans all laugh about it. American kids grow up eating Hershey bars and they think that is chocolate. Clearly Europeans have a different taste.

It will not be so difficult to make Russians, Poles and others in the East realize that the chocolate that we deliver is better than what they tasted before. But I do not think we will ever convince the mass of the Americans. Chocolate does not taste the same in Europe and in America. They do not like our *tablettes* and we think their chocolate tastes awful. Such differences reduce our chance to sell global products.

European firms expanding in the US have to adapt their products to meet particular regulations, for instance chocolates filled with alcohol are forbidden and the formula has to be modified so that products have a longer shelf life.

Americans have a different perception of quality for a retail product. We went to America with what we thought was a very high class, a very nice tasting candy as they call it. But it did not sell. We had no recognition. Recognition is extremely important to the Americans and the packaging and the marketing of the product also. Our shops were spread all down the East Coast, and that gave us great problems with supervision, with delivery, and with quality control. The lawyers took us for a ride, the merchandisers took us for a ride, the marketing people took us for a ride. I think it is a very tough world and I think one needs to understand the scene very closely in order to succeed.

There is also great diversity across European countries.

International characteristics are often determined partly by taste, partly by legislation and partly by received custom. It has long been the custom in the United Kingdom, Ireland and Scandinavia to include in your chocolate coating something like 5 per cent of vegetable fat [cocoa butter equivalents]. This does have certain technical advantages and also economies can be made. This is not regarded as real chocolate in France and in Germany. British chocolate is regarded on the continent as being rather sweet. There is a bias in favour of the domestic product. I might even be able to undercut the domestic manufacturer, but there is a natural bias.

The countline is a very British thing. In the biggest chocolate market in Europe which is Germany, countlines are of no particular significance. Here in Britain boxes are very much gift giving and terribly seasonal. There is seasonality on the German market, but far less. Typically on a Saturday afternoon if you watch football in front of the TV and you are feeling a bit peckish, in Britain you will raid a multi-pack of KitKats. The average German consumer in similar circumstances will also go and raid their kitchen but he/she will get a box of chocolates and eat part of the box. Also in the UK we are great 'on the hoof' eaters. You will see people walking along eating Mars bars whereas on the continent consumption is far more in the home. I do not know what is the cause and what is the

> effect but in Britain roughly half of all countlines are sold in what are called CTNs [confectionery, tobacco and news agents]. A CTN does not really exist on the continent. You do get news vendors and they might sell a few confectionery lines but it is a tiny business.

Europe could be divided between the UK, the Swiss-Germanic image ('Alps, cows and milk'), the French-Belgian image ('maître chocolatier'), and Southern Europe. In the North people prefer sweet and chewy products whereas the Latins prefer bitter, lighter and crunchier chocolate. Dark bitter chocolate represents more than 40 per cent of French consumption; that is chocolate with high percentage of cocoa (at least 50 per cent). The British prefer a weak percentage of cocoa (about 20 per cent on average) and they like mints. The Germans love chocolates with marzipan fillings, the taste of milk and a white colour. Scandinavians add caramel to their chocolate to get a caramelized taste. The Spanish have many specialities that do not sell abroad, for instance chocolate *turrones* and *chocolate a la taza* (bitter melted chocolate for drinking). Traditions remain strong and education transmits specific tastes from one generation to the next.

Beyond taste differences, there are also different consumption behaviours:

> In Latin countries sugar confectionery is a reward, a gift; in Northern European countries it is often a complement to a meal. There is the notion of pleasure on one hand and utility on the other hand; depending on the country, the mix between these motivations is different.

Confronted with such market diversity international players tend to expand through *international mergers and acquisitions*. General Food adopted this strategy to form Kraft Jacobs Suchard, Nestlé acquired Rowntree to broaden its product range and take a significant share of the British market. After merging, the strongest national and regional brands are maintained and a few international brands are developed.

> We have brands that we advertise throughout Europe. Milka is one of them. Milka was a Central European brand: Austria, Switzerland, Germany. We expanded it to a European scope: expansion into France and Spain, market introduction in England. Suchard products are more regional – Switzerland and Austria – and many products are specific to a country.

Such dual brand strategies were also implemented in consumer (decorative) paints (for instance by ICI) and in footwear (for instance by Eram).

Smaller firms may adopt *an international niche strategy* and target a particular market segment in search of exoticism.

> Until the end of the 1970s we exported to the United States. During the war and just after the war there was a population shift from Central Europe to the United States. These people brought a little bit of their European tradition with them. When they arrived in the States they wanted to find products reminding them of the old country, nice candy boxes. The following generations forgot their roots and turned to American products. Then the Brazilians started up a sugar confectionery industry with their excess sugar cane, with second hand equipment bought from the Germans, and with West European technicians. With their low-cost production they killed us on the North American market.

The same company had success in Japan with its luxury candy boxes sold for Saint Valentine's Day. The celebration of Saint Valentine's Day came from the United States and invaded Japan.

> On St Valentine's Day girls buy presents for boys, and not only for their boyfriend: you can buy gifts for several boys if you like them. Chocolate and candies in small red boxes have a lot of success. When you receive a Valentine gift you have to respond. So, one month after, for the Break-Day [14 March] boys buy presents for girls. Department stores in Tokyo have entire floors selling gifts with nice ribbons and white packaging. The gift should be a bit more than what was received one month before, but it should not be much bigger so that the girls are not offended. For the Break-Day, chocolate and candies in small white boxes have a lot of success.

This is a particular case of globalization of customers' behaviour. The rules may change slightly when crossing borders. For instance one should remember that 'In France, Saint Valentine protects *lovers*: if you give presents to two Valentines one of them may slap you.'

The third strategy, *global brand advertising*, is costly but it can create a global niche in a multidomestic industry, as in the case of Chupa Chups' lollipops in the sugar confectionery industry.

> I think that if one has a good product one can succeed on a global basis like Coca-Cola or the Mars bar. You may well educate foreign people in what is a new taste to them. I think that has proved to be very possible. To succeed in doing that, one has to have a vast marketing budget and great marketing skills.

Sometimes marginal product adaptations are still needed to please local taste:

> The famous chocolate powder brand Nesquik looks the same everywhere, but it is not. There are different formulae depending on the country. In Italy Nestlé adds a significant quantity of milk powder, in Spain they do not.

As they travel more and more, consumers become more and more cosmopolitan. Central and Eastern European countries slowly come to adopt Western European consumption patterns and new products start to cross continents.

> There were no jelly candies in North America 15 years ago. European firms created a market there, they had big success for some years. But then the Americans started to build their own factories. Now the Asian market is discovering jelly candies, there are opportunities there for anyone who will solve a few problems: distance, heat and humidity.

Different business cultures

Managers sometimes mention the intangible barrier of business cultures – the difficulty of managing a foreign business in a radically different institutional and cultural business environment. Cultural differences sometimes create cultural clashes, particularly during post-acquisition integration.

> We work in a different way in different countries. We do not have such a strict hierarchy in Scandinavia. You find more hierarchical structures when you go south. For instance we made our first acquisition in France 15 years ago: there we found a rigid hierarchy . . . you cannot take these structures down right away otherwise the turbulence will be incredible. You have to adjust to them and evolve slowly. In Sweden we have a very open debate and we do not necessarily believe that the boss knows best. (Paint)

However, issues of cultural compatibility often dissimulate political struggles which are much harder to solve.

As they are aware of differences between national cultures, managers put a great deal of effort into achieving international post-merger integration.

When there are equally attractive opportunities for foreign direct investment, executives tend to select the countries that are close to their home business cultures, for instance Spanish firms have a preference for South America, British firms have a preference for the Commonwealth and the USA, Scandinavian firms feel at home in the new Baltic republics. Although English can be used as a lingua franca for international business, language barriers are significant. Indeed the combination of geographical distance, political risk, language and cultural differences creates agency problems and requires high local responsiveness from international competitors in most industries.

Coordination: the way to manage diversity

Coordination is viewed as the best way to manage diversity, differences in distribution systems, customer behaviour and business cultures. Policies are discussed and defined at the centre but coordination is preferred to centralization:

> Manufacturing, logistics, procurement, management control and strategy are coordinated at the international level. Current investments aim at improving the present fragmented configuration in terms of manufacturing, logistics and purchasing. But this does not mean that these activities are being centralized. Far from it, it means that policies are discussed and defined in common. (Cables)

Headquarters staff is small, and diverse geographical units have a coordination role, depending on their expertise.

> Our central office is very light. It includes the president, two general managers, three coordinators for R&D, strategy and international activities, three coordinators for finance, human resources and communication. This small team coordinates all the operations. In the cable business there are five persons responsible for a geographical sector. We meet, spend a day together, we discuss and refine our strategy, then they go back to their respective locations and implement it. My R&D colleague does exactly the same. He has designated 15 competence centres worldwide, each one focused on a type of product or a research area. Each one has the responsibility to put competences together and to work for the other units. Research is coordinated worldwide through a number of meetings for each theme.

When forces driving global integration are strong some upstream activities may be centralized while downstream activities are decentralized and coordinated.

> In procurement we have to be able to use our total strength; in research and development we have to use our total competence. Then you still have to remember that all business is local when it comes to marketing and sales.
>
> Research and development are centralized. The production is less centralized, we have local and regional plants. Sales are really managed locally. The strategy is decided at the centre (targets, product positioning) but the rest is local. There is some international coordination in the automotive paint business and for monitoring international customers such as UPS or Shell, but in principle sales and after sales services are managed locally, because mentalities are different. At the moment logistics is decentralized: we have a German organization and a Dutch organization.

> Inside the EU, borders are becoming blurred, so we started to coordinate logistics and we will probably centralize decisions in the future in order to optimize logistics and reduce costs. (Paint)

Decision-making autonomy may be given to regional units, between headquarters and different countries.

> In Italy, strategies, finance and personnel policies are coordinated. But the whole company is quite decentralized. There are three regional units – Europe, USA, the Far East – which have approximately the same size. Each regional unit is quite self-sufficient. For instance the American region deals with product development and marketing in the zone. It is listed on the New York stock exchange. The Asia unit is based in Hong Kong, it deals with product supply (95 per cent of manufacturing is done in the Far East) and with marketing and distribution in the region. (Footwear)

Generally foreign units are managed by nationals:

> In the United States I work with an exclusive American agent who thinks like an American. In Germany I sell in Deutschemarks with a German. In Italy I sell to an Italian and in England I work with an Englishman. (Footwear)

In the chocolate and sugar confectionery industry international players base their international strategies on coordination.

> We need to maintain open communications. Our people meet frequently. Our global design council meets three times a year either in New York or in Brussels or in Tokyo. We let our own sales people get on and do their own thing in each country and the R&D people meet to make sure our recipes and formulas are up to date and exchange information on what is working and what is not working. (Chocolate and sugar confectionery)
>
> Our policy is to leave each country with a significant market share with a great deal of decision-making autonomy. The corporate level is responsible for profits and losses. International headquarters has the goal of facilitating strategic thinking on a European or global level and to facilitate the essential elements of coordination. (Chocolate and sugar confectionery)

Webster's Dictionary defines the verb 'to coordinate' as follows: 'To place in the same order, rank' [. . .] 'To bring into proper order or relation; adjust various parts so as to have harmonious action' (1994: 306). These definitions emphasize three key success factors in managing international diversity: the centre does not overdominate foreign subsidiaries, the different geographical units are related to each other in order to form a harmonious whole, and management by council plays a major role in coordinating diverse activities.

From practice to theory: a summary

Two structural forces restrain the international development of industries: *high transportation costs* (relative to the added value of the product), and *protectionist policies* set up by national governments or regional trade blocs (tariff barriers, quotas limiting imports, minimum level of local content in foreign transplants). These forces create barriers to international trade (product flows). In such international settings, when foreign markets are attractive enough, international competitors may turn to foreign direct investment and set up manufacturing units abroad. However, given the local scale, they may not enjoy a cost advantage over national players.

Several structural forces drive international players to be locally responsive. Specific *local regulations and technical norms* may create the need for specific product development, manufacturing and marketing. *Chauvinism* may protect national players against foreign intrusion and force international players to become market insiders. When *services* are an important component of the business and when time and face-to-face interactions are key success factors, international players have to set up local units and provide local services. Adaptations to local market conditions are particularly important when distribution and sales represent a significant part of the product added value and when the structures of distribution are very different from one country to another. High *distribution intensity and diversity* delay the expansion of international players, as they have to build relationships with distributors and learn local practices. High *international diversity of customers' behaviour and preferences* drive international players towards local adaptations of products and/or packaging, and/or different promotion and/or pricing policies. In such circumstances an international scope may not generate economies of scale; moreover, in each local market an international competitor may find a strong national player with a significant market share and products/services perfectly adapted to local demand. *Different business cultures across borders* (norms of behaviour in the workplace) often require local adaptations of leadership styles and human resource management practices. This may cause agency problems, particularly in businesses which are labour intensive.

When the structural forces that drive local responsiveness are high, international mergers and acquisitions (M&As) are the preferred mode of international expansion. International M&As make a firm a market insider, they speed up access to distribution and provide a portfolio of products, brands and services that are already adapted to local demands. After the merger, the strongest national brands are maintained and a few international brands are developed.

Alternatively some firms may focus on a particular market segment and try to turn it into a global niche: luxury or global brand advertising.

International players who have dispersed assets (resulting from logistical constraints, protectionism, and international acquisitions) are faced with the challenge of rationalizing the international *configuration* of their activities. When the need for local responsiveness is high, *coordination* is the preferred mode of international control. Coordination is achieved by several management practices: the geographical units discuss policies and strategies with headquarters, some geographical units have the role of international coordination in their domain of expertise, downstream activities in the value chain enjoy high decision-making autonomy, regional (continental) coordination is achieved by council, and foreign units are managed preferably by nationals.

This set of structural forces that (1) restrain international development and (2) drive local responsiveness is parsimonious and comprehensive. The framework relates structural forces with competitive actions: international acquisitions strategies and specific international coordination practices.

Bibliography

Economic theory sees transportation costs as impediments to exchange; however, high transportation costs may stimulate foreign direct investment in attractive markets (Kindleberger, 1969). Contributors to the global integration/local responsiveness framework tend to consider high transportation costs (relative to the added value of the product) as a factor limiting the international development of an industry (Roth and Morrison, 1990; Porter, 1986). Transport costs can make it inefficient to concentrate activity in one location, and geographical dispersion may counterbalance integration economies (Porter, 1986). Several authors take a positive view and mention 'advances' in transport and communication as favourable to global integration (Prahalad and Doz, 1987; Bartlett and Ghoshal, 1992; Yip, 1992).

Economic theories view governments' interventions and industrial policies as major market imperfections. Multinational enterprises must respond to changes in government positions that may affect their firm-specific advantages (Rugman, 1985). The political activity of firms is part of their international strategy to balance the negotiating power of states (Morrison and Roth, 1992). Several authors mentioned host government demands – in terms of industrial policies, local content, plant location and protectionism – that hinder the global integration of industries, particularly the development of international trade (Perlmutter, 1969; Prahalad and Doz, 1987; Bartlett and Ghoshal, 1989; Roth and Morrison, 1990). However, Yip (1992) noted that government intervention is sometimes directed at stimulating foreign direct investment, which is a substitute for international trade (Mundell, 1957). Specific regulations and norms are also seen as barriers to international trade: they tend to maintain the international fragmentation of industries (Porter, 1986; Bartlett and Ghoshal, 1989; Roth and Morrison, 1990). The same arguments have been developed concerning tariff barriers. In many industries, public purchases are significant. There may be a preference for national champions in public sector purchases (the European Community tried to abolish these practices in 1992). Public sector purchases tend to maintain the fragmentation of competition and influence firms' localization policies (Porter, 1986; Prahalad and Doz, 1987; Dunning, 1993). Perlmutter (1969) argued that economic nationalism in host and home countries is a major obstacle to the development of the geocentric form of multinational (which is a worldwide integrated network). Numerous cases of economic nationalism are documented in the business press, and market studies show that country of origin affects product evaluations (Kaynar and Cavusgil, 1983).

The importance of proximate customer service requirements determines local responsiveness (Roth and Morrison, 1990). According to Porter (1986), when 'downstream' activities are important, particularly the interface with clients, industries tend to remain 'multidomestic'.

Differences in distribution channels force firms to be locally responsive and adapt their distribution strategies (Prahalad and Doz, 1987). Research in marketing demonstrated the relationship between the fragmentation of markets and differences in distribution and logistics (Bello and Dahringer, 1985; Cooper, 1993). Inversely, the emergence of international distribution networks can stimulate global integration (Yip, 1992). Access to distribution channels is often a major entry barrier. Porter (1986) made this argument in the case of global strategies. Difficult access to distribution channels is a challenge for international marketers. Barriers may be cultural (resistance to foreign suppliers) or, as documented in the case of Japan, they may stem from the strength of relationships between suppliers and distributors.

Cultural differences reflected in nationally differentiated consumption patterns (tastes and preferences) push firms to be locally responsive (Bartlett and Ghoshal, 1989). This factor is widely recognized by scholars who have contributed to the global–local paradigm (Prahalad and Doz, 1987; Roth and Morrison, 1990): it is opposed to the existence of universal needs.

The same authors also consider cross-national differences in purchasing behaviour (Bartlett and Ghoshal, 1989) that force firms to adapt their market strategies (particularly advertising and pricing) to the specificities of the country or the region.

Cultural differences across borders may also be reflected in the effectiveness of different organizational forms and management systems (Bartlett and Ghoshal, 1989). Perlmutter (1969) identified differences in business cultures as favourable to polycentric forms of organization. For Simon (1993), multinational corporations have to adapt their management practices to the heterogeneity of national cultures; international integration is then so costly that global integration economies cannot be reaped. Johansen and Widershein-Paul (1975) argued that the 'psychic distance' between nations determines firms' international strategies.

The relationship between the need for local responsiveness and the level of international M&As activity is not much documented in the literature except in the form of case studies (Haspeslagh and Jemison, 1991). The level of international 'coordination' is one of the two variables that define generic international strategies in Porter's framework (1986). The concept of international coordination is close to the definition of the 'transnational form' given by Bartlett and Ghoshal (1989): an 'asymmetrical integrated network'.

4

Structural Forces Driving Global Integration

Roland Calori, Paul Emmanuelides, Egbert Kahle, Leif Melin and Juan José Renau

A set of structural forces drives the international development and global integration of firms and industries. Firms extend their geographic scope to sustain growth and to exploit and strengthen competitive advantages. Global integration is the process by which competitive advantages based on a broad geographic scope are created and sustained. Managers make a subtle distinction between two phenomena. Some structural forces stimulate the international expansion of firms and industries, but do not necessarily stimulate integration. For instance the emergence of high growth markets in Asia and in South America attracts foreign direct investments and/or trade flows. Some structural forces foster international development *and* drive the global integration of firms and industries. For instance potential economies of scale may drive firms to expand *and integrate* their activities across borders: concentrate research and development, centralize procurement, concentrate manufacturing in some locations, organize international key accounts management, etc.

International competitors enjoy superior competitive advantages to national players when they integrate their international activities. *Webster's New World Dictionary* defines 'integrate' as: 'to put or bring parts together into a harmonious whole'. Integration can be achieved by three main mechanisms: concentration, centralization or coordination. An international company may decide to *concentrate* logistics for Europe in a single location and close down local depots in several European countries, to *centralize* decision-making concerning research and development projects at the headquarters, and to *coordinate* the marketing of European brands (for example each national unit has high autonomy in defining operational marketing plans, but brand managers meet every quarter and harmonize their strategies). Coordination can be achieved by different mechanisms: a hierarchy (e.g. European headquarters), horizontal coordinators (e.g. a product manager for Europe), or a council (e.g. regular meetings between brand managers from the different countries). Such formal coordination mechanisms are complemented by informal ties: socialization processes.

The purpose of this chapter is to uncover the structural forces that drive firms to:

- expand their geographic scope;
- integrate (concentrate, centralize, and/or coordinate) their international activities.

Based on discussions with top managers in cables, paint, footwear and confectionery, these structural forces can be grouped into four categories: technological intensity, economies of scale and scope, comparative advantages, and international customer base (see Figure I.2, p. 12). Most of these forces are specific to some industries or to some product-market segments within an industry. For instance comparative advantage based on labour cost is crucial in the footwear industry, significant in low voltage power cables, and unimportant in the paint industry and in the chocolate industry. Some forces are common to the four industries in this study: the international scope and negotiation power of clients and the emergence of high growth markets.

The concept of *technological intensity* encompasses several aspects. In some industries product and process innovations are paramount: the technologies involved are at the leading edge of scientific knowledge. Research and development is the key success factor: R&D budgets are very high, both in absolute terms (critical size) and relative to sales turnover, state of the art knowledge is rare and firms compete to attract the best engineers. Competitors with a global scope can amortize R&D budgets quicker, before the next generation of products comes on to the market. They can also tap knowledge wherever it is located: for instance they recruit from the best universities worldwide. Indeed they enjoy a significant competitive advantage over local players. Technological intensity also includes capital intensity. In some businesses, sophisticated machinery, industrial processes and production plants require high investments that may not be amortized when sales are limited to the domestic market. Industries such as civil aeronautics and electronic components are technology-intensive, both in terms of R&D and manufacturing. Clearly no firm can compete successfully without a global scope in such industries. Managers view high technological intensity as the main structural force driving global integration (cf. Kobrin, 1991).

In many industries unit cost depends on *economies of scale*. A broad international scope provides the terrain for a larger-scale business. There may be potential economies of scale at different stages of the value chain: in research and development, procurement, manufacturing, and marketing (advertising and sponsoring). Economies of scale (and scope) in R&D are a facet of technological intensity (as mentioned above). Large-scale purchases often reduce the unit cost of inputs – raw materials, components and sub-systems – due to the negotiating power of large competitors *vis-à-vis* their suppliers. Large-scale manufacturing may also be a source of cost competitiveness: it may be a necessary condition to amortize highly productive process technologies, and long production runs may lower unit cost. However, there are several limitations to the effect of scale economies. Once a critical size has been reached in manufacturing, marginal economies of scale may become insignificant. High transportation costs may limit the accessible market and the optimal size of a manufacturing unit. Flexible manufacturing processes may reduce the need for long production runs. And in labour-intensive industries the competitive advantage of cheap labour unit cost can be more significant than economies of scale in manufacturing. In some businesses, advertising and sponsoring expenses represent a high percentage of sales (up to 10 per cent). When advertising and sponsoring campaigns can be the same across borders (i.e. when consumers have similar motivations and behaviours), economies of scale in advertising and sponsoring may have a strong impact on unit cost. Many sponsoring opportunities are open to global competitors. For instance sponsoring global events such as the Olympic Games or the World Formula One Grand Prix is so costly that firms need a worldwide presence to amortize such budgets. In the end, the cost of advertising per unit sold can be lower for global players than for regional players. Finally, fashion products are characterized by a short life cycle. In this case a broad geographic scope is a necessary condition to reap economies of scale (in product development, procurement, manufacturing and advertising), before the next season.

The sources of competitive advantage that are specific to a location, country or geographic zone are known as *comparative advantages*. There are several types of comparative advantage: firms located in certain countries may benefit from a relatively low unit cost of labour (a significant advantage in labour-intensive businesses when productivity levels are similar). In certain countries firms benefit from the relatively low cost of capital (low interest rates, low taxation, etc.). Access to rare raw materials or components may be easier in some locations. Also certain countries may have developed a superior knowledge base in a particular business. When there are such asymmetries in production factors between countries, competitors try to capture comparative advantages by locating their activities in attractive countries. Competitors who benefit from comparative advantages also exploit their superiority and expand their international activities through exports.

International players who can reap economies of scale and benefit from comparative advantages often compete on prices. Strong *pressures on prices* drive further cost reductions and stimulate international strategies. The spiral of price competition and cost cutting is accelerated when customers have high negotiating power and operate on an international scale.

Powerful international customers prefer cost-competitive international suppliers who can provide consistent quality across borders. When customers expand their geographic scope, the best suppliers seize growth opportunities and follow their clients. *Emerging high growth markets* also create new opportunities for international development, particularly when traditional markets have become mature. Growth opportunities attract international competition and broaden the geographic scope of the industry. The international development of an industry is driven by the international development of its customer base. Figure 4.1 summarizes the forces that drive global integration and/or international development, and indicates their influence on competitive actions.

The following sections report top managers' views on the forces that drive global integration in the four industries: cables, paint, footwear, and chocolate and sugar confectionery.

Technological intensity

Technological intensity drives international development and global integration in the paint industry and in the cable industry; its influence is less significant in the other two industries in this study.

Car finishes and can coating (for beverages) are two technology-intensive businesses within the *paint industry*: they also are the most global. Technological innovation creates the need and the opportunity to expand the geographic scope of the innovator.

> Size helps you to cope with technological jumps. We have developed water-based paints for car finishes. Up to now only four international competitors have mastered this new technology, all of them from Europe. The others have no access to this technology for the moment. This technological advantage contributed to globalize competition. Thanks to the new technology, Europeans increased their market share and American customers started to work with European suppliers. Since 1 January 1994 only water-based paints have been allowed for car repairs in the region of Los Angeles [this was the most advanced regulation worldwide]. We already sell there. One day San Francisco will follow, and California, and Texas, and the rest of the United States. As a consequence PPG and Dupont lost market share in their home market; they responded by attacking Europe and Asia through acquisitions and with an aggressive pricing strategy.

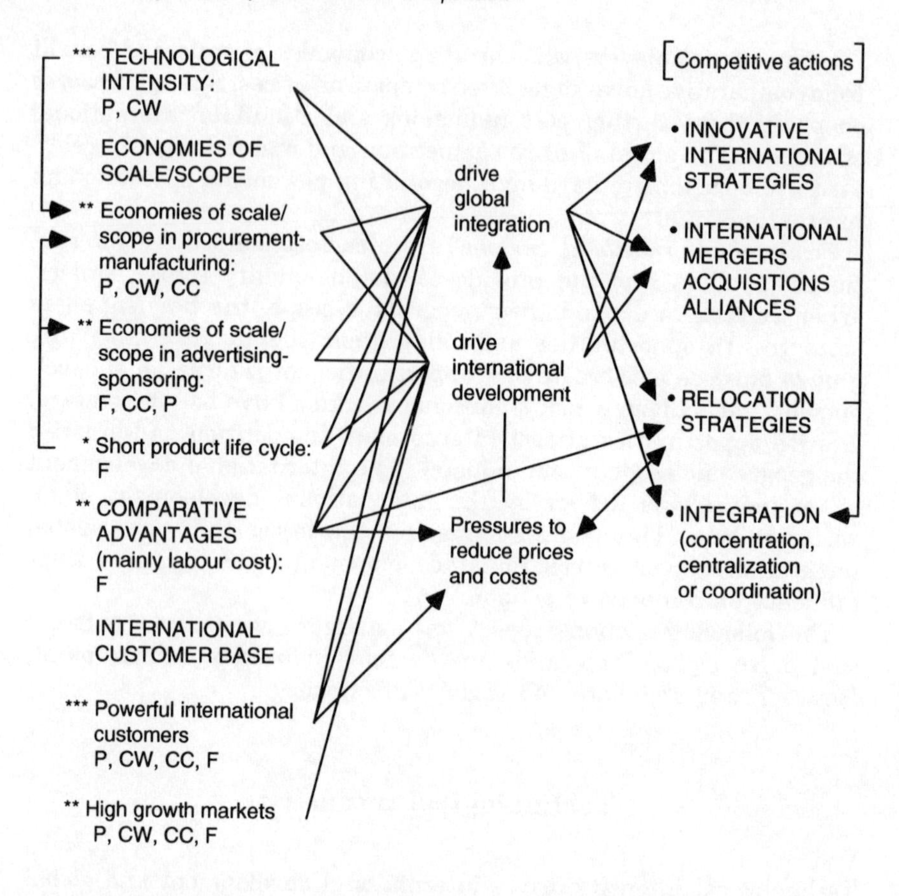

Figure 4.1 *Structural forces driving global integration and/or international development*

Sophisticated industrial customers stimulate technological innovation that creates the basis for international development.

> IKEA manufactures bookcases consisting of chipboard, glue and varnish. All these materials contain some formaldehyde. IKEA got into trouble in Germany with those Billy bookcases and they expressed their wish: 'We want a varnish free of formaldehyde.' They cancelled their agreements with some suppliers and finally they got their formaldehyde-free varnish. We were one of the winners in that game. By doing that they pushed the technology into a new area, causing a technological transition and setting a new trend.

As far as the paint industry is concerned, technological jumps have been driven by the new demand for 'green products':

> What has arrived with great force over the last ten years is the awareness about environmental issues in the paint industry. Today, when we develop new products the strongest driving force is probably care for the environment. The whole thing originally came from the workers' unions who would not accept that their members had to work with solvent-based products. Then there was the awareness among the end-consumers, particularly women: they make sure that the men buy environmentally friendly products. Then there were regulations. [. . .] The technical content has increased significantly. The products are more complex and with the environmental demands the level of investment has increased dramatically. It takes a certificate from the country administration and the [Swedish] National Franchise Board for Environment Protection to manufacture, and they are so strict that you have to invest an awful lot in purification plants, which makes it more difficult particularly for small local companies.

This trend affected all the market segments within the paint industry, even the most multidomestic activity: decorative paint. Thirty years ago anyone could start a business in decorative paint in his/her garage, buy and mix resins, pigments and solvents and fill containers. Research and development and manufacturing are much more complicated for making water-based paint and user-friendly products for handymen. The substitution of water-based paint for solvent-based was particularly quick in Northern Europe and in North America. For instance in the mid-1990s water-based paints represented about 90 per cent of the British market, as compared to 50 per cent in France and even lower percentages in Southern Europe. As a consequence competitors in Northern Europe (such as Akzo Nobel, Alcro Beckers and ICI) developed an expertise in water-based paints, and they relied on it for their international expansion.

In the *cable industry* managers point out the strong relationship between the level of technological intensity and the geographic scope of the business.

> When you deal with very high technology products, for instance high tension power cables, the market is global. A company located in one country can manufacture for the whole planet.
>
> No one would bury a 110 kilovolt cable without knowing who was behind the technology. The manufacturer must achieve perfect purity. It is hard to make joints and ends for high voltage cables: there are only a handful of qualified manufacturers to do that.
>
> In our three-year plan I proposed a product-market segmentation including about 50 products in significant market segments. No more than 10 of these were marketed internationally and these were the most technologically advanced.

On the one hand exclusive technological competence creates opportunities for international expansion. On the other hand leading edge technology requires enormous R&D budgets that can only be paid back by global markets.

> There will be new technological developments in the future: glass fibres and superconductors will play a role in energy distribution. Pirelli and a US firm have an R&D alliance to bring superconductors to market on a global basis. Within ten years it will make sense to use superconductors for high voltage cables [110 kV and more]. With superconductors the wires will be thinner and the heat would be reduced during energy transport. With this technological jump competition will become more global.

Finally, global scope allows economies of scale in research and development.

> A company like ours has the ability to be a technical leader: we feel that you can earn better margins if your technology and your customer service are leading edge. This is expensive, but all good things tend to have a cost. Now, we did not want to change our credo but we did want to make industry-leading returns and to keep costs down. So we decided that the way to go was to concentrate on a limited number of products and sell in all the major markets of the world so that we had a large litrage over which to spread these basic costs. (Paint)

Economies of scale in procurement

There are significant economies of scale in procurement in the *paint industry*.

> The driving force behind the concentration of the paint business is economies of scale, and economies of scale start in procurement. When we have procurement under control we will buy raw materials at prices 10 per cent lower than mid-sized companies, and that is 5 per cent profit already.

A broad geographic scope is generally associated with a large size, and the cost of purchases depends on the size of orders.

> We negotiate in Barcelona and they negotiate in Leverkusen [Germany], and the prices are not the same. I am talking about 10 to 20 per cent difference in the cost of raw materials and the cost of raw material is 70 per cent of the total cost of varnishes.

Big international competitors may have a sufficient base to integrate the production of raw materials.

> Scale economies are important above all when they allow a paint manufacturer to integrate upwards, for instance in the production of resins

> when you make varnish. The leader, Milesi, have their own company to produce resins, they do not have to buy their resins from Bayer or BASF.

However, this is an exception; the reverse is more frequent: chemical groups that produce raw materials (Hoechst, BASF, ICI or Total) add value to their activities by launching or taking over a paint business.

Economies of scale and scope in procurement rely on the negotiating power of the firm.

> In order to develop and sell new environmentally friendly products you need new materials and research laboratories. Research laboratories belong to multinational companies that produce raw material. If these multinationals decide to sell at 10,500 lire per kilo, you have to pay this price, there are no alternatives. Therefore internationalization is probable, many small companies will close down and the strongest will go on.

Paint manufacturers increase their negotiation power when they can coordinate their international orders.

> The advantage of being an international company is clear in terms of purchasing power. When I buy titanium, when I buy resins, when I buy packaging, the fact that we have production sites in France, in England, in Hungary, in China, in Vietnam . . . all this gives a significant negotiating power. We do centralize purchasing in order to cope with international suppliers: they know that our paint division is international. Being big helps a lot.

Economies of scale in manufacturing

A business with a broad international scope may benefit from scale economies in manufacturing and, in turn, low manufacturing costs will help it compete on foreign markets. There are significant economies of scale and (geographic) scope in three of the four industries: cables, chocolate and paint.

In the *cable industry* a few big competitors expanded their international scope by taking over local businesses. Fifteen years ago the market was multidomestic: strong connections between local telephone companies or utilities and local cable manufacturers limited international competition. In the 1990s international competitors started to restructure their operations.

> Large international competitors have rationalized manufacturing, they closed down old factories and built specialized units in large countries such as Germany and France. They decided on the best places in order to serve the market in the best way.

> Small cable makers will have a hard time competing with the big ones who enjoy economies of scale. Moreover there is an overcapacity of production. Close-downs are coming. We shall have to close down some factories because they no longer have the critical size, and many small companies will have to focus on niche markets.

The international challenge is to reach a critical size in manufacturing, given the size of the market and transportation cost.

> When you manufacture a cable like this, you start up a line that is 200 metres long, and the waste from starting and stopping represents a considerable cost. You really get the costs down when you run a 100-kilometre cable as compared to a 4-kilometre run. However, you cannot make it too long, you must be able to sell what you produce. I hope that within ten years we will have a reasonably standardized range of products across Europe. Several competitors would benefit from that: Alcatel have manufacturing units in all of Europe, BICC also; Pirelli are in Southern Europe, ABB is in Northern Europe. All of us would prefer to use our units optimally. So the base for restructuring is there.

Critical size in manufacturing should be compared to the total size of the world market. When there is room for only a few competitors, the scene is set for the globalization of an industry.

> Nowadays most cable makers have become fibre optics manufacturers. But there are very few of them because the manufacturing of the fibre is a heavy investment. Today in order to reach the market price you need high productivity factories, you need to reach a critical size, let us say more than a million kilometres a year. This is high compared to the world market which is about 11 million kilometres a year. So the potential number of factories is limited.

Economies of scale in manufacturing drive the concentration of the *chocolate industry* and the global integration of international players. Economies of scale are significant with high volume products such as *tablettes* and countlines. Products such as chocolate boxed assortments or specialities are more diverse and small flexible production sites are still competitive.

> Scale economies are driving the concentration of production. When the main multinationals hold two-thirds of the world market you will see the same products in the kiosks everywhere. The only solution for local companies will be to focus on specialities; they will not be able to compete with multinationals otherwise. Moreover, multinationals will progressively concentrate manufacturing. Of the multinationals operating in Spain only one, Nestlé, has some local production. The other ones, Suchard and Lindt, closed down their factories in Spain, and most of these international products are imported.

> If you want to be efficient you need to reduce your product range from, let us say, 100 products down to 40, then you can rationalize manufacturing. Then you need longer production runs, a larger market and that leads you to sell abroad. One of the driving forces behind international development is economies of scale in production.

International players, such as Nestlé or Kraft Jacobs Suchard, rationalized their manufacturing sites across borders. By doing this they reaped economies of scale and changed the rules of competition.

> The production sites that we have result from our geographic situation, our product categories and past acquisitions. It is part of our history, and it is being modified within the process of rationalization and specialization of our factories . . . toward factories specialized in one product category.
>
> We have a plant in Loerrach that produces chocolate *tablettes* for the whole of Europe. A lot of chocolates are manufactured in Strasbourg or Berlin, which are focal points: marketing is local, production is international.
>
> Nestlé have built a fantastic new Lion bar facility in France, which now makes Lion bars for the whole world. Incredible economies of scale. I presume that if they are making Lion bars for the UK and for France in this factory they are using English style chocolate for British consumers. But still, they probably exploit huge economies of scale: an all-singing, all-dancing totally automated production line. Similarly I know they are putting huge investment into the Rowntree's York factory, so my guess is that they will partly relocate the production of After Eight to this site.

Nestlé, Kraft Jacobs Suchard, as well as Mars and Ferrero, contributed to an increase in the level of capital intensity in the chocolate industry. Nowadays it costs several million US dollars to start a new product line.

> Most chocolate factories use robots, for instance to recognize the shape of pieces and the size of nuts before covering them.

Sufficient scale is needed to amortize sophisticated equipment, and international scope is needed to reach sufficient scale.

According to managers, economies of scale in manufacturing are less significant in the paint industry, particularly for low added value products that cannot be transported a long distance. Economies of scale in manufacturing are also less significant in the footwear industry because it is a labour-intensive business in which manufacturing cost depends on the unit cost of labour.

Advertising intensity

Advertising intensity drives international development and global integration in several product-market segments: sport-leisure footwear, countlines and a few global brands in the chocolate and confectionery industry. These products and brands have been adopted by consumers worldwide. The competitive actions of a few innovative manufacturers and marketers shaped the globalization process. By spending massive amounts on advertising and sponsoring programmes they invented new rules for competing in their industries: in brand image and economies of scale and scope in advertising.

In *sport-leisure footwear*, Nike created a global image with massive advertising and sponsoring for several years.

> There is no European firm, even Adidas, who can compete with people who spend 10 billion pesetas a year on their European advertising. It became a real dictatorship, number one in tennis, number one in basket ball and number one in all the most popular sports.

Being the market leader with a global coverage helps amortize enormous marketing budgets. High growth in sport-leisure footwear attracted other competitors: Reebok and Adidas followed similar strategies. A significant exception in this gigantic mass marketing battle was Fila, a smaller competitor with a differentiation strategy. However, Fila also relied on TV advertising for its international expansion.

> The leisure footwear business has many analogies with the music industry, the main consumer target is the same. So we use an American music TV channel with a European base in London for advertising. It is costly but it yields very positive returns.

International TV channels are the main vectors in the globalization of this business.

> There are significant economies of scale in advertising. There is a tendency to launch advertising campaigns that cover many countries. Nowadays even the Koreans watch Eurosport. Communication is more and more global.

The international development of sport-leisure footwear belongs to a broader sociological evolution of consumption patterns:

> Young people are consuming more and more, they tend to behave in the same way around the globe. Means of communication broadcast the same

image, the same fashion, the same ambience, the same heroes – rock stars or basketball players – and behaviour becomes universal.

The same phenomenon is taking place with *countlines* in the chocolate industry.

TV commercials will increase and that is favourable to the big companies with large-scale advantages. You can produce TV commercials in one place and show them in a number of countries: sometimes you just dub the voices, or have Swedish subtitles. Snickers is one of the main sponsors of the soccer World Cup and Mars spent over US $100 million to gain this position. The reason why they do this of course is to reach consumers all around the world via TV. After all the cost per customer for such an advertising campaign is relatively low. When your products are distributed everywhere in a foreign country you can afford TV advertising.

I see more future in internationalization than in local action and something that will help us to be international is mass media. They are themselves becoming more and more global. If you advertise on MTV, Eurosport, people from 20 different countries will watch you at the same time. If you are the sponsor of an international sport event also. Sports and television will make internationalization much easier for the ones who can pay.

Marketing skills and economies of scale in global brand advertising have become the key factor of success in the last 20 years.

The chocolate business has become very much a brand business. Brand marketing investments are huge if you want to expand worldwide. Some companies have chosen to focus on a small number of products in order to afford heavy brand building, for instance Mars with Mars bars, Snickers, M&Ms, and Wrigley with its chewing gums. In chocolate today it is not enough to have a good product: there are thousands of good products, the good product is a prerequisite, everybody expects that you have a good product. In addition you need marketing skills and investment, and then you make economies, because it is very expensive. Building the brand is at least as expensive as building the factories.

A few innovative international competitors have shaped the new rules of the game. Mars was one of them.

[. . .] A Snickers bar is as applicable to a Russian as it is to a North American. It tastes great, gives lots of energy and is made of good quality ingredients, and if people are hungry and want something nice to eat as a snack, they will buy it and eat it. So I think one of the major drivers of internationalization is acceptability of established products. If you have to reinvent or design a new product every time you go somewhere, it will slow the whole process down.

In sugar confectionery most products are generics, for instance cooked sugar candies or jelly candies. Advertising and marketing intensity are lower than in the chocolate industry. However, a few innovative competitors relied on massive advertising and created international brands: Chupa Chups lollipops (originally from Spain), Haribo jelly candies (originally from Germany), TicTac sweets from Ferrero (originally from Italy). Advertising and sponsoring intensity became a significant structural force driving global integration, under the pressure of innovative competitive actions.

There is a similar evolution, less significant and more recent, in one market segment of the paint industry: *decorative consumer paint.*

> The costs of marketing have a tendency to increase. That has a lot to do with more and more advertising on TV, and that is a bloody expensive media. You could say that you reach a large number of customers. I am still not sure that TV advertising is efficient for selling paint. I hope we can increase the total consumption of paint per capita, otherwise it would mean that we have increased our costs of marketing.
>
> Competitors try to increase their market shares and expand internationally in order to benefit from scale economies, at the manufacturing level and mostly at the marketing level: advertising. For instance Dulux originally was the British brand of ICI; now we see it everywhere in Europe.

Some remarks about marketing intensity

Scholars use the concept of marketing intensity to capture the relative importance of marketing in the value chain.

Economic and strategic theories reach inconsistent conclusions about the effect of marketing intensity on the international dynamics of industries. On the one hand Levitt (1983) suggests that global marketing brings cost advantages when marketing expenses are high relative to sales and when the transfer of marketing practices across borders is possible. Bartlett and Ghoshal (1989) argue that global brand policies are efficient because they fully exploit economies of scope, and some economic theories view product differentiation (measured by the ratio of advertising expenses to sales turnover) as an oligopolistic advantage that drives the international development of firms (Lall, 1980; Caves, 1981). On the other hand, marketing intensity is also seen as a sign of market heterogeneity and a characteristic of multidomestic industries, and Kobrin (1991) found a negative relationship between marketing intensity (measured by the ratio of advertising expenses to sales turnover) and a global integration index. Managers' views clarify this debate: *marketing intensity has a dual effect.*

Downstream activities are multifaceted; sales and distribution are dependent on local market conditions, whereas communication (advertising, sponsoring) may allow economies of scale and scope. When sales and distribution costs represent a high percentage of total costs in the value chain (high marketing intensity) international competitors are forced to duplicate sales and distribution and their competitive advantage over local competitors is not significant. Hence high sales and distribution costs and the diversity of distribution systems across countries create entry barriers, drive local responsiveness and preserve local firms, as shown in Chapter 3. When communication costs (advertising, sponsoring) represent a high percentage of total costs in the value chain (also high marketing intensity) *and* when universal needs can be met or created, global communication generates significant competitive advantages (economies of scale and scope) for international competitors. Hence marketing intensity is a dual concept with a dual impact on the international development of industries. As high sales costs and high advertising costs generally go together in consumer goods industries where downstream activities are paramount, it is crucial to differentiate between the two effects and to assess their combined impact. When the effect of sales and distribution dominates the effect of global communication, marketing intensity drives local responsiveness, and when the effect of global communication dominates the effect of sales and distribution, marketing intensity drives global integration. Such a context creates more freedom for firms: some adopt global brand strategies, others prefer to focus on a geographical zone, while others adopt a dual strategy (global brands and local brands).

Short product life cycle

When technological intensity or advertising intensity is high or when unit costs are driven by economies of scale, short product life cycles drive international development. A broad international geographic scope opens up market opportunities to pay back product development and launch before the next generation. Short product life cycles may result from frequent technological innovations or from fashion cycles.

Short fashion cycles drive international development in women's luxury *footwear* and among young consumers.

> The main factor in women's luxury shoes is fashion, which is now international, not Italian or German or French any more. With seasonal fashion the life of the product becomes shorter and shorter. It must be

> renewed continuously and the cost of amortizing new products is much higher than before. On the other hand fashion allows you to sell all over the world without local adaptation, and indeed you *have* to sell worldwide.
>
> Young people represent a growing market segment, they are sensitive to fashions that emerge in an unpredictable manner. Manufacturers can hardly follow these aggressive fashions that the young people like. For example, young Afro-Americans made working boots popular among the youth of the planet. In order to catch up with this phenomenon, the big footwear companies such as Nike had to replace some of their traditional production of sports footwear by worker boots; they had to quickly follow the fashion. Anything can happen at any moment.

Manufacturers and marketers have set up coordination mechanisms in order to organize fashion: worldwide professional fairs in Düsseldorf (twice a year, in March and September), in Milan, Paris, Las Vegas and Tokyo. Between fairs, manufacturers prepare their worldwide 'collection'.

> There is some coordination between fashion committees, on shapes, on colours. National fashion committees sit first. Then the international committee tends to stay in the middle of the road. Afterwards there are some moves to the left or to the right, at a country level or at the company level, muddling through. [. . .] We aim at a worldwide collection. We get the ideas and the desires from our local branches and we consider them in making the collection, but the output is a worldwide collection.

Given the geographic dispersion of manufacturing sites (in order to benefit from low labour costs) and consumption areas, international competitors have to integrate and coordinate their activities on a global scale in order to shorten cycle times.

> We shall have to find more effective solutions to improve just-in-time production to catch up with fashion trends. At the moment there is a lot of what we call 'shoe tourism'. We use satellite communications to send production designs to our foreign plants in Portugal. Some parts are made in India, some others are made in Italy and then sent to India via Frankfurt. The upper parts of the shoe are manufactured in India and sent to our operations in Portugal for assembly. Then they come back to us in Frankfurt . . . a worldwide trip.

Comparative advantage

Among diverse sources of comparative advantage, labour cost appears to have a major impact on the international development of the footwear industry. Other types of comparative advantages are seen as less significant: cost of capital, access to supply sources, and to superior local knowledge. This may be because international markets of capital, raw materials and knowledge have become more fluid in the last 15 years (whereas cheap manpower cannot be massively moved across borders).

In *footwear* labour cost represents about 40 per cent of total cost (on average). There is a ratio of about one to ten between hourly wages in Brazil and in the US and a ratio of about one to thirty between hourly wages in mainland China and in Germany. As a result the manufacturing of shoes has been relocated to countries with low labour cost.

> The footwear industry is not driven by technology. Technology is simple and accessible to everyone. On the other hand it is a labour-intensive activity, therefore manufacturing has migrated from country to country in search of the most competitive costs. The first relocation wave was toward Southern Europe: first to Italy, then to Spain, then to Portugal and Yugoslavia, and also toward Brazil in the region of Porto Alegre. When hourly wages increased in Southern Europe a second wave of relocation took place toward Korea and Taiwan. But nowadays wages in Korea are higher than in Portugal. I read that a Korean shoe manufacturer was studying the opportunity to set up a production site in England to benefit from lower cost and social flexibility! The third wave of relocation was toward Indonesia and Thailand. Later on the Taiwanese moved manufacturing to mainland China: they provided management skills, equipment and design and paid hourly wages of less than 50 cents. A few other Asian countries joined the late third wave: Malaysia, the Philippines, Laos, Cambodia and Vietnam, which started four years ago and is making giant strides. India combines cheap labour and first quality leather, it has a great future in the industry. Where will the migration stop? I do not know – probably one day in the deep jungle of Borneo.

The first relocation wave was initiated by European manufacturers (toward Southern Europe) and US manufacturers (toward Brazil). The second wave (toward Asia) was initiated by competitors in sport-leisure footwear: Nike and Reebok, soon followed by manufacturers involved in mass market shoes. The higher the sensitivity to price and cost the stronger the impulse to relocate manufacturing.

> Their strategy is quite simple, they manufacture in countries with low labour cost and sell in countries with high purchasing power. There is some sort of gravity law depending on the level of economic development. For instance French manufacturers export footwear to Benelux, to Germany and a little to Scandinavian countries; they relocated part of manufacturing to Southern Europe but they do not export to Spain, Italy and Portugal. Within Europe there is a dominant stream from the South to the North.

In some countries this process transformed the whole industry. For instance in the mid-1990s less than 20 per cent of manufacturing was done in Germany, and this was for shoes that were priced above DM 200 a pair. Under this limit the German unit cost of labour was too high to be competitive.

> German companies relocated production to Portugal and more recently to Slovakia, the Czech Republic and Hungary. The parts are purchased in India and in the Far East. The leather is purchased in Italy, in India and in Pakistan. At the end of the 1960s the German footwear industry employed about 110,000 persons and manufactured 170 million pairs. In 1993 it employed about 23,000 persons and produced 53 million pairs.

Within Europe there are still significant differences in manufacturing costs, but these are narrowing. For instance the difference between Portugal and France (wages and all taxes included) was one to four in 1995. There is still a shadow economy that makes it cheaper in Spain and in Italy. The stitching of shoes can be done at home and a lot of Italian small factories (with about ten employees) work without overheads. However, Spanish and Italian manufacturers suffer from Asian competition on the mass market. In 1995 Spain exported 15 million pairs to the USA, as compared to 45 million pairs ten years before. Indeed it is very hard to compete with the Chinese factory:

> I believe that China exports about 600 million pairs of shoes to America a year, their average price is about US $1.80. What do they sell for US $1.80? Socks? Thongs? I do not know!

The European Commission has imposed quotas on the amounts that can be manufactured in China and imported by Europe. The quota for 1994 limited imports (in 12 countries) to 96 million pairs as compared to 132 million pairs in 1992 before the quota existed. However, the lobby of sport and leisure footwear manufacturers cleverly managed to argue that 'highly technical sport shoes' should not be concerned with this quota. They decided to call 'highly technical sport shoes' any pair sold at a price above 79 French francs to the retailer. Given such a low price, most imported sport shoes could escape quotas.

About 90 per cent of sport footwear is manufactured in Asia, but

> The best price is not always the best option: you can buy shoes for 400 pesetas in China . . . but you have to buy at least 50,000 pairs, pay for them in advance, wait for them to arrive in good condition and then check their quality.

As short delivery times become a key success factor, relocation to the Far East may be questioned, at least for products with high added value.

> From the supply side, I think that once you have done Vietnam, Laos and Cambodia there are very few other places to go. I think that proximity to market will become more important. As retailers become more sophisticated they will demand faster response, and I think the future of the European footwear industry is one of being able to compete on a fast response basis. Once you move off-shore to the Far East, you cannot be fast, the shipment times are too long.

For instance some American distributors such as Wal-Mart and Gap set up a system to improve response time to demand fluctuations with their manufacturers and subcontractors. In this system regional production is preferred to overseas production.

The dynamics of relocation depend on the characteristics of each product-market segment. Relocation is significant in sport and mass-market footwear. However, the strongest international brands and distribution networks still belong to North American and European competitors. The split of their value chain activities between different locations (so as to exploit comparative advantages) has required tight global integration in order to compete on time and quality.

Pressures to reduce prices and costs

The combination of several forces drives a general reduction in prices and costs.

The emergence of new competition from low labour cost countries drives price wars. For instance, China and tomorrow India will probably dominate the footwear industry.

> The level of productivity that we have reached in Europe is not much higher than in the Far East. We do not compete with people working in dusty workshops, among bamboo. The factories in the Far East will soon be as modern as those in the old world. The only significant change in competition could come from political decisions, but protectionism is not the dominant economic doctrine nowadays. (Footwear)

In the cable industry new low-cost suppliers have entered the low end of the cable market: they compete on price and improve their level of quality.

Overcapacity leads to price competition before the industry becomes concentrated, and there has been overcapacity for several years in Europe.

> In telecom cables, the volume of copper cables was cut by half within the last five years. That has put an enormous pressure on that industry. Everyone moved to fibre optic cables, and believed that demand would

> explode. But everyone increased production capacities in optofibres. . . . So now there is an enormous overcapacity in the entire world, in both Europe and the US, in both opto and copper cables. There you can now see why the price level has been cut by half over a few years. In this context firms start buying each other right and left.

In turn, overcapacity stimulated international expansion.

> At the beginning of the 1990s the recession led to an intensification of international competition: we had to go out to look for markets, prices kept falling every year, we had to improve productivity. (Cables)

When cross-border trade increases, international harmonization of prices can take place. For instance in the chocolate industry prices tend to be lower in Germany and in the UK than in the rest of Europe. Within the European Union such differences will not last for long; prices will probably be harmonized at the lower level.

> The growth of jelly candies attracted many competitors. A couple of years ago, with devaluation and industrial overcapacity, the prices fell. The Spanish lowered their prices, so did the Belgians and the Scandinavians. The general trend in Europe is a decrease in prices and a general harmonization of quality. When everyone does the same thing as their neighbour, prices fall.

In brief, high pressure on prices and costs is both a cause and a consequence of the globalization of an industry.

More and more consumers have become sensitive to price:

> The consumer philosophy is changing. Now people prefer to buy four pairs of shoes in one year instead of one. They like to change, follow fashion, and they buy cheaper products in order to afford variety.

Increasing negotiation power of distributors also helps to drive prices down.

> The growth of private labels drives prices down, particularly in the *tablette* and chocolate box businesses. Pressure on prices will also come from the internationalization of distributors and the harmonization of prices across countries at a lower level.

Under these forces the strongest competitors expand their international activities to get access to low-cost production or to reap economies of scope and reduce unit costs. The weakest competitors cannot survive: they close down, leave room for the others, or are taken over by international players. The concentration of the industry goes hand in hand with its international development.

Powerful international customers

International customers drive the international development and global integration of their suppliers. This is the case in the *paint industry*, where car finishes is a global segment because clients (car manufacturers) are becoming global and because technological intensity is high. The dynamics of can coating is similar:

> There is a global battlefield characterized by a few big suppliers and a few big customers: can coating. In this case the formulation is standardized, more than in any other area of the coating industry, because you have to adapt yourself to powerful global customers. If Coca-Cola have a canning plant in Shanghai, Berlin, London or New York, they want the can to be the same colour, same type of coating, so you have truly global specifications in that area.

Suppliers follow their clients wherever they go.

> For industrial coatings it all depends on the geographical scope of the client. The scope of competition depends on the customer. Industry customers who operate worldwide force suppliers to adopt a worldwide strategy.

The same mechanism applies to high temperature resistant *cables* for home appliances.

> Our clients are merging; large groups are developing, e.g. Electrolux, Bosch, Siemens, the Italians (Merloni, Nomicelli, Candy), the American giant Philips-Whirlpool, and concentration is not finished yet. In these groups production can easily migrate from one country to another, and there is a battle between subsidiaries for the right to produce. The first consequence for us suppliers is that we have to lower prices, increase volume, and reap economies of scale, otherwise we may lose a client. Second, our clients are relocating their manufacturing operations: from France they moved to Italy where costs are lower, so we have to go and sell our products in Italy.

When original equipment manufacturers act global, suppliers also have to act global.

> Many of our customers started to expand around the world. Everybody goes to China – most car manufacturers do – and we make wire for them. It is better to accompany them to new countries and to cooperate with them globally, not just at the regional level.
>
> One reason for becoming global is that our clients are multinationals, we negotiate with plants that may be located in Scotland, the USA, South Africa. For instance, after deciding to buy our cables, IBM told us to deal with their procurement department in Paris. This is the way the market

becomes global. [. . .] Working for such clients is very interesting because manufacturing operations can be focused on a single type of cable and be more efficient.

As far as consumer products are concerned, the high negotiation power of retail chains and their recent international expansion drive the international development and global integration in *decorative paint*, *footwear* and *chocolate and confectionery*.

The customer base becomes more international. Big 'do it yourself' retailers expand from the US into Mexico and Canada, so they are covering the whole of North America. In Europe large DIY stores move out of their national base into other European countries. It is early days, some have done more than others. Castorama and Carrefour are moving outside of France, German retail chains for building materials are also expanding their territory, Bricola and G&B from Benelux are moving into other European countries. We think that retailing will become more international and that decorative paint manufacturers will accompany them.

Retailers bring with them their basic product range. They start to negotiate on an international level, which means new opportunities but also an increased pressure on prices and more international competition. (Paint)

In the footwear industry distribution is organized in two main channels. On the one hand there are strong brands of high quality, high added value and high price which are distributed through wholly owned or franchised retail shops or by small multibrand specialized boutiques. On the other hand there are anonymous products, low priced, distributed by large specialized retail chains or by discounters. The most influential evolution in this industry has been the drop in the number of independent retailers down to 30 per cent of the market.

The major development over these last ten years is not the growth in the supermarkets which have, at best, maintained their position. The most influential development is the advent of what we call in our jargon the specialized supermarket stores, in particular Les Halles de la Chaussure and in sportswear Decathlon. Some of these powerful retail chains have started international expansion. (Footwear)

Competition is shaped by the clients. They come here with a pair of shoes and say: 'Look, I need this', and you give them a price. Then they go to another factory in another country to ask for lower prices. Customers are going to clean up the footwear industry. Giant distribution companies are pushing the industry towards globalization; we depend on them for the mass market.

The negotiation power of retail chains also is significant in the chocolate industry, where there has been considerable concentration in retailing. In many European countries the top ten food retailers have 80 per cent of the market.

> The power that you have against the power of the grocer is actually very important. And if you are number four you have not the power of number one and you tend to lose out. (Chocolate and sugar confectionery)

In France, about 25 per cent of chocolate *tablettes* are sold under private labels:

> International competition may manifest itself through the growth of private labels or own-label merchandise where Sainsbury, Tesco, Safeway [retail chains] will be quite happy to talk to anybody who comes along with a quality product, prepared to give a good price and meet their requirements in terms of agreement, packaging and that sort of thing. (Chocolate and sugar confectionery)

Competition is more and more at the European level because modern distribution is organized on a European scale. Supermarkets and discounters have a European strategy. Each tries to select the best supplier abroad.

> German discounters are quite powerful now, firms like Aldi, Lidl, Norma. They now expand over Western Europe to Benelux, to France, to England; they are starting to go to Italy. Austria also has a strong discount business which is expanding towards East European markets. Scandinavia is catching up, Rema in Norway is starting to go abroad. The manufacturers follow the discounters where they go. (Chocolate and sugar confectionery)

Emerging high growth markets

Emerging high growth markets attract foreign competition, particularly when traditional markets are mature. This is the case in the four industries that we studied. Growth potential is located in two main areas: the Far East and some Eastern European countries.

> Paint consumption per head is very closely linked to gross domestic product per head, so as prosperity increases then consumption of paint increases. The highest per capita consumption of paint is in Paris and in Switzerland and the lowest in Somalia and Ethiopia. The tigers of Asia are grouped in the lower half but are moving up that course very rapidly. Asia Pacific is all about growth and development, whereas the sophisticated Western markets are mature.
>
> We believe in the growth of consumption in the Eastern European countries in the next 15 to 20 years, in countries like Hungary, ex-East

> Germany, the Czech Republic, Slovakia, Poland, the Baltic countries, even Russia and the Ukraine. In countries like Bulgaria and Romania it will be more difficult.
>
> When a country opens up economically it starts to paint houses. The look of Eastern Europe is starting to change, thanks to paint. Paint is symbolic: a touch of white paint in a town that has been torn apart by war is a symbol of revival – take Vietnam for instance. . . . A touch of paint is good for the morale.

The same evolution is taking place in the cable industry:

> The industry becomes global because the growing markets are somewhere else than in Europe. If you want to grow and play a bigger role in the industry you have to go out from Europe. The Far East, and Asia and South America are growing markets. China and India will be; Russia is a big promise.

In the footwear industry several Eastern European countries and Asian countries such as Japan, Korea, Singapore, Hong Kong and Taiwan attract Western European manufacturers involved in upmarket fashion footwear. Latin America, particularly Brazil and Mexico, also offers growth potential in the cable industry, upmarket footwear and chocolate and confectionery.

> I think that the scope for geographic transfer of Western parts to Central and Eastern Europe, to Asia and to places in South America is in. The potential is mindblowing. These people are getting disposable income. Even if only 10 per cent of the population has an income, they want those products. (Chocolate and sugar confectionery)

Foreign competitors move into emerging high growth markets with a long term strategy.

> The competition will take place in the East and in Asia. We will try to set up strong positions in all the Eastern countries as quickly as possible. This is now the battlefield for food companies. There is always a premium for the first entrant; brand reputation has to be built as early as possible. We are not the only ones – all the big groups with international strategies are doing this. The potential of the Far East is so enormous that we must be ready. (Chocolate and sugar confectionery)

They are driven by growth ambitions that cannot be fulfilled in their traditional mature markets.

> What is behind this is a human desire for growth and development. Company managers behave as [the King] Gustav Adolf and Napoleon. More peaceful methods, for sure, but the same desire to expand and to win. (Paint)

In chocolate and sugar confectionery there are different expectations, depending on the region.

> The big change will be the development in Eastern Europe and in Asia. Talking about Eastern Europe, international Western companies will establish themselves with modern production systems. European know-how will spread throughout all these countries and the international brands will gain market share, but the consumption per capita will not rise dramatically. In Asia the picture is different: the market will grow thanks to increased purchasing power. Imagine how much it would represent to move from an average consumption per capita below 1 kilogram to 2 kilograms, and multiply this by two billion people. (Chocolate and sugar confectionery)

Growth in Eastern Europe

In the paint industry Eastern Europe is seen as a natural expansion area for competitors established in the West.

> American companies may be interested to grow in Europe through acquisitions. Those who are not yet present in the European market see that the East is opening up, the whole area will be the largest market in the world, much bigger than NAFTA.

In the cable industry there is local competition on power cables but high growth opportunities in fibre optics and high technology systems.

> The cable industry is strong in some Eastern European countries and it is underdeveloped in some others. They are stronger in the power cable markets than in the telecommunication side, especially in fibre optics. There we will see strong growth over the coming years in the area of fibre optics. The problem is the financing and that is really what sets the limits on how fast the building can go on in these countries. It is of course about support from the World Bank and others.

Some developing countries in Eastern Europe have started to manufacture electrical appliances with French, or German or Dutch specifications: East Germany, Poland and Russia have become potential clients for makers of high temperature cable.

There are growth opportunities for upmarket fashion footwear in Eastern Europe. Fashion did not fit with socialist ideology, and it was hard for local manufacturers to switch to fashion in the 1990s.

> After the fall of the Berlin Wall it took some time for the market to take off. This was because purchasing power was low and no local organization had sufficient financial resources to import foreign products. Now for a couple of years there has been a market, maybe small compared with the

> percentage of the population, about 4 per cent on average, but these people can buy and they want designer label products because for them it is a status symbol to show their own products that not everyone can afford.

For chocolate and sugar confectionery Russia is the third-largest market in the world, and the Ukraine is in the top ten countries for consumption.

> The opportunities in the former Soviet Union and the Eastern bloc generally are absolutely huge. Hundreds of millions of people who have not grown up where they have learnt to like that taste. What they have grown up with is awful poor quality state-produced stuff . . . and that is a wide open market for the people who have the courage to tackle it . . . a major push towards globalization.
>
> Eastern Europe, including Russia, represents a gigantic reservoir of new consumers. And I think that all the global firms are in the process of organizing themselves for it, either by building production units in these countries or by exporting. I am talking about Eastern Europe but in China there are also some very important operations that are going on. The idea is to grow on a global level in zones that have largely been overlooked, rather than trying to reanimate consumption in countries like the United States or Western Europe: there consumption has reached a plateau. (Chocolate and sugar confectionery)

There are some risks, but also a lot of advantages, in moving early into these markets.

> We have to tap Eastern European markets. The costs of advertising media are accessible, they are still cheap. It will never be so cheap to set up a brand in East European countries. Marketers in large companies laughed at the prices announced for TV advertising in Poland or in Russia. At the beginning, and still now you can set up a new brand. On the other hand logistical and trade structures are insufficient but you cannot have it all pink. (Chocolate and sugar confectionery)

Growth in Asia

Paint producers from developed countries set up local operations in Asia in order to follow their customers to these expansion areas (car manufacturers and other industrial clients) and to tap high growth local markets in decorative paint.

Asia has become a prioritary target in the cable industry: 'Today we are in the process of setting up joint ventures in China, in Vietnam and in India . . . just like everyone else.' In these developing markets customers ignore traditional copper cable and go straight on to fibre optic cable.

> Asia will be the most important market for growth for us for many years. We have started up our own manufacturing of fibre optic cable in India and we will do the same in Malaysia. In Thailand and in China we started up the manufacturing of network material and cable-ends.
>
> In the new developing markets, in Asia for instance, they cannot wait for a local supplier to be able to provide a complete package: technology, a system (including all sorts of equipment) and access to the funds needed to set up the whole business. In those countries the availability of funds for financing the project can be a key factor when choosing between a local supplier and an international one. (Cables)

Managers consider that they have to set up local operations because the distance between Europe and the Far East does not allow significant synergies and the local markets for cables are large enough.

In the footwear industry several Asian countries import upmarket fashion products which they are not able to design and manufacture themselves.

> In the 1950s we exported mainly to Europe. When the European market became stable we started to do business with South East Asia in the 1960s, particularly Hong Kong and Japan. In the 1980s we expanded our sales to Singapore and to Korea. Today Korea is a very interesting market for us, not so much for Korean consumers but for tourists. The Japanese fly to Korea for the weekend, they buy four pairs of shoes and the price difference pays for their plane ticket. Just as people go to Paris and come back with Vuitton bags.

In the chocolate and confectionery industry there are growth opportunities for global brands and upmarket niche players.

> For our high quality expensive chocolates the most interesting markets are in the Far East: Japan, Hong Kong, Singapore, Taiwan. Over there the population understands quality. Besides this priority zone we can find some pockets of demand in the USA and in Canada, among the ethnic German population. On the other hand the average American or Canadian does not understand our concept of quality.

When products have a relatively low added value, local manufacturing operations are set up.

> Three years ago we started to produce in Russia, and on 20 November this year the first lollipop came out of our Chinese production line. Suppose that we could sell freely in China and without currency problems, and imagine that a billion people start buying [our brand], then we would have difficulty in delivering from Spain.

However, there is tough competition in these emerging high growth markets, precisely because they attract a lot of international players.

> In Asia and in Eastern Europe you find all the biggest world manufacturers of high voltage cables: Alcatel, BICC, Pirelli. . . . We meet them everywhere and everybody fights vigorously.

International players consider that the level of risk is still high in countries such as Russia.

> We have a foothold in Eastern Europe already, and we are selling to Russia. We sold rather a lot last year and it looks very interesting. But this could end any time. A few months ago they suddenly introduced customs duties in Russia, which made things much more complicated. You have to be careful when you are dealing with these countries. (Chocolate and sugar confectionery)

Competition will increase as soon as local production grows.

> Germans have looked to the East and benefited from a new demand, particularly from Russia. German production has really picked up. Companies like Bahlsen worked at full capacity just to respond to the first Russian orders. But there will be a moment when companies will settle there, the Russians are going to progressively structure their industries and trade will slow down a bit, then the fight will be even tougher. (Chocolate and sugar confectionery)

In the footwear industry Asian and Eastern European manufacturers dominate their domestic markets and compete in the mass market worldwide. Local businesses are very active in decorative paint, where growth opportunities are moderated by increasing local competition. Generally foreign direct investment is welcome but imports are limited by protectionist policies. In the future it is also expected that these countries will compete back and sell their low-cost products to Europe and North America. For instance for enamelled wires:

> It is quite possible that companies from the East or from Asia will come into Europe. China, for example, is very well prepared with new and modern machinery and, although they have to supply their own growing market, one day they may start selling abroad at competitive prices. (Cables)

Managers also mentioned a relatively high level of financial risk in Russia and in some Asian countries, but at the time of the study (1995) they did not anticipate the financial crisis in Thailand, Indonesia and South Korea (1997), the recession that followed the period of overheating of the economy and financial speculation, and the financial crisis in Russia (1998).

In spite of all these risks, taking a long range perspective, emerging high growth markets are so tempting that they drive international ventures and can change the geographic scope of industries, particularly when traditional markets are mature or declining. Moreover the case of emerging economies *vis-à-vis* traditional markets may be a particular scenario of a more general law: the international expansion of firms is driven by market-growth differentials across borders.

The history of international business gives ample evidence of the impact of monetary conditions on international trade and investment. Managers are concerned with monetary fluctuations. On the one hand some currency stability is needed to stimulate international trade; on the other hand currency fluctuations (such as the devaluation of the Italian lira and the Spanish peseta at the beginning of the 1990s, and the fall of several Asian currencies in 1997) influence relative product flows across borders and some international companies are tempted to disperse production sites throughout regions in order to average risk. However, monetary conditions are not considered a major structural force, they are viewed as moderating variables.

Throughout the discussion of structural forces that drive global integration a number of related competitive actions have been mentioned, for instance differentiation strategies based on R&D in relation to technological intensity, volume strategies in relation to economies of scale, global brand advertising, relocation strategies in relation to comparative advantages, price cutting, and new ventures in emerging markets. The following chapters analyse international competitive actions in more detail and provide a typology of international strategies.

From practice to theory: a summary

Several structural forces drive global integration. *Technological intensity* is viewed as the strongest driver of globalization, in line with the literature (for instance Kobrin, 1991). High technological intensity includes economies of scale and scope in research and development and relates to economies of scale in manufacturing. *Economies of scale and scope in manufacturing* have a moderate to strong impact on internationalization depending on the industry; in some industries such as paint they are combined with *economies of scale and scope in procurement*. *Economies of scale and scope in advertising and sponsoring* also drive global integration, contrary to the conclusions of Kobrin's study (1991). A *short product life cycle*, such as in fashion footwear, stimulates internationalization: a large market scope compensates for the short time frame. *Comparative advantages*, mainly labour costs, drive the global integration of upstream activities, and relocation strategies in some industries such as footwear and low technology cables. Competition from low labour cost countries, overcapacity, cross-border trade, the negotiation power of customers and so on create *pressures to reduce prices and costs*, which stimulates international expansion, further relocation and integration so as to reap economies of scale. *The international nature of customers* offers opportunities for international expansion and requires some international coordination of marketing and sales. The *emergence of high growth markets* stimulates international strategic moves, particularly when traditional home markets are stagnant.

When the findings concerning the effect of advertising intensity (this chapter) and the effect of distribution intensity (Chapter 3) are considered together, one comes to the conclusion that *marketing intensity* is a dual concept and *has a dual effect* on the global integration of industries. High advertising-sponsoring intensity stimulates globalization, whereas high distribution-sales intensity stimulates local responsiveness. This duality resolves the paradox of contradictory findings and arguments in previous research (Levitt, 1983 vs. Kobrin, 1991).

The concept of technological intensity encompasses supply and demand factors: economies of scale and scope in R&D, exclusive knowledge that may be located in specific countries or firms, and worldwide high growth demand for new and better products. Economies of scale and scope and comparative advantages relate to costs and economic theories. *Practitioners draw our attention to a set of factors related to demand: in so doing they complement mainstream theories*. Managers consider the *geographical scope and negotiation power of clients* as one of the major forces driving global integration in the four industries studied. The influence of international customers is direct (suppliers have to follow them) and indirect (suppliers have to grow in order to balance the increasing negotiation power of customers). Indeed the combination of two forces – high technological intensity and powerful international customers – creates the most dramatic globalization scenarios, such as the globalization of can coating, car finishes or high voltage submarine cables. The *emergence of new high growth markets abroad* is also perceived as a strong force driving international development in the four industries that we studied. New high growth markets in Asia, in Eastern Europe and in South America attract foreign firms, particularly when demand stagnates in traditional developed markets (North America, Western Europe and Japan). High-growth countries stimulate product flows and foreign direct investments, until they get equipped with a local industry. This is a particular case of a more general phenomenon: the stimulating effect of differences in market growth across borders.

These structural forces drive international development and global integration when, and only when, firms exploit a set of favourable conditions and venture across borders.

Bibliography

Technology is a source of innovation and competitive advantage, and economic theories consider that foreign investment relies on competitive advantages that local firms cannot acquire (Kindleberger, 1969; Hymer, 1976). Technological innovators exploit their competitive advantage across borders (Vernon, 1966) and they implement technological transfers between their international operations (Teece, 1976; Rugman, 1981). Technological advantage is one of the ownership advantages in the eclectic paradigm (Dunning, 1988, 1993). In transaction cost theory, technology and know-how are sources of market imperfections that stimulate international investments (Buckley and Casson, 1976; Teece, 1986). High R&D cost can be amortized when firms have a wide geographical scope (Porter, 1986; Prahalad and Doz, 1987; Bartlett and Ghoshal, 1992; Yip, 1992), so technological intensity is viewed as a strong determinant of global integration. Kobrin (1991) measured technological intensity by the ratio of R&D expenses to sales turnover and found a significant relationship between technological intensity and a global integration index.

Concerning access to scarce material resources, Porter (1986) argued that the bargaining power of international suppliers pushes firms to coordinate or centralize purchasing in reaction to the pressure exercised by these suppliers. This factor is particularly important when the cost of raw material is high or when prices fluctuate in world markets (Prahalad and Doz, 1987). In the eclectic theory, the power of international suppliers is one of the location-specific variables (Dunning, 1981).

Economies of scale have been widely recognized as a determinant of the international development of industries, both in the economic and in the managerial literature. In economic theory, scale economies are one of the four oligopolistic advantages that explain foreign direct investment (Kindleberger, 1969) and multinational development (Hymer, 1976). In the strategic management literature, a broad geographical scope creates opportunities for scale economies, and the perspective of scale economies drive firms to expand across borders in order to access a larger potential market. Scale economies create a need for global coordination (Bartlett and Ghoshal, 1989, 1992) and lead firms to concentrate an activity in one or a few locations to serve the whole world (Porter, 1986). Authors generally think in terms of economies of scale in production. As far as manufacturing is concerned, the challenge is to reach a critical size for a production unit to be competitive. The ratio of critical size to the size of the world market determines the level of pressure toward globalization. Kobrin (1991) retained manufacturing scale as a variable explaining global integration; however, he did not find any significant relationship and concluded that the importance of this factor has been over-emphasized in the literature.

Concerning the dual effect of marketing intensity and economies of scale and scope in advertising, Prahalad and Doz (1987) noticed the ambiguity of the relationship and suggested that the causes of the high advertising to sales ratio be analysed. A high ratio may result from a duplication of marketing expenses in several different countries; it may also result from expensive global brand advertising campaigns. When universal needs exist, economies of scale in advertising drive international development and global integration.

According to Bartlett and Ghoshal (1992), short life cycles of products and technologies drive worldwide innovation. The perspective of a short cycle increases the need for companies to seek global volume in order to amortize their investments (R&D and manufacturing) as quickly as possible. Yip (1992) argued that short market life combined with high cost of product development stimulates global strategies.

Since the theory of comparative advantage (Hecksher, 1919; Ohlin, 1933) the development of international exchanges has been explained by the asymmetrical distribution of resources across countries, more precisely the repartition of production factors: labour, capital, and scarce material resources. More recent theories concluded that comparative advantages stimulate both exchanges and foreign direct investments (Mundell, 1957; Vernon, 1966; Kojima, 1978; Dunning, 1981). Most strategic management scholars also retained comparative advantage as a major determinant of the international dynamics of industries and of firms' strategies (Perlmutter, 1969; Kogut, 1985a; Prahalad and Doz, 1987; Roth and Morrison, 1990; Bartlett and Ghoshal, 1992). However, Porter (1986) suggested that comparative advantages are eroding.

Intense rivalry and/or low growth in key countries creates strong pressures on prices. According to Porter (1986, 1990) strong competition on prices pushes firms to extend their geographical scope in order to maintain growth and to exploit scale economies. Strong pressures on prices also drive firms to relocate their activities in order to exploit comparative advantages. Prahalad and Doz (1987) retained the pressure for cost reduction as one of the four factors influencing global operational integration.

The influence of international customers has been overlooked by the economic theories of multinationalization. Several authors who helped to develop the global integration/local responsiveness framework argued that the international coordination and/or centralization of customers' purchases drives the international development of suppliers (Porter, 1986; Prahalad and Doz, 1987; Ghoshal, 1987; Roth and Morrison, 1990; Yip, 1992). Perlmutter (1969) saw international customers as one of the environmental forces favourable to geocentric organizations.

5

Competitive Actions

Tugrul Atamer, Roland Calori, Gianluca Colombo, Sarah-Kathryn McDonald and Martine Menguzzato-Boulard

Structural forces create opportunities and constraints, but change happens when firms implement new competitive actions. Firms may or may not exploit structural opportunities for international development, they may or may not be constrained by structural forces. The international dynamics of industries is a continuous interaction between structural forces and competitive actions. Competitive actions can be stimulated by structural forces, but they can also shape new structural forces.

Innovators exploit their ownership-specific advantage worldwide and accelerate the globalization of their industry. When effective international strategies are imitated, collective strategic moves further transform the competitive system. The theoretical foundations of this perspective were laid down by Vernon (1966), but the importance of competitive actions has been underestimated in research on globalization (Birkinshaw et al., 1995).

This chapter reviews the set of significant actions that drive or restrain the international development of an industry, according to top managers. We start with the most conservative force: the presence and defensive strategies of national players, and progress toward the most revolutionary force: innovative international strategies.

International development and global integration are restrained when *national players hold and defend significant positions in their home market*. Local competitors may combine several strategies to delay or to block foreign intrusions: gain a high share of their domestic market, hold local distribution channels, create and maintain local preferences (differentiation) and strong brand image, exploit cultural proximities in a limited geographic area, lobby for protectionistic policies, etc. Such strategies preserve the multidomestic or mixed character of an industry when they are implemented in key countries or within a trade bloc.

On the other hand three main categories of competitive action drive international development and global integration: relocation strategies, mergers-acquisitions-alliances, and innovative international strategies.

When several *key competitors relocate activities* of the value chain abroad, particularly manufacturing and R&D, the amount of foreign direct investment and international trade (components, products) increases and international coordination mechanisms have to be implemented. By exploiting comparative advantages in some countries firms accentuate asymmetries; however, comparative advantages based on labour cost tend to decrease over time with the economic and social development of host countries.

International mergers, acquisitions and alliances are critical events in the dynamics of globalization. They increase the level of foreign direct investment and cross-border trade quicker than organic growth. When major competitors merge, the rules of international competition may change dramatically. Industry concentration and international development drive each other. When an industry is mature and when national champions hold significant market shares, M&As are the only way to achieve quick and massive international expansion. In high growth and technology-intensive industries international alliances reduce R&D risks and pay-back times by giving access to larger markets.

Some competitors are strong or creative enough to *change the rules of international competition in their industry*. According to top managers who participated in this study, innovative international strategies play a significant role in the dynamics of competition. A single firm often is at the origin of major changes. Further on, when the new strategy has proved successful, imitations contribute to a collective shift. By definition each innovative international strategy is unique, but six generic strategies can be identified: product innovation and global brand responding to or creating a universal need, transnational restructuring, worldwide exclusive technology, worldwide luxury niche, product differentiation, and low-cost international operations.

Figure 5.1 summarizes this set of competitive actions.

Defending one's home market

When national competitors hold significant market shares in a key country with a large domestic market, they may block foreign intrusion and thus hinder international development.

In the *paint industry*, in 1995, the Japanese market represented 800 billion yen with an average yearly growth of 2 per cent. There were

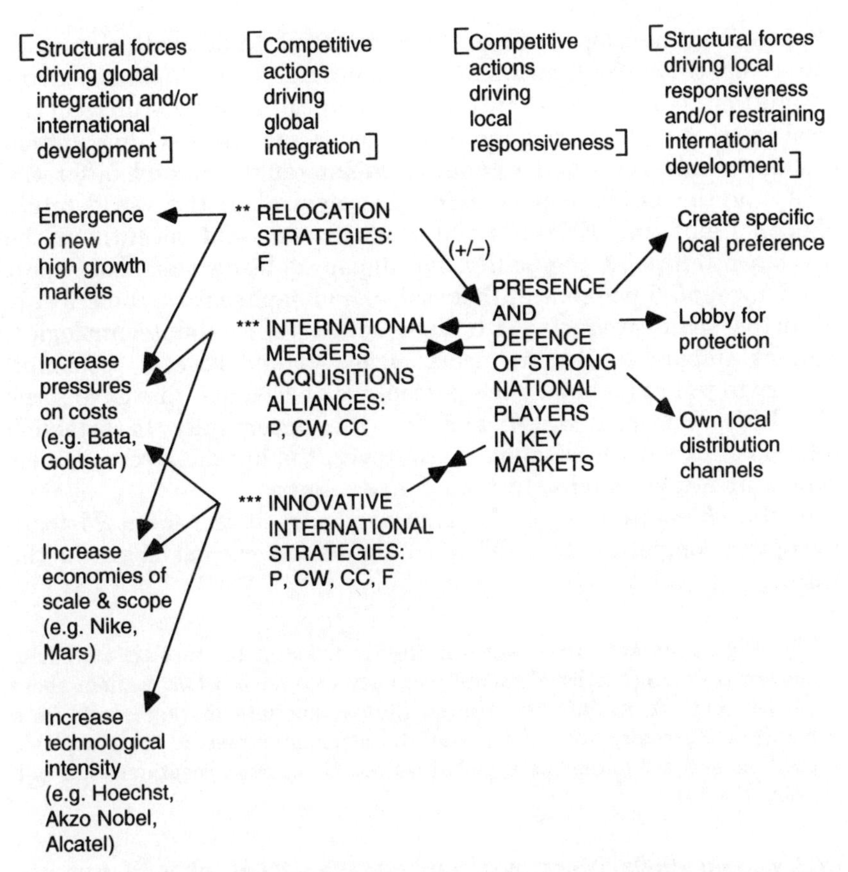

Figure 5.1 *Competitive actions and their effects on structural forces*

about 200 paint manufacturers, most of them Japanese; the first three held more than 50 per cent of the Japanese market. Kansaï Paint (20 per cent market share) belonged to the Sanwa Group and was integrated upstream in chemicals. Nippon Paint (20 per cent market share) belonged to the Sumitomo Group. The number three Daï Nippon Toryo (10 per cent market share) belonged to Mitsubishi. Nippon Paint and Kansaï Paint together held more than 90 per cent of the market of car finishes. Clearly it was very hard for a foreigner like PPG or Dupont to penetrate this market, particularly since customers require just-in-time delivery and quick services. When foreigners develop superior skills and are tempted with reciprocal agreements, national players may agree to cooperate. For instance in automotive coatings Kansaï Paint made a joint venture with Dupont, Daï Nippon Toryo made a joint venture with Herberts (Hoechst), and

Nippon Paint developed cooperation with PPG. In decorative coatings the competitive configuration was similar, three Japanese firms (Asahi Pen, Nippon Paint and Atom Chemical) held two-thirds of the local market, which was protected by a complicated distribution system (wholesalers and retailers). Japan ranked second (after the USA) for the production of paint (18 per cent of the world total), Nippon Paint and Kansaï Paint ranked sixth and seventh in the world top ten paint companies, but Japanese leaders did not export much (around 5 per cent of their sales) and Japanese customers only imported some products with high added value and technological content. Japanese manufacturers lagged behind several occidental leaders in the reduction in the percentage of solvents; this gave firms like PPG, Hoechst, BASF and ICI the opportunity to establish relationships with local players. However, the latter preserved their dominant market shares in their home country.

In the *chocolate and confectionery* industry it is very hard for a European competitor to build up a significant market share in the USA.

> The largest market in the world is the United States: there the chocolate market is dominated by Mars and Hershey who have between them about 80 per cent. To go into the United States chocolate market would be a mistake. Therefore whilst we want to consider ourselves from a global position and set ourselves a global target, there are exceptions that will prove the rule.

In the mid-1990s Mars was one of the global players but the American leader Hershey was still focused on North America and its sales in other continents were relatively small. In the case of Hershey and the two geographic zones of America and Europe, differences in consumers' tastes added an invisible barrier.

Managers believe that national competitors create specific tastes.

> In the Nordic countries there is a preference for the taste Marabou has in its chocolate. I do not believe that it is because it lies in our genes that we prefer a chocolate with a particular taste. Instead it is because these products have existed, have been produced and sold by a local company for decades, the company had success and created the taste. It is much the same with liquorice products. They started in England and in Denmark then in other Nordic countries and the people got accustomed to the taste. Salt liquorice for instance is a product that astonishes a lot of people. But when one has been eating salt liquorice since one was a child, then the product tastes good.
>
> When it comes to milk chocolate I think Marabou has become the norm for the Swedish. Swedish Marabou has a milder, vanilla taste and a softer texture than, say, German chocolate. We and the other Scandinavian companies have strong positions in our countries because our brands are

> leading. In Sweden chocolate coated biscuit bars are expected to taste like Cloetta's bars. So when Nestlé launches KitKat, which is a global brand, the Swedes think it has a strange taste. So it is hard for Americans and British companies to break into our markets. One way of course is to take over Scandinavian companies.

Strong national brands and strong national players die hard; some consumer products and brands even become part of the cultural heritage of a nation, they survive and coexist with global brands which are part of the TV heritage of the world.

> Each country still has its own dominant national brand that historically imposed a formula and a taste preference on consumers: Côte d'Or in Belgium, Cadbury in England, Verkade in the Netherlands. [. . .] In Japan there are a few strong local competitors, Lote, Gluko, Meidi, they innovate a lot in flavours and packaging. For instance they have chocolate with different flavours such as orange, mint, banana, kiwi. The only way to penetrate Japan is to be different and perceived as a luxury product.

National players also defend their positions by expanding within a limited zone of influence: old colonies or neighbouring countries, which may share some cultural traits with their home country.

> Spanish companies are active in Chile and in Argentina. [. . .] Germans have a foothold in Eastern Europe given that the ex-East Germany had business relationships with this zone. Even if they do not like each other very much, they work together.

National players may be in danger when comparative advantages call for a relocation of manufacturing abroad. Paradoxically, relocating critical upstream activity is a way to defend home-based activities (product development, marketing and sales). For instance in the footwear industry many firms still have national brands, design, distribution and sales; they can still be competitive thanks to relocation of manufacturing to foreign countries with low labour costs.

> Take for instance the UK, and Germany, and Italy, all three of which have some domestic businesses. They are competitive, they just rely on sources elsewhere for their footwear industries.

> There will be a stabilization of the better products in the Netherlands. The assembling of quality products, I mean assembling the upper leather on the sole, the heel, will stay in the Netherlands for a long time, because with that you have your quality insurance for high quality products.

Finally, national players can take an active part in raising and/or maintaining governmental protectionistic policies: they may lobby for specific regulations and norms.

> In the area of paint for roads, France stands out in terms of the quality of its products. However, we run into barriers. In Spain clients do not require certification but we do not sell a kilo of paint because they prefer to buy Spanish. In Germany the market is protected. Public purchases represent about 80 per cent of this business. The other way around, it is very difficult to enter the French market that represents 20,000 tons of paint spread on the roads every year. Two big paint manufacturers already share the French market and the certification process is very difficult. In France we have on-site certifications, for instance we need to test our paint on a road for 24 months if it is to be certified for 24 months. We measure everything and if the results are not good enough we start another test for 24 months. In Germany they have a different system of specification called the 'turning table', a 15 day simulation, of course it is much quicker than the French system. Whatever, the Germans still prefer to buy their German road paints.

National competitors may discreetly encourage national preference in public purchases.

> Key accounts represent a high percentage of the turnover in a given country: electric utilities and telecoms companies. Until now they have always given priority to local manufacturers. Privatization will change the rules of the game. Also, trade barriers were the main reason why we did little business, let us say, on the German market. The European directive now gives equal chances to foreign manufacturers; it will take time but changes are on the way. (Cables)

They may lobby for radical measures such as high tariff barriers or quotas. In the paint industry high tariff barriers protected national competitors in developing countries, in the footwear industry quotas were set up to protect European manufacturers from Chinese competition. National players may also influence commissions that are responsible for mergers and monopolies when decisions have to be made concerning international takeovers.

When they are strong enough in their home country and when their domestic market is large enough, competitors with a national scope can resist international competition for a long time. When structural forces and competitive actions driving global integration increase and when structural forces driving responsiveness decrease, the question is: for how long can they defend their home market?

National companies with high market share and/or strong national brands tend to become priority targets for international takeovers, unless they decide to venture into international takeovers themselves. Part of the answer depends on competitive actions that drive global integration: relocation strategies, mergers-acquisitions-alliances, and innovative international strategies.

Relocation strategies

During the last 20 years relocation strategies have changed the geographic configuration of the footwear industry. Changes in the cable industry are more recent: they are related to deregulation in traditional markets and quick industrialization in Asia, South America and Eastern Europe.

Relocation strategies in the footwear industry

The footwear industry has had a tradition of international sourcing since the beginning of the twentieth century, purchasing the best leather in India, in Morocco, in Italy or in South America. After moving from Czechoslovakia to Toronto, the 'Western' Bata was the pioneer in relocating manufacturing to low labour cost countries (mainly Asia and Africa). This was just before World War II. Bata's strategic intent was to 'put shoes on people', and low cost was a necessary condition to sell low-priced mass market footwear worldwide. The first wave of massive relocation started at the end of the 1970s in the low-priced segment and in sports-leisure footwear.

> If we go back ten years ago, to 1984, there were 408 shoe manufacturers in France. There are now only 274. The 1984 production was 201 million pairs, it is now only 154 million. There was a workforce of 54,000, it has fallen to 32,000. The coverage of home consumption was 62 per cent ten years ago, it will be 46 per cent in 1994. It is no longer a crisis – it is extinction. That is what I told you on the phone: 'hurry up and do the interview', because if we wait, there soon will be no interviews to be done in France. The reasons are simple: high relative labour costs in France and a free trade policy. There you have the formula explaining the massive arrival of the Far East over the past ten years. In addition to that, all those countries sell in dollars, and as you know, the dollar tends to be undervalued.

Falling numbers witnessed firms' exits due to insufficient competitiveness and relocation of manufacturing. In the 1990s a high percentage of manufacturing was located in low labour cost countries. The percentage depended on the market segment: very high in sport-leisure footwear (above 90 per cent), high in mass-market and lower in upmarket footwear. Relocation strategies are determined by several parameters: product added value, manufacturing-delivering cycle time, and quality control.

For luxury shoes (high added value, quick cycle due to fashion and importance of quality) relocation strategies tended to be limited to Europe.

> With luxury shoes, you can relocate to Europe, for instance you can manufacture in Italy, it is just next door. Italy makes the same quality

> shoes as we do and has tanneries; the processing of skin-hides does not cause any problem. As far as we are concerned this is relocation within the Common Market. I do not believe that a radical relocation of the production of luxury shoes will happen for some time. On the other hand, in the 'cheap' segment, relocation is much easier.

For mass-market footwear, particularly sport-leisure, relocation was radical and directed to the countries in the Far East with the lowest labour costs.

> The big names – Nike, Reebok – are pure marketers, they do not produce in their own countries, they design their products, they have them manufactured in several low-cost countries (generally five or six), and they ship them to the markets they target worldwide. Most of all they spend billions in advertising and sponsoring.

Spain and Portugal attracted a lot of French companies in search of low-cost manufacturing, for instance Eram the French leader. Italy and Spain attracted upmarket brands such as Bally (from Switzerland), and luxury brands such as Charles Jourdan for a small percentage of their production (men's shoes). German companies also turned to Eastern Europe: Slovakia and Hungary. Eastern European countries could offer geographic proximity and still relatively cheap labour. Italian manufacturers themselves made agreements with Romania, they provided raw materials to the Romanians and paid for the manufacturing.

In the 1990s trade flows between North America (design, brands, distribution) and South America (raw materials, manufacturing, subcontracting) were significant. However, North American footwear companies turned to manufacturing in Asia earlier than their European counterparts.

There is a widespread consensus on the importance of containing labour costs in the footwear industry. Whether this general objective is best met through automation, (re)locating production of finished products abroad, and/or locally assembling 'foreign' components, and how important quality considerations may be in selecting among these alternatives, will vary from segment to segment. Moreover, the extent to which concerns with distribution costs, and/or market perceptions of the significance (if any) of the country of 'origin' on the image (ultimately the desirability) of the product also varies from one segment of 'the footwear industry' to another.

Containing labour costs

Costs are a matter of considerable concern in almost all segments of the industry, the high-priced segment of the high fashion niche being the most notable exception. Costs are key to the development of strategy and the configuration of the footwear industry internationally.

> We have to remember that the raw materials cost the same throughout the world; this is clear, and relatively normal. The difference lies in the different cost of labour, which is very high for our product. We believe that on average it is about 40 per cent of the final cost of the product: not the final cost to the public, but our final cost.
>
> It is very labour intensive, and, when you are stitching together uppers it requires a lot of patience, semi-skilled work, it takes a long time to learn. [. . .] Labour is the most important element of shoes. [. . .] When we make a pair of shoes, there are over 60 operations. [. . .] And we are no different, basically, to many companies. The people who are making the fine welted men's footwear that the Americans like so much, there are nearly a hundred operations in that, a lot of which are still done by hand.

The automation alternative

Technology can usefully be applied to automate a variety of production and related (e.g. design, purchasing, warehousing) processes, and therefore to reduce staff costs. This is an option which has met with some success.

> You would be very surprised going around a shoe factory just exactly how many components and operations there are in making a pair of shoes. So we have had to look at ways in which that can be less labour intensive, to make sure the footwear prices do not get out of all proportion, because clearly there is a big labour cost involved in a pair of shoes. [. . .] We have had to look at things like automatic stitching machines. We have had to look at computerizing warehousing – all the things that help you to save time and money, and make you more efficient, we have had to invest money in that, and every shoe company has had to do the same thing. [. . .] It is very much a matter of looking at a pair of shoes and just seeing how efficiently you can produce it.
>
> Computerization has revolutionized the shoe industry. [. . .] We are using computer aided design. We are designing shoes on television screens. I mean, we do not have to create a shoe now. We can draw a picture of it on a screen and see whether we like it, and if we like it we can manufacture it and produce samples of it, whereas previously we would have had to go through all the processes of making a shoe to see whether it was viable. Now we can do that on the screen, and the cost savings on that are quite dramatic.

Other managers are less optimistic about the cost savings that can be achieved through the introduction of technology to the production process. For some (particularly speciality footwear manufacturers) production runs are not large enough to warrant (or for them to be able to afford) the introduction of new technologies. Others argue that the nature of the footwear manufacturing process is such that, often, automation is not an option. The result is that the 'introduction of advanced technology in footwear is more or less important depending on the type of business'. Overall the consensus seems to be that this is – and is likely to remain – a labour intensive industry.

> If you want to mechanize you have to make a lot of pairage to support the mechanization. [. . .] If you could see our factory working, you would see there are people that actually pick shoes up, with a brush and adhesive, and brush the bottoms. Now you might look and say, 'There must be a better way of doing it'. Yes, there is, but you have got to be making 70,000 pairs a week and not 7,000.
>
> In the shoe industry, we have to deal with a pretty marginal industry. That means that the level of investment is rather low. If we talk about renewal of technology, then in general we are talking about expensive investments. In view of the generally small scale of the shoe companies it is only possible for a few companies to make such investments.
>
> [Despite automation to] close uppers by computer stitching . . . you cut the leather – still by hand because that is a skilled job. Leather being a natural substance, certain parts of the leather are used for certain parts of the shoes. You get wire marks, you get scratches – that has to be cut out, so you cannot computerize that.

Relocating production

If automation is not an option or if it cannot sufficiently reduce labour costs, questions are often raised about the desirability, if not the necessity, of relocating production. Thus, some notable exceptions notwithstanding, in the 1990s much footwear manufacturing, of major components, if not of finished products, was sited in relatively low wage rate countries or regions.

> When you see that today, a worker in China earns the same a month as a German worker earns an hour, the trend is tied down in advance.
>
> Over the last ten years, the shoe business has, or such a major part of the shoe business has, moved to Asia. [. . .] Quite simply it is a question of the price, labour cost. You cannot produce shoes in Europe any more. At least not in Northern Europe. You can still do it in Southern Europe but not in Northern Europe.

As the preceding remarks illustrate, while Northern European footwear manufacturers 'historically moved production more and more towards the South', a much larger and more general exodus of production occurred from Western, including North American, to Eastern, notably South East Asian, countries. Production continues to be mobile within that region, as footwear firms struggle to keep pace with the rapid development of its local economies, the skills and thus the quality of product its workforce is capable of producing, and – ironically to many – the trade barriers being erected to protect their own home countries from being flooded by products of the lowest wage-rate countries.

> Ten years ago [. . .] South East Asian production was based in South Korea and Taiwan. They hardly make any shoes there now. It moved from there to Thailand and Indonesia. Thailand has become too expensive, so the Thai industry is in decline. [. . .] Then it moved to China. The European Union imposes ridiculous quotas, which have just made everybody move again to Vietnam, and Laos, and Cambodia and everywhere else. So now, basically, at the sharp end, at the very price competitive end, of certain types of footwear, the industry has followed low labour cost.
>
> In Far East Asia, there were two phases. First of all what people refer to as the 'Four Dragons', made up of Korea, Taiwan, Hong Kong and Singapore. [. . .] But since then the labour costs have gone up. Right now wages in Korea and Taiwan are too high. [. . .] Now even these countries are undergoing intense competition and the shoe industry is in decline. Even these countries have relocated production.

Thus the development of many national economies in the South East Asian region (and associated increases in wage rates) is leading to yet another relocation of production. Central and Eastern European countries, India, and possibly countries in Northern Africa are identified as likely future sources of components and/or production sites.

> The industry is moving. [. . .] The huge shoe giants are constantly looking for the lowest point concerning wages. So that means that one year they are located in a certain developing country and the year after they are located in another developing country if that is cheaper.
>
> The next ones could be North Africa, India, which have not been explored much, and in the near future all of Eastern Europe.
>
> Eastern Europe has very low manufacturing costs and in some countries they have adequate quality. The East European countries are awakening from their decade-long torpor and are going to become significant players on the international market.

Assembling components

Of course, it does not have to be the whole shoe that is manufactured abroad. Considerable cost savings can often be achieved by producing or sourcing major components abroad, and assembling them domestically.

> Ten years ago most of the domestic production in the UK would have been in the UK, and now it definitely is not. I mean, it is not uncommon for a lot of uppers to come in from India, or from the Far Eastern countries, and then they will be made up in the UK as UK-made, manufactured shoes, with a lot of the labour being done elsewhere. [. . .] That is a major change. And it has had to be that way, because of the pressure to provide retail prices that people can afford to pay.
>
> The German shoe industry has gone in the last 30 years, particularly in the last 20 years, through a tremendous declination process, because the consumer in the men's shoe segment is not willing to pay out far more [than a given price] for a shoe. It is not possible to manufacture [. . . domestically] more cost effectively. You must go abroad with the production of the labour cost-intensive part, the shaft, that is the upper part of the shoe.

Given the pressure which price and cost considerations place upon manufacturers, why is it that some continue to follow the typically more expensive process of sourcing components abroad and assembling them locally, rather than (re)locating production of the finished good abroad? Two major factors, singly or in combination, argue in favour of the outsourcing alternative: quality considerations and transportation costs.

The quality factor

When demand does not support premium prices, thus allowing for higher manufacturing costs, some manufacturers feel pressured, but at the end of the day do not feel able, to (re)locate production abroad. Poor quality can be a major consideration. The quality of product that the managers believe a given labour force can produce, the 'value for money' criterion, has encouraged some manufacturers to purchase components abroad and assemble them in local facilities, where the workforce may be more skilled in certain aspects of finishing and assembling the product, and/or where it may be easier to control this aspect of the manufacturing process.

> We manufacture exclusively fashionable shoes in the more sophisticated area of consumption. On the basis of prices demanded here, we are forced to relocate parts of production to more cost-effective countries in order to make a marketable offer. We follow a strategy to get high-grade shoes in conformity with the market price in the long term. The strategy is to produce parts where they can be manufactured cost-effectively, taking them back to the home market to complete the manufacturing process using the know-how and qualifications of our staff.

Controlling transportation costs

The preceding discussion has focused on the importance of labour costs in deciding where in the world footwear manufacturing should take place. Yet labour costs are not the only factors taken into consideration in deciding where to produce footwear and still deliver finished products to local retailers at prices 'people can afford to pay'.

Another expense one might expect to be critically important in calculating breakeven points, especially when one is weighing up the overall attractiveness of manufacturing half-way around the world, is the cost of transporting components or finished products to their final destination. For some industry segments, notably sports shoes and unbranded mass-market items, the costs of moving product from, for example, South East Asia to Western Europe are not a matter of concern. For others, notably fashion footwear segments, they are critical, and effectively block organizations operating in these segments from taking advantage of low wage rates around the world.

Interestingly, the key difference between the two groups is not distance *per se* – it is time. Thinking about the 'how to move footwear from South East Asia to Western Europe' scenario, several respondents pointed out that, relative to many products which are routinely transported over land or sea, shoes 'are not very heavy, nor do they take up much space'. Provided speed of delivery is not critical, the cheaper land and sea container methods of transport can be employed. In such situations, distribution costs are not a barrier to European footwear firms wishing to locate production in remote, low wage rate arenas. Such is the case with sports shoes.

> Sports shoes are not, in general, a product of fashion. [. . .] They do not fall out of fashion in two or three months' time. Consequently, you can plan several months ahead of time.

Thus designs can be agreed and advance orders placed with relatively long lead times – lead times that are at least long enough to allow mass production in areas with labour cost advantages and distribution to intended markets using the relatively inexpensive land and sea routes. Fashion footwear segments, on the other hand, by their very nature are subject and must respond to rapid changes in the designs, colours, materials, etc. desired by consumers. In these segments, rapid response to the vagaries of fashion is essential. The only way in which such rapid response could be provided from remote production locations would be to fly goods from manufacturing facility to market, a prohibitively expensive exercise.

> I was saying a moment ago that transportation costs by boat are not very significant in the shoe sector. If you were to take the cost of air transport, that changes the equation. So there are certain types of products that can be planned well in advance, and that consequently can be manufactured far from their market without there being any impact. On the other hand, for (some) women's shoes, there are a lot of different varieties, a lot of

> different colours, fashion changes quickly – it is much more difficult to plan ahead and consequently to have them manufactured far from the market.

So managers' cost containment options may be limited by market or segment-specific supply time parameters. Even if costs of production are lower somewhere in the Far East than in Southern Europe, for example, the shorter distance and correspondingly faster delivery times (key when one is dealing with fashionable footwear items), makes Southern and, increasingly, Central and Eastern Europe the production site of choice for many European companies in the fashion segments of the industry, as the following comments illustrate:

> If you must react quickly to the latest fashion you cannot transport shoes by ship for four weeks around half the world. That does not work [. . .]; this means ultimately I cannot go to for example Vietnam only on the basis of price, putting up with six weeks to transport shoes.
>
> We are always in search of favourable procurement markets and there is a lot of movement. [. . .] Relating to Eastern Europe, definitely there is the advantage of shorter distance in comparison with procurement markets in the Far East. That means lower freight cost and faster reaction times. This is important in fashion.
>
> One of the important things is the ability to respond quickly to fashion changes, to demand changes, to swings and demand, and really you can only do that by having local supply. Local does not necessarily mean within the country. But it certainly means within the region. Within Europe, you can be fast. Once you move off-shore to the Far East or to South America, you cannot be fast, the shipment times are too long. You cannot fly shoes anywhere, because it is too expensive, they are too heavy and too big.

So we see that, just as quality considerations sometimes stop managers from taking advantage of the lowest possible wage rates on offer around the world, the importance of being able to respond quickly to market demands can also affect decisions about the location of production when pursuing a cost containment strategy.

> You must try always, as a shoe manufacturer, to manufacture most cost effectively. But you cannot have the factory so far abroad, in such a remote country, that you have no market proximity any more. [. . .] You cannot go to the other end of the world; the logistics do not admit that at all.

Equally, it appears, one cannot pursue a cost containment strategy if the decisions one makes about where to locate production to minimize costs affect the price one can charge for the product. For ultimately it is the relationship between total cost and price (notably the size of the gap between the two which can be maintained) with which many managers are concerned. Indeed, of the factors affecting their pricing strategies it is the one which emerges as the third important influence on decisions about where in the world footwear production should be located: the 'value' that consumers place on products manufactured in (or otherwise associated with) particular markets; the 'cachet of the country'.

The 'cachet of the country'

The image associated with, notably fashionable, products manufactured in particular countries can be critically important both in footwear manufacturers' decisions about where to locate production, and in decisions to source only components, rather than manufacture finished products, abroad. Shoes that are assembled in one country can often be effectively marketed as 'made in' that country, even if a significant part of the manufacturing has actually taken place abroad. Of course, products do not have to be produced (or even assembled) in one country in order to be perceived as originating there. As one respondent pointed out, what one perceives as being, for example, 'American' shoes may actually be footwear sold by an organization 'based in' or 'owned by' Americans, not footwear 'made in' America:

> American companies export a lot, but most of the time with products that are manufactured under their supervision in South East Asia. [. . .] What is sold as an American product and manufactured in South East Asia represents an enormous part of the market.

Such national images are identified as extremely important to some segments of the market. Most generally, our managers noted the tendency for many customers around the world to associate a high fashion, high quality image with (notably leather) footwear 'from' France and Italy.

> There is a certain cachet to a brand which manufactures its products in one country. [. . .] Particularly strong at the moment are American brands that manufacture in America. There is still a 'made in the USA' cachet. I think there is a 'made in Italy' cachet.

Often the desire to purchase a product with the 'made in . . .' cachet translates into willingness to pay a higher price. Conversely, premium prices are unlikely to be happily paid by consumers who perceive goods produced in some countries as lacking a 'made in . . .' cachet.

Such perceptions serve to limit further managers' abilities to pursue generic cost containment strategies by maximizing the amount of manual labour associated with the production (including the assembly) of footwear products in low wage rate areas. As noted, one common compromise is to source components abroad and carry out just enough of the production process in a given country to warrant the coveted 'made in. . .' label. When demand for the 'cachet of the country' premium does not allow prices to be set much higher than, or as high as, the cost of providing such a product, the assembly alternative can be very attractive indeed.

At this point one is left with the clear impression that it makes more sense, at least from the managers' perspective, to talk not about 'factors affecting the location of production in the footwear industry', but of factors affecting decisions about where different kinds of footwear products can efficiently and effectively be produced to meet the needs of various segments of the market.

Relocation strategies in the cable industry

In the cable industry there is more and more competition on cost, particularly when product and process technologies are accessible.

> Ten years ago we sourced cables from Germany or from the country where we operated. Now more and more international players manufacture cables in new countries where production costs are lower. We have a cable operation in Germany but we try to develop low-cost sites in Europe: in Spain, in Portugal, in Turkey. . . . We are looking at Russia.

After a period of international acquisitions in most key countries, a few multinational competitors started to restructure their manufacturing operations. Production plants were closed down and some production was transferred to developing countries, particularly China.

> Factories built in China, Malaysia, Indonesia, India, will start manufacturing high voltage cables; most of them in some form of joint venture with established manufacturers.
>
> The American cable industry is moving towards South America, they are attracted by labour cost which is much lower than in the USA. There is pressure from host governments to add a significant share of local content to the products, and new infrastructure is being built. It has become worth settling there, transferring technology and getting back part of the profits.

In the case of the cable industry, developing countries are both attractive places for manufacturing and attractive markets: a lot of local production is sold to local customers. In general, relocation strategies contribute to the development of host countries' local revenues, purchasing power, availability of foreign currency, and technological knowledge. Consequently competitive actions (relocation) have a significant indirect impact on a structural force that drives global integration: the emergence of new high growth markets. Relocation strategies are achieved in different ways: by purchasing, subcontracting, greenfield affiliates, joint ventures with foreign local partners or international acquisitions.

International mergers, acquisitions and alliances

In the *footwear industry* relocation strategies based on cooperation (agreements, subcontracting, joint ventures) and relatively low capital intensity have put off the need for mergers and acquisitions. In upmarket segments, manufacturers expanded through networks of wholly owned or franchised retail stores. International expansion was incremental and very few big bang mergers took place. However, there were some exceptions.

> There is a sort of comeback of North Americans today in the Cholet region (France). Not in the form of industrial operations. They really have nothing to teach us. Their shoe industry is not more modern than ours. We are clearly more productive. The Americans spotted a few performing small firms to invest in, and they were federated through American capital. The American group is called Polygone, it includes small businesses such as Francelor, Chenet, Poupelar. Altogether the French operations of the group now employ about 1,300 persons.

In paint, cables, chocolate and confectionery, mergers and acquisitions have driven international development.

M&As in the paint industry

Over the last 15 years the concentration of the paint industry has been very quick and a few international leaders have emerged.

> If you look at the way that merger and acquisition activity has altered the structure of the industry you will see that there has been really a tremendous amount of change, and broadly what is happening is that the big are getting bigger and more international, the medium-sized companies are feeling the squeeze and unless they can be strong in a particular region, are tending to lose out. And then if you are very focused on a particular segment or you have a particularly good cost base because you are small, your overheads are low . . . smaller paint companies occupying niches continue to flourish. However, broadly, the number of paint companies has come down very rapidly over the last ten years. For example in the US it came down something like 9,000 to 2,000, and in Europe from something like 6,000 to 1,500: that is a very big contraction while volumes have gone up. The other thing that has happened is that the top ten

> companies are taking more and more of the total market and so we now have ten companies that cover about one-third of the free world coating industry.

This trend will go on and lead to a polarization of the industry with multinational companies on the one hand and small focused businesses on the other hand.

> In ten years' time four companies will be dominating the market. It is not that bad to be small: you can be small locally and you can specialize, at least as long as the governments are not too tough on the small companies when it comes to environmental policies. But the medium-sized ones will have a hard time, they will be squeezed, they better sell themselves to the bigger ones now, otherwise they will be stuck somewhere in the middle. The driving force behind this is economies of scale. [. . .] There will be two types of company left, the very big and the small local ones. The big thanks to their resources and the small thanks to their low overhead structure. To survive in the future you either have to be Pan-European, or you have to have a very strong local position, or a strong international position in a niche. In such positions you are able to free resources for product development, this is the condition if you are to keep your place and not to become a market follower, low price producer who is altogether in the hands of the big ones.

The international development of technology-intensive businesses such as car finishes or can coating has not been based so much on acquisitions. On the other hand significant M&As transformed the other businesses in the paint industry. For instance one of the world leaders, Akzo Nobel, was formed after successive mergers and acquisitions. Casco, a Scandinavian glue company, entered the paint business in 1982. They merged with Akzo from the Netherlands and formed a SKr. 30 billion paint company. Then Akzo merged with the Swedish Nobel in 1992 and acquired several other businesses, for instance Sadolin in the UK, Astral in France, Ivanoff, Brueguer and Procolor in Spain. In the mid-1990s the group was in the process of rationalizing its international operations.

> The concentration of paint manufacturers has been particularly strong in Northern Europe. In the consumer paint business in England, for example, you have two main players who took 50 per cent of the market. In France there still are five or six significant players. In Spain the leader, a family-owned business, Titan has 30 per cent of the market but the rest is fragmented. The Italian market is still fragmented.

In 1995 American competitors ranked fourth (PPG) and fifth (Sherwin Williams) worldwide, behind three European groups (ICI, Akzo Nobel and BASF). Most of the leaders belonged to large chemical groups.

> A lot of acquisitions have been achieved by chemical groups integrating downstream. When you are ICI, a manufacturer of resins, it is in your interest to be involved in the paint industry that consumes your resins. The logic is based on the industrial vertical chain. When you have brands downstream you can relax a little, even if your captive market only represents 20 per cent of your sales. . . . It helps you finance your research.

In the UK, ICI and Courtaulds; in Germany, BASF and Hoechst; in France, Total chemicals, dominated and restructured the paint industry.

In 1995 the business of decorative paint represented about 50 per cent of the whole market and was still relatively fragmented as compared to other market segments. In this activity mergers and acquisitions were the best vehicle for international development because structural forces driving local responsiveness were high and traditional markets were saturated.

> The dilemma is that if you want to grow in this business, then you really have to acquire companies and buy market share, because this is a mature industry and it really is difficult to get a massive increase otherwise. When you acquire a company, you pay an awful lot for the distribution. When you buy market you pay for the distribution of a local brand name. If you want to develop Pan-European brands it means that you have to kill the local brand names that you paid for. And this is a real economic dilemma: to kill or not to kill.

After international acquisitions, the buying firms tend to preserve the strong brands of their partners and they often add one global brand to the portfolio.

> ICI acquired Glidden, Grow Group and thereby became number three in the US. That means enormous volumes. Then they would enter and make changes and tell everyone that Glidden has now changed its name to Dulux. That would be extremely risky since there are a lot of buyers loyal to the brand name Glidden and there is also the relationship between the retailer and the brand name and that means you cannot always do it.

Such intercontinental acquisitions were exceptional in the paint industry, but intercontinental agreements were made for instance between occidental and Japanese manufacturers. In order to expand their geographic scope several competitors redefined their portfolio of businesses and concentrated on a few activities for which they could achieve international coverage and sustain competitive advantage.

> Often when you discuss acquisitions, you are tempted to swap businesses with each other. If we are discussing with BASF for example, they have a coil coating business in Germany and nowhere else, they could be

> interested in swapping it for another business, say in automotive finish, in order to strengthen their international position. In doing so they would please an international player who wants to strengthen its leadership in coil coating.

International mergers and acquisitions are not all pink; clearly there are severe post-acquisition integration problems related to the rationalization of operations.

> There are serious post-acquisition problems. Many people are fired. The morale of the ones who remain goes down, the sales people are less enthusiastic, some leave the company. In the end I am not sure that market share and profitability improve.

After redundancies and international restructuring, managers suggest that the autonomy of acquired subsidiaries should be preserved and that coordination should be preferred to centralization, particularly when forces driving local responsiveness are significant.

> Many technological breakthroughs come from small and medium-sized companies. I do not want to say that small is beautiful and big is ugly, but I hope that not everything will become global. Paint is a business that needs imagination and intuition beyond chemistry. If I were the managing director of a big company I would give maximum freedom of action to the companies acquired, within a few common goals and minimal rules. There should be great freedom of action in a market that is not global.

The age of mergers and acquisitions has not yet come to an end in the paint industry.

> The attractive companies on the market, small and independent, who succeeded in surfing the waves will be the targets for future takeovers. Marriages will be celebrated; concentration is the major trend for the future and the most attractive matches will happen first.

The next stages of international development will depend on the competitive actions of a few large multinationals that have already transformed the industry in the 1980s and the 1990s.

M&As in the cable industry

In the 1980s the cable industry was fragmented by national protectionist policies in telecommunication and power. A few competitors overcame these barriers by taking over foreign companies and by preparing the ground for future deregulation.

There have been a lot of acquisitions, a quick concentration led by large groups: Alcatel Cable, Pirelli, BICC, Sumitomo. . . . They came out of their countries with all their power, they took over market shares and the weakest local firms went bankrupt.

Within the last four years many medium-sized German cable makers, were taken over by the largest European groups, for instance Alcatel.

Market leaders settled in several continents and in most key countries (except the Japanese market, which was still controlled by Japanese groups).

In the USA distributors became more and more powerful, and American cable makers became less and less profitable: the majority went bankrupt. Foreign competitors who wanted to settle in the USA, took over US cable makers. Today the leaders are Alcatel Cable, Pirelli and BICC, three Europeans, who benefited from their comfortable positions in their home market, and took over and restructured the American cable industry. The evolution that took place in the USA prefigures what may happen now in Europe.

Recent deregulation within Europe should stimulate further international acquisitions in the late 1990s.

In Portugal the two or three remaining local cable makers will be taken over soon. Look at Sumitomo – they keep on growing through takeovers. Alcatel and Pirelli do the same, and in the USA companies are merging. Restructuring will continue, especially in Europe. There will be fewer global players, medium-sized firms will disappear, there will be some niche players, and some local firms will survive in a few large protected markets.

However, the harmonization of norms is a long process and global players still have to manage diversity.

The large are getting bigger, there will be more mergers because there are still many cable companies in the world. But first, conditions should be created to take advantage of scale economies. Today the potential of scale economies is still limited because of all these variants and norms.

International players also have to reduce overcapacity in order to reap the benefits of their acquisition strategies.

We are now restructuring production capacity in Italy and in France where we had acquired too many operations. In the past the obvious way to grow was to buy market share and production capacity. As demand fell drastically, now everyone is restructuring to reduce overcapacity.

M&As in the chocolate and sugar confectionery industry

International takeovers also transformed the chocolate and confectionery industry in the 1980s.

> There has been consolidation. If you think about Jacobs Suchard acquired by Philip Morris and if you think of the things Nestlé did acquiring Rowntree, you are seeing two or three world players.

Numerous mergers and acquisitions also restructured upstream businesses such as cocoa butter and cocoa powder.

Market share growth is the goal that drives international acquisitions.

> There are three companies, that is Nestlé, Mars and Philip Morris, who have each about 10 per cent market share worldwide. The next batch, Cadbury, Hershey and Ferrero, have about 5 per cent each. That tells you two things. One is that the world market for confectionery is still fragmented. The biggest single player, Nestlé, only has 12 per cent. If you track back over a number of years you see that the fragmentation was incredible and that consolidation has happened apace over the last four or five years and therefore you project that the consolidation will continue. To be in the first division, the mathematics tell you that you have to achieve something around 10 per cent market share. Generally speaking one of the golden rules is that in a country you either want to be number one or a strong number two to drive high profit levels.
>
> In 1986 the top seven companies made up 32 per cent of the world market. In 1992 the top six made up 45 per cent, by the year 2000, the top five will make up more than 50 per cent. The remainder of the market will remain very fragmented. Consolidation happens mainly within the top few. And of course part of this consolidation has been the big buying. Many of the small companies will go into niche activities to survive.
>
> Market share is a big thing. Now we cannot prove to you scientifically that there is an absolute linkage between that market share and our profitability. We are confident enough that it is true. Now the question is, how do you actually do it? Practice has suggested that half of our total growth comes organically. The gap is really a sort of acquisition target and that nails us to a certain number of tons worldwide that we need to acquire over a period of time. What we do then is look at a map of the world, and that very quickly focuses you on certain areas of the world that become of strategic interest.

International development through acquisitions is quicker than organic growth; it requires strategic direction (priority targets), opportunism and perseverance.

> What we wanted to do was to go to Spain and buy the number one company, or at worst the number two, or the number three. In reality we

> had to buy a smaller firm probably number six or seven, which was the first one available. Availability is the key. This was a company called Hueso we bought about four years ago. We knew that we were going to have to buy another company in Spain to bolt on to it and we were seeking that company until very recently, when we bought one: Dolce. We have now got two companies in Spain which together make the second biggest.
>
> Acquisitions are the only way to quickly get a significant market share in countries where local competitors have strong positions. This was the case in Scandinavia. Marabou and Freia were acquired by Kraft Jacobs Suchard, but there are still a few strong local competitors such as Fazer, Cloetta, Thoms. These could be targets for multinationals which do not want to start from scratch.

Before taking over Marabou, Kraft General Food had tried to enter the Nordic market for years with their Suchard brand, but they failed. Local players were strong enough to defend their market share. Moreover, after the merger, Kraft could bring some interesting products from Marabou into foreign markets.

Indeed international players tend to adopt dual brand strategies after an acquisition.

> We deliberately have a stance which is decentralized: when we acquire a foreign company we protect their local brands, and we layer on our global brands on top of their local brands.

As in the case of Kraft and Marabou, a global player can turn the best local brands of its partner into global products.

> After the acquisition of Rowntree, Nestlé took those elements of the Rowntree business where there was potential for globalization: After Eight mint chocolates and Lion bars. By owning companies in many countries, Nestlé was able to achieve a better globalization job than Rowntree was ever able to do, as essentially a British company.

As the result of international acquisitions, in the mid-1990s local markets were dominated by multinational companies, both in chocolate and in sugar confectionery.

> In France the leader in confectionery is Kraft (Philip Morris), the number two is 'La Pie Qui Chante' from the Danone Group, and Lami Lutti now belongs to the American group Campbell.
>
> Here in Spain Cadbury bought Hueso, Jacobs Suchard bought El Almendro which makes *turrones*, including chocolate *turrones*. Twenty years ago regional Spanish brands dominated the market; for instance in the region of Valencia there were about 50 factories in Torrente and about 30 factories in Villajoyosa. They all closed down and now you can find some national brands and the multinationals. In Spain Nestlé, Cadbury, Lindt and Jacobs Suchard represent about 60 per cent of the market.

Managers expect a future polarization of the chocolate and sugar confectionery industry: big players will get bigger, and small businesses will focus on niches. It will be difficult to play in the middle unless a firm has a very strong position in a few selected countries.

> Concentration will go on in the chocolate industry. Multinational companies will continue with mergers and acquisitions. This is the first strategy. The second strategy is for medium-sized firms: manufacture chocolate and candies for the retailer – private labels, the share of private labels increases all the time. The third strategy is to focus on specialities and provide excellent service to customers, because the larger the multinationals become the more they leave niches for the small firms. Small ones will survive and succeed alongside big ones, but of course there will be a selection process, and many will fail.

In 1995, there were still a few very interesting targets in Europe for further massive restructuring: Cadbury in the UK and the old British colonies, or Lindt in Switzerland, France, Spain and Italy. Hershey, the North American leader, had acquired a couple of small German companies, and was tempted by more intercontinental ventures.

> Hershey is trying to buy everything that moves, they are trying to get into Europe. The European groups do not want to see Hershey in Europe. They have their foot in the door just about everywhere. If they are able to get in, they are going to have a major impact.

In the chocolate industry a firm can be viewed as a portfolio of brands (for instance Milka, Côte d'Or, Suchard, and Marabou from Kraft). Therefore there is always room for further acquisitions that would add strong new brands to a portfolio.

In three of the four industries in this study international mergers and acquisitions drive international development and strengthen structural forces. As far as *global integration* is concerned, the post-acquisition period is characterized by incremental restructuring: first logistics and manufacturing are rationalized and control mechanisms are set up, then international brand strategies are developed and international knowledge flows are stimulated. However, coordination and networking are generally preferred to centralization and concentration (see Chapter 3). This is partly because there is a need for local responsiveness, and partly because post-acquisition integration should reduce the risk of major political or cultural clashes. International mergers in particular may raise specific agency problems as they mix different national cultures and different organizational cultures. International players learn to deal with such problems from experience: in this domain awareness and commitment are key success factors.

Innovative international strategies

Innovative international strategies stem from the creative mind of ambitious entrepreneurs and flourish in flexible organizations. There are several cases where a single firm changed the rules of the international game in its industry. Innovative *international* strategies can be viewed as a sub-set of innovative strategies, i.e. strategies that 'create the future' (according to Hamel and Prahalad, 1994). International pioneers disregard conventional wisdom about structural forces, or they see opportunities where others do not. Their strategic move across borders may create a new structural force which is strengthened when other competitors imitate the first mover. The long term effect of innovative international strategies was significant in the four industries in this study: Nike in footwear, Alcatel in cables, ICI in paint and Mars in chocolate are famous cases, but the study reveals several other innovative players who had or are having an impact on the international dynamics of their industry: for instance Bata, Fila and Charles Jourdan in footwear, the Taiwanese and Koreans in the cable industry, Akzo Nobel, Hoechst and Dyrup in the paint industry, Ferrero, Godiva, Haribo and Chupa Chups in the chocolate and sugar confectionery industry.

Innovative international strategies in the footwear industry

In the 1930s the footwear industry was multidomestic: local markets were served by local manufacturers. Structural forces driving local responsiveness were much stronger than structural forces driving international development and global integration. International activities mainly consisted of imports of the best leather from Morocco, Southern Europe, South America or India.

One emigrant to Canada invented Bata's global strategy concept:

> Originally Bata was a Czech company and when communism settled in the country, Bata was dispossessed of its assets. The son of Bata moved to Toronto and set up a new company with new headquarters: the Western Bata. Before World War II, they established manufacturing sites abroad, in Africa and in Asia. The strategic intent of Mr Bata Jnr. was to 'put shoes on people', everywhere in the world, at low price and low cost for the mass market. Location of manufacturing in low labour cost countries was part of this strategy. Actually Mr Bata Jnr. got himself killed in 1940, going to visit a Bata factory in Morocco. While the Western Bata was becoming the world leader in the footwear industry, the Eastern Bata was selling shoes on the other side of the Iron Curtain. They still exist, their headquarters are in Zlin, Czechoslovakia, their factories are running at half their capacity.

In the mid-1990s Bata had about 80 factories across the world, mainly in Asia and in Africa, and they had one factory in the east of France, in 'Bataville', which served as a laboratory for technical and management development and training. Bata was the first mover, opening the way to international development in the footwear industry. Their low-cost products changed competitive rules in several key markets, and pushed other firms to follow them and relocate manufacturing. To some extent they also opened the way for another major strategic innovator 40 years later: Nike.

Nike created a new concept of sport-leisure footwear, originally North American, and made it universal.

> The revolution came in 1979 from the USA and with the jogging fashion. When companies like Nike and Reebok arrived on the European market 15 years ago people did not believe they would succeed. In fact they did impose their marketing and their American concept became universal. American culture is based on sports, and sport is accessible to everybody. [. . .] Nike grew from $100 million sales to US $3 billion. They could grow so quickly because they are not manufacturers. They were no longer interested in the production aspect of their business and they had their products manufactured in the Far East.

Nike invented a concept of 'marketing company', a 'wandering enterprise' in search of the lowest costs, and pushing towards a worldwide 'Darwinian survival of the fittest'.

> Today Nike employs about 3,000 people with sales of US $3 billion [estimated by the interviewee in 1994; in 1997 Nike had a turnover of about US $9 billion], and of those people about 60 per cent work for marketing. Advertising budgets represent about 12 per cent of sales. They establish manufacturing in a low-cost country, they stay there for three years, labour costs become too high, they leave the country and go elsewhere. . . . Production is wandering. Indeed they have disconnected manufacturing from marketing, both in space and time: for instance orders are made in September 1994 for the year 1995.

This strategy was also adopted by Reebok and, later on, by Adidas. The fittest survived, and from a local sport footwear market created a global sport-leisure business. Nike's innovative international strategy transformed the competitive system and created new structural forces: high advertising intensity, extreme relocation, and universal needs. However, Nike did not win the game for ever. In the late 1990s they faced new challenges. They had problems with long transportation times between distant production and consumption areas, and they were accused of exploiting low-cost labour in Asia. Customers expected more innovations and were more and more demanding: for instance Reebok developed a product that could be recycled, Nike and Adidas had to respond. New trends also brought in new competitors from adjacent market segments.

> Nike and Reebok are having a hard time in reacting to the new trend promoting nature more than sport. In the future they will probably need to respond to competitors such as Timberland who have this positioning from the start. So Nike's marketing message will probably have to change. There are some signs that they have understood this.

A few other firms have led the international development of leisure footwear since the beginning of the 1990s (leisure is close to but different from sport-leisure). Timberland is one of them, they grew fast on the American market, with young people as their primary target. Their image was based on nature and ecology. The globalization of their brand was very quick and their target was broadening.

Fila is an Italian company from Biella, a traditional textile area. It started in 1930 with manufactured woven textiles, particularly undergarments for men. In 1972 Fila launched a line of tenniswear, they sponsored famous athletes such as Borg and Panatta and were the first to put colours on tennis shirts. In 1982 they gave the manufacturing licence for their sport footwear to an American company. Fila's footwear benefited from the strong image of Fila's tennis shirts and was quite successful. In the following years Fila took back the licence, as footwear had become a core business.

> Fila also launched a line of outdoor leisure footwear. The trend for outdoor footwear is recent and came from Britain. Outdoor products are linked to nature whereas sport footwear is linked to tennis or basketball athletes with an American look. Distribution channels are the same for leisure-outdoor footwear and sport-leisure footwear but the images are different. Also, the potential market for leisure footwear could be larger than for sport-leisure as it includes consumers of all ages. [. . .] Fila's image is based on aesthetics and style, on top of high technical quality. [. . .] They chose an American music channel with a European base in London for TV advertising.

In the mid-1990s Fila was organized as a transnational company: strategy, finance and personnel policies were coordinated in Italy but decision-making autonomy was given to three regional units in Europe, the USA and the Far East. The American region dealt with product development and marketing in North America; it was listed on the New York stock exchange. The Asian regional headquarters, based in Hong Kong, dealt with product manufacturing and with marketing in Asia, and supplied 95 per cent of Fila's footwear.

Further upmarket, a few companies pioneered the globalization of women's luxury footwear and opened wholly owned or franchised stores in large cities across the whole planet. For instance Charles Jourdan from France or Pollini from Italy.

> As a company we tend to look at the world as a whole. I start with the assumption that the world is one. I do not care about differences. I make my product for those who like it around the world.

Innovative international strategies in the cable industry

In the 1960s the cable industry was multidomestic. In the 1970s the first signs of global integration came with a technological innovation developed by Corning Glass Works: optofibres for telecommunications. However, the increase in technological intensity did not upset national firms who were still protected on their home market: CGW licences were sold all over the world.

In the 1980s a world leader emerged with an innovative international strategy: Alcatel Cable. In 1985 Alcatel acquired Thomson's cable division and started to take over local cable businesses all around the world. In the mid-1990s Alcatel cable owned (or had majority stakes in) more than 70 companies worldwide and had become the number one with a US $8 billion sales turnover (as compared to US $4 billion in 1990). Other major competitors followed Alcatel's extensive acquisition strategy: Pirelli (number two), BICC (UK), AT&T (USA), Sumitomo (Japan). Alcatel was part of the Alcatel-Alsthom Group involved in communication systems, energy and transport, electrical engineering, batteries and services. The other facet of Alcatel Cable's innovative strategy was to be a system provider and achieve full horizontal integration. A system provider has significant competitive advantages in foreign developing markets where customers are looking for complete and consistent solutions to their communication needs.

> When your phone rings, a machine somewhere has picked up and is transmitting the call. The companies which make this kind of equipment, Alcatel, AT&T, Northern Telecom, Ericsson, Siemens, Italtel, etc. deal with the valuable and intelligent part of a telecommunication network. In the past, they only sold the part of the system which corresponded to their core technology. Now some of them sell the whole range of components and services in the system. Siemens sells equipment and cables, Alcatel sells equipment, cables, network engineering, project design, and so on. For Alcatel the trend is going toward more and more horizontal integration. [. . .] Alcatel took over and continues to take over cable manufacturers in Germany. This is because East Germany is being equipped. Cable manufacturers make money where investments are being made in infrastructures with complete systems.

The third facet of Alcatel's strategy came with deregulation within Europe. After a wave of international acquisitions, they started to rationalize manufacturing and logistics across borders.

All major competitors turned to emerging high growth markets: Eastern Europe and Asia. In Asia, Taiwanese and Korean cable manufacturers invented a simple new international strategy to penetrate the Chinese and the Malaysian markets.

> One option is to follow the Taiwanese–Korean model. There, the factory manager, who also owns the firm, sells the products, keeps the accounts, has slaves working under him, turning out a product which is a commodity (as cables now are). He manages to make a profit on the cables because he has no fixed costs.

The other option was the one adopted by Alcatel: high added value. This is the world of system providers and firms involved in high technology segments (submarine cables, high voltage power cables, special applications), and growth through international acquisitions. The two strategies changed the international scope of the cable industry between 1985 and 1995. They shaped new structural forces driving global integration: increasing pressure on costs in low-tech segments, increasing technological intensity, and the harmonization of norms.

> The cable industry became more international because some leaders decided to go international. They drove the industry behind them. Alcatel goes to India and to China, and now everyone is going to China.

Innovative international strategies in the paint industry

In the 1980s a new European leader emerged from successive large-scale international mergers. Casco (Swedish-Danish-Norwegian) merged with Akzo from the Netherlands, then Akzo merged with the Swedish group Nobel in 1992, and, since then, further acquisitions (particularly in the UK, in France, in Spain and in Italy) formed the first transnational group in the paint industry.

> We have a good market share in Europe, twice as big as our closest competitor, so we can stay in front and decide on which way to go when it comes to restructuring the European paint industry. [. . .] Being the leader means setting the pace, and he who sets the pace sets it at his own rate, and the rest have to follow.

Akzo Nobel sold its car finishes business and was particularly strong in decorative coatings, which represented half of the paint division within the group. They based their international development on a differentiation strategy: environmentally friendly products in which they had strengths.

> The difference between a low-price supplier and a quality supplier is that the low-price suppliers cannot afford new product development, they are market followers and they tend to be local. The high quality suppliers can afford product development, they are the ones who expand across borders. Most of the international evolution of an industry is about offering the customers something that they do not already have.

The third step in Akzo Nobel's international strategy was to rationalize manufacturing:

> There will be one manufacturing unit in Sweden, one in Holland, one in France, a couple in England, maybe one in Italy. . . . Then we will have some satellite operations. Each unit will be specialized and produce large volumes of standardized products sold throughout Europe in order to improve efficiency. It is difficult to implement because Europe is not homogeneous yet, but we will benefit from substantial economies of scale in manufacturing. Manufacturing costs could be reduced from 15 per cent of the sales turnover to 7 per cent.

Clearly in the 1990s Akzo Nobel was pushing towards the Euro-globalization of the paint industry. The company had adopted a transnational model of organization that combined global integration and local responsiveness. At the corporate level Akzo Nobel was divided into four groups: fibres, chemicals, pharmaceuticals and paint. Each group had its own board and its own strategy, but there was significant communication between the four. As far as the paint group was concerned, the central unit consisted of a research and development manager, a technical manager, a marketing manager, a human resources manager and a controller: their role was to *coordinate*. In order to use the total competence of the group in research and development, the R&D manager coordinated the various centres of expertise of the paint division. For instance the managing director of the Spanish unit was considered a member of an international network.

> We do not receive instructions from Holland telling us what to do. We make strategic decisions *jointly* with the management from Holland, in a meeting every quarter. We have some autonomy but it is coordinated and controlled. Moreover, information permeates local units and helps synergies. For instance we know exactly who are the suppliers of the other companies in the group, the prices, the quality. . . . It adds strength to flexibility.

The other world leader in the paint industry was ICI. In the 1990s ICI grew by acquisitions, both in Europe and in the USA, where it took over Glidden, Grow Group, Fuller O'Brian Paints in 1995 and then became number three in North America. ICI's intercontinental position was unique in the business of decorative paint, and it showed the global ambitions of this chemicals group.

> We formulated a long term plan which was designed to reduce the diversity of our product range and to concentrate on three areas of the world – Europe, North America, Asia Pacific. When we started we had something like 27 per cent of the coatings in that 'others' category and it is now 5 per cent. We ended up with three core businesses – decorative paint, car refinish and packaging coatings. [. . .] Our strategy for the future is to continue to drive down that three-core business base and to expand geographically into markets where we think we can be a market leader. In the decorative paint business we push towards standardization. If we are doing colour cards for a lot of people they are cheaper than if you are doing specific ones for each country. Even in the decorative area, which earlier on we talked about as being mostly regional and national, the degree of coordination is increasing all the time. So I think that if we had this conversation in another three years' time I would have many more examples of how we successfully coordinated, standardized and yet maintained the appropriate sensitive bit to local customer needs.

Can coating and car finishes were considered global segments that called for global strategies. But, as far as decorative paint was concerned, ICI's innovative international brand strategy drove global integration and shaped new structural forces.

> There are signs of major changes. Some international brands are starting to emerge. Most notably the Dulux brand of ICI is spreading. ICI has had a subsidiary in France for a few years, the French brand was called Valentine. ICI added Dulux to Valentine and the brand became Dulux-Valentine. They thought twice before killing a brand name such as Valentine. Now the Dulux brand is sold in the Benelux and in Germany, although the products are adapted to each country. So we are just at the beginning of the Europeanization of the brand.

In the market for car finishes and car refinishes other companies pushed toward globalization: PPG (originally from the US) and Hoechst (from Germany). Hoechst based its international development on technological innovation. The group had two main subsidiaries: Herberts, the European leader in OEM (for original equipment manufacturers) car finishes, car refinishes, powder paint and industrial varnish, and Spies Hecker in car refinishes and industrial varnishes. Hoechst was viewed as a technological innovator in water-based paints for car refinishes. Thanks to this advance and with these environmentally friendly products Hoechst could gain significant market share in California, a bridge to North America. This was done at the expense of PPG and Dupont.

Akzo Nobel, ICI and Hoechst were powerful industrial groups with a base in chemicals, but smaller firms also had a significant influence on the international development of the paint industry. Dyrup, a Danish company, invented wood-treatment products that protect from humidity and are substitutes for varnishes. Their international strategy relied on this technical innovation and on strong international promotion of their brand, Bondex. Then they acquired several other small competitors in neighbouring countries (Germany, England and France) and added their best brands to the portfolio (for instance Xylophène). They built an image of technical speciality which protected them from the intrusion of large chemical groups. In ten years' time they created a Euroglobal niche in the paint industry.

The combination of all these innovative international strategies transformed the competitive system and increased structural forces driving global integration: technological intensity, advertising intensity, and economies of scale.

Innovative international strategies in the chocolate and confectionery industry

The three world leaders in the chocolate industry played a significant role in transforming the competitive system from a multidomestic business to a mixed industry.

Kraft Jacobs Suchard (Philip Morris) relied on acquisitions to form an international group. In the mid-1990s global integration was based on umbrella brands.

> Now we use umbrella brands to launch a product under Milka as a *tablette*, as a countline, as a praline and as a seasonal. This is our strength. The umbrella strategy helps you to use and strengthen the brand while spending less money on each product. We do it for Milka, Côte d'Or, Suchard and Marabou.

Nestlé started with a broader international base, but also relied on acquisitions to expand its portfolio of brands: Perrugina in Italy, Rowntree in the UK.

> Nestlé was present in the chocolate industry mainly by selling chocolate *tablettes*, the most traditional business. Some years ago Nestlé made a decisive move in the chocolate industry in Europe and worldwide: we took over the British company Rowntree and, through Rowntree, global brands like KitKat, After Eight, Smarties and Lion. We understood that the most promising business was the countlines segment and for that you need

> strong existing brands. Nestlé started with the marketing base of Rowntree and developed the brands internationally. It basically remains the current strategy. Moreover it is clear that Nestlé is present in all product categories in the chocolate industry. We concentrate our attention on countries where chocolate consumption is low as compared to potential: Southern Western Europe, Eastern Europe, China, South America.

In the mid-1990s the breakdown of sales turnover – 50 per cent in Europe, 25 per cent in North America, and 25 per cent in the rest of the world – showed that Nestlé was on the way to achieving global market coverage.

However, among the three leaders, Mars is considered the firm that transformed the chocolate industry with its innovative international strategy. Mars focused on a few products and brands, which became universal.

> We have over the last ten years invested a lot in making our brands truly global. So in other words anticipating the world of global sponsorship and the world of moving products from one place to another. We changed things like Marathon in the UK to Snickers. We changed Raider to Twix and we did that not just on a European basis, we did that on a worldwide basis. A major plank of our strategy is global brands. Six of our brands are truly global, Snickers, Mars, M&Ms, Whiskas, Chum (they are pet food brands), Uncle Ben's rice. Each of those particular brands has a turnover in excess of $1 billion. [. . .] An important part of the worldwide strategy is that if 15 per cent of the world's population consumes 85 per cent of our products and sales, the other 85 per cent of the world's population is starting to become more affluent and have a disposable income to consume our products in the future.

Manufacturing was organized to achieve maximum efficiency.

> Western Europe is organized as one business with plants located in the UK, in France, in Germany, in Holland, in Austria. We integrated the business five years ago in anticipation of the European Union: for us there is one market. We may produce product A and product B in Germany and ship it to the other members of the Community, and product C might get made in England and the same thing happens.

Mars also had plants in Eastern Europe, in Poland, in Hungary, in Russia, and they were building new plants in other high growth areas in Mexico and in Korea.

> We get efficiency from the way we run plants. We make very small margins on our plants, deliberately to give the consumer good value for money. That is our basic philosophy. We do that, we work our assets to

> death, 24 hours a day, seven days a week. And we also make sure they are the most modern assets and that is where we get our money.

In the mid-1990s, Mars combined tight control and regional autonomy.

> There is a president for each of the product sectors [chocolate, pet food, rice] in each region, the whole thing is not more than 40 people at our headquarters office in MacLean, Virginia. Everything else is decentralized into the business, within a matrix framework. [. . .] Internationally we integrate or coordinate just about every single function. We have a single set of integrated accounting structures on a worldwide basis. Our personnel practices are exactly the same worldwide. We all operate within a framework and policies are written down. We live within these policies and sometimes we revise them. This is the way to coordinate our functions on a worldwide basis.

With their innovative global strategy, 'Mars made countlines a global market'. In this business they showed the way to Nestlé with Lion and to Kraft Jacobs Suchard with Milka bars. In the late 1990s, given the increasing competition in countlines, Mars started to have problems with its costly one product/one brand strategy. They learned from KJS-Milka and Ferrero-Kinder the benefits of umbrella brands, and they launched Milky Way as an umbrella brand for children.

The Italian family-owned company Ferrero is less well known than its international brands: Kinder, Mon Chéri, Rocher and TicTac. Ferrero's innovative international strategy is considered a success story in the chocolate and confectionery industry. Ferrero started with a new concept: the Kinder-Surprise egg. It is an old Italian tradition to offer children an egg with a small present inside for Easter. Ferrero launched Kinder-Surprise eggs in Italy and in Germany. The light milk chocolate (brown and white) of the Kinder egg corresponded to children's taste and to German taste. Further international development relied on the success of Kinder-Surprise: Kinder became an umbrella brand for children's products such as Kinder-délice and Kinder-Bueno. Ferrero chose to make light products that correspond to Italian taste and are easily accepted in any foreign market: Mon Chéri is a light praline with cherry and liqueur, Ferrero's Rocher is lighter than others: lots of milk, wafers and hazelnuts and a limited amount of cocoa.

> Ferrero's strategy is to grow on the market through products that are exclusive, different from the competition, and even technologically innovative. This is where we are making great investments in R&D. Ferrero's international strategy is to gradually conquer new markets with products that already exist and have proved to be successful on certain markets. If

> our Rocher has been successful in Italy, Germany, France and England, it will eventually penetrate Latin America and the United States.

Ferrero clustered its products and brands according to consumers' behaviour: for pleasure, for a gift or for a snack. They spent massive amounts on advertising (about 300 billion Italian lire a year, as compared to a sales turnover of about 1,300 billion lire in 1994). However, they believed that 'a unique, exclusive product was the best weapon to increase market share'. Their products were sold through a worldwide network of subsidiaries and became universal, 'from America to China'.

Further upmarket, Godiva created a worldwide niche for luxury chocolates (priced at over 1,200 Belgian francs per kilogram, with a shelf life of 12 weeks as compared to 30 weeks for other competitors). They first expanded into France where there is a tradition of gourmet chocolates, and through duty-free shops. The financial and commercial strengths of the American Campbell Group, which acquired Godiva, fostered further international expansion.

> In the States Godiva did a great marketing job from scratch where they created a luxury gift which happened to be chocolate. They put it in a very expensive package and charged $25 per pound weight. They went into Nieman Marcus, Bloomingdale's, they created their own shops in Fifth Avenue and they created an image of very much a Cartier, Dunhill, very expensive luxury product. Nowadays Godiva has about 100 retail shops and another 400 wholesale points of display in the USA. In Japan it started about ten years ago and it is also extremely expensive, $50 per pound weight.

In sugar confectionery, a few companies created global brands. Wrigley turned chewing gum into an international business, Ferrero succeeded with Tic Tac, low-calorie mint and orange sweets, Haribo managed to develop an international line of candies, and Chupa Chups imposed a global brand of lollipops.

Haribo started with a large domestic market with little competition: Germany. They innovated by marketing their top quality jelly candies all over Europe:

> Haribo had a consistent pricing policy: rather low prices that allowed them to grow and acquire volume. They were then able to produce a very wide product range and this very wide product range, in turn, gave them greater volume. They expanded in several countries, particularly France; they also took over some companies in Germany and in England. That is the way they became European.

Then Haribo introduced jelly candies to the USA and created a new market, which attracted followers.

Chupa Chups is an exception in the sugar confectionery industry: they started in Spain in 1958 and at the end of the 1990s they sold their exclusive lollipops in 164 countries. Original Chupa Chups have a ball shape, a milky taste, some sophisticated flavours, funny advertising, and a premium price. Until 1991 most of the manufacturing was done in Spain (90 per cent) and in France (10 per cent). Chupa Chups started production in Mexico and in Russia in 1992 and in China in 1994. Other production sites were planned in India and in Brazil. In 1997 the sales turnover was about US $200 million and 4 billion Chupa Chups were sold worldwide.

Clearly, innovative products and strong brands are the key to international development in the chocolate and sugar confectionery industry. Innovative international players transformed structural forces: advertising intensity and economies of scale increased dramatically in the 1980s and early 1990s. As a consequence, in the late 1990s the industry was divided between a few international competitors and a number of local players.

From Bata in the footwear industry to Chupa Chups in sugar confectionery, each case presented here is unique. All these innovative firms contributed to the international transformation of their industry. However, it is tempting to reduce complexity and propose a simplified categorization of innovative international strategies. Table 5.1 presents six types of innovative international strategies identified in the study.

The first category includes companies who are the first to create universal products, based on a new concept, and develop global brands with massive advertising budgets: Nike, Mars, and to some extent ICI in decorative paint, and Ferrero in the late 1990s.

The second category includes companies who restructure their industries through extensive mergers and acquisitions: Alcatel Cables and Akzo Nobel are typical examples. Each of these innovators added another unique characteristic: 'being a system provider' (Alcatel), and 'superior environmentally friendly products' (Akzo Nobel). Nestlé and Kraft Jacobs Suchard are in this second group. All of them belong to large diversified industrial corporations that could provide resources (if not synergies) to foster international development.

The third category includes technological innovators who exploit their technological advantage across borders. Hoechst in car finishes and car refinishes is a typical case. More cases could be found in high technology industries.

The fourth category, luxury global niches, includes firms like Charles Jourdan, Pollini and Godiva.

The fifth category includes a number of firms who base their international development on product differentiation and premium prices:

Table 5.1 *Innovative international strategies*

Type one:
- Create universal products and global brands with massive advertising budgets
- Innovative concept

Cases: Nike, Mars

Type two:
- Extensive mergers and acquisitions
- First mover to a new competitive advantage
- Resources from a large company

Cases: Alcatel, Akzo Nobel

Type three:
- Technological innovation

Cases: Hoechst

Type four:
- Luxury global niche
- Involvement in retailing

Cases: Charles Jourdan, Godiva

Type five:
- Product differentiation
- Premium price

Cases: Timberland, Fila, Dyrup, Ferrero, Chupa Chups

Type six:
- Low-cost manufacturers with worldwide ambitions

Cases: Bata, Goldstar

Timberland and Fila in footwear, Dyrup in coatings, Ferrero and Chupa Chups in chocolate and confectionery belong to this group.

The sixth category includes low-cost manufacturers who target large markets: Bata in the footwear industry (with relocation of manufacturing and volume effects) and the Koreans in the cable industry (with low overheads and highly productive labour).

International strategic innovators often become market leaders in their industry or in the particular segment they target. As leaders they keep on setting the pace; they are also imitated by followers, and the collective actions that result from imitation further transform the competitive system.

From practice to theory: a summary

A set of related competitive actions – innovative international strategies, mergers-acquisitions-alliances and relocations – drive the international development and the global integration of industries. National players defend their positions as long as they can, and move towards local responsiveness. The tensions between these competitive actions transform structural forces. In this field of force, transformation is the rule, and the diversity of international strategies that we observed reveals that there are significant strategic degrees of freedom.

Strong national players, with a high share of their domestic market, restrain the international development of their industry in several ways: they control distribution channels, they create and maintain local preferences and strong brand images, and sometimes they lobby for protectionist policies. When their domestic market is large enough strong national players can resist foreign intrusion for a long time. When the forces driving global integration increase, some of them become targets for international takeovers and some of them get actively involved in the international consolidation of their industry.

In some industries (in our study, footwear and cables) firms contain labour costs by *relocating their manufacturing* in low labour cost countries, and coordinate their value chain across borders. The decision to relocate production depends on several parameters which are industry-specific: for instance in the footwear industry, automation alternatives, the level of quality, the image of the country, transportation costs and delivery times; and in the cable industry, host government policies and high growth of local demand. Within a given industry relocation strategies differ from one product-market segment to another (depending on the set of the above parameters). The case of production can be extended to other activities in the firm's value chain (R&D, marketing, etc.), thus raising the question of the international configuration of value chain activities.

International mergers, acquisitions and alliances drive the international development and the global integration of industries (in our study, chocolate confectionery, cables and paint). International mergers speed up the consolidation of industries and give birth to international leaders (such as Alcatel Cable, Kraft Jacobs Suchard or Akzo Nobel). They lead to a polarization of the industry, with multinational companies on the one hand and small focused businesses on the other hand. When the forces driving local responsiveness are significant the buying firms preserve the strong brands (products) of their partners and often add one or a few global brands to their portfolios. Post-merger rationalization and integration enhance the firm's competitive advantage and market power, and foster further international expansion.

Innovative international strategies are viewed as a major force driving global integration (in the four industries in our study). Managers refer to 'first international movers' who 'change the rules of the game', exploit or *create* the potential for globalization in the industry. Firms such as ICI, Akzo Nobel, Hoechst and Dyrup in the paint industry, Alcatel Cables in cables and wires, Bata, Nike and Timberland in footwear, Mars, Ferrero, Godiva and Chupa Chups in the chocolate and confectionery industry have transformed competitive systems: they turned multidomestic businesses (in the 1970s) into mixed industries or global product-market segments (in the 1990s). Each case is unique, but innovative international strategies can be clustered into six broad groups: product innovation and global brand responding to or creating a universal need, transnational restructuring, worldwide exclusive technology, worldwide luxury niche, product differentiation, and low-cost international operations.

Some economists (Schumpeter, 1954; Vernon, 1966), and strategists (Baden Fuller and Stopford, 1992; Hamel and Prahalad, 1994), have pointed out the role of strategic innovators who create new norms in their industry. The resource-based theory of the firm (Penrose, 1959; Wernerfelt, 1984) offers a solid base to explain why some firms are unique and how unique combinations of resources produce innovative strategies. Managers agree with these theories: they rejuvenate models of international competition and put innovative entrepreneurs in the picture. International strategic innovators rely on firm-specific competitive advantages. They are then imitated by followers, and the collective actions that result from imitation further transform the competitive system. This is to say that *the first step in Vernon's theory of internationalization is crucial: the individual action of an innovative firm.*

The competitive actions of international strategic innovators shape new structural forces. In the cable industry strategic innovators increased the pressure on costs in low-tech segments, they increased technological intensity and stimulated the harmonization of norms. In the paint industry competitive actions shaped new structural forces: technological intensity, economies of scale and advertising intensity. Advertising intensity in sport-leisure footwear is the legacy of Nike's innovative strategy. In the chocolate and confectionery industry innovative international players transformed structural forces: advertising intensity and economies of scale increased dramatically in the 1980s and early 1990s.

The 'mixed' character of the four industries studied probably offers more strategic freedom than in global or multidomestic industries. However, a historical perspective shows that cables, paint, footwear and chocolate and sugar confectionery were all multidomestic businesses before innovative entrepreneurs turned them into mixed industries. As far as global industries are concerned the set of innovative international strategies may be limited to two categories: major technological innovation and mega mergers and acquisitions (transnational restructuring). This proposition could be further explored in industries such as semiconductors, civil aeronautics or pharmaceuticals. In spite of the limitations of the present study, top managers' espoused theories seem to confirm integrative models of competition (Astley and Van de Ven, 1983; Hrebiniak and Joyce, 1985): international competition evolves from the interaction of environmental determinism *and managerial voluntarism*. Recognizing the influence of innovative international strategies is a necessary step towards a holistic framework.

Bibliography

In the literature concerned with the international dynamics of industries, the competitive action perspective is much less developed than the structural perspective (Birkinshaw et al., 1995). The need to distinguish between the two was pointed out by Ghoshal (1987) and Kogut (1989).

Economists are mainly interested in the collective strategic moves that affect the international development of an industry, some of them, for instance Knickerbocker (1973) and Hymer and Rowthorn (1970), argue that oligopolistic reactions dominate the process of international development.

Strategists are interested in the respective positions and the strategic moves of international players in 'key markets' (Birkinshaw et al., 1995; Roth and Morrison, 1990; Prahalad and Doz, 1987). Strong local positions and defensive strategies of national players in several 'key markets' restrain global integration (Prahalad and Doz, 1987). Bartlett and Ghoshal (1989) and Roth and Morrison (1990) mentioned the actions of some companies that influence the standardization of customers' preferences across borders, Porter (1986) and Yip (1992) mentioned the influence of international networks of alliances, and Porter (1986) noted the emergence of new global competitors, principally from East Asia.

Relocation strategies can be analysed within a broad framework that maps the international configuration of all value chain activities (Porter, 1986). This framework considers cost advantages *and* differentiation advantages related to location (for instance access to a superior local knowledge base).

The role of mergers, acquisitions and alliances in global integration has been recognized (Bleeke et al., 1990) and documented through case studies (Haspeslagh and Jemison, 1991; Bartlett and Ghoshal, 1992).

The competitive action perspective may focus on the 'collective' strategies of businesses, and rely on *population ecology* – firms have to adapt to environmental forces or fail (Hannan and Freeman, 1977), and on *neo-institutional theory* (Oliver, 1991) – a firm's (international) strategy is influenced by 'strategic norms' in the industry (Knickerbocker, 1973). Such norms result from a process of imitation of effective (international) strategies. A competitive action perspective focused on collective strategies is biased toward determinism. On the other hand, a competitive action perspective also interested in first international movers, the firms who *create the new norm*, can reconcile determinism and voluntarism. Vernon (1966) proposed such an integrative framework. The internationalization of competition is tied to three distinct factors: the individual action of an innovative business, the presence of favourable international structural conditions, and the collective reaction of numerous other businesses.

Within the set of economic theories that explain the international dynamics of industries, many have a strong deterministic bias but some have opened the way to the concepts of strategic choice and strategic innovation: Schumpeter (1934, 1954), Penrose (1959), Hymer (1960) and Vernon (1966).

Strategic management theories generally try to reconcile determinism and voluntarism. Many case studies describe innovative international strategies (see for instance Bartlett and Ghoshal, 1992). The recognition of strategic innovation as a central concept is a recent phenomenon. Best-selling books such as *Rejuvenating the Mature Business* (Baden Fuller and Stopford, 1992) and *Competing for the Future* (Hamel and Prahalad, 1994) imposed the idea that some firms change the rules of the game in their industry, and that strategy is about doing things differently.

6

International Strategies

Tugrul Atamer, Roland Calori, Peter Gustavsson and Martine Menguzzato-Boulard

The study revealed a very diverse set of international strategies in the four mixed industries. According to industrial economics, within an industry, the variety of firms' strategies corresponds to the heterogeneity of supply and to customers who value variety. Barriers to mobility preserve differentiation, and firms that exploit market imperfections generate rents (i.e. above-normal rates of return).

The 'resource-based' theory of the firm suggests that differentiation stems from unique combinations of resources at the firm level (Penrose, 1959; Wernerfelt, 1984; Barney, 1991).

The products, the services and the rents that unique resources will yield depend upon the dominant logic of the top management team (Grant, 1988). Also, the development of the dominant logic of the top management team is partly shaped by the resources with which they deal. According to this cognitive perspective, top managers' mental maps of (international) competition determine their (international) strategies (Calori et al., 1994). Hence strategic variety can be explained by the variety of individual maps.

Moreover, the implementation of strategy relies on idiosyncratic organizational abilities. Bartlett and Ghoshal (1989) have shown that international strategies are determined by a firm's specific administrative heritage. Part of the heritage is shaped by the administrative culture of the home country, and part by the specific history of the firm. Hence strategic variety can be explained by the variety of firms' administrative heritages.

Variety may also result from specific conditions in the home country: industry structure and institutional influences.

Finally, economic theories (Samuelson, 1948) suggest that countries with superior production factors endowments, create the opportunities for firms to develop location-specific advantages. As a consequence, differential access to resources creates high strategic variety.

All the above factors – market imperfections, unique combinations of resources, cognitive diversity, diversity of administrative heritage, the influence of the home country, and location-specific advantages – contribute to the diversity in international strategies. To some extent each international strategy is unique, but it is useful to simplify complexity and reduce the set of international strategies to a smaller number of categories (or configurations). *Categories complement the whole set of unique cases*. The logic behind the analysis of strategic configurations relies on contingency theory (Lawrence and Lorsch, 1967), population ecology (Hannan and Freeman, 1977) and institutional theory (Di Maggio and Powell, 1983). These theories suggest that there is a limited number of viable strategies that match a given environmental context. Moreover, strategy types result from the imitation of strategies which are viewed as the most effective.

Previous research adopted three different approaches to the classification of international strategies.

The first approach relies on a theoretical construction of discriminant dimensions. Fayerweather (1969) and Doz (1980) identified two key concepts: 'geographic scope' (broad vs. narrow) and 'standardization' (vs. fragmentation). The geographic scope of a firm was defined as the set of targeted key countries. Standardization was defined as the homogeneity of the firm's competitive weapons across borders. The opposite concept, 'fragmentation', was later renamed 'local responsiveness', and complemented by a third dimension: the level of 'integration or coordination of activities' across borders (Bartlett, 1986; Prahalad and Doz, 1987; Bartlett and Ghoshal, 1989). Kogut (1985a, 1985b) and Porter (1986) suggested that another dimension be added: 'the geographic configuration of value chain activities'. According to this view, firm-specific competitive advantages are related to the competitive (or comparative) advantages of nations. Firms may locate (disperse or concentrate) the various activities of their value chain (R&D, manufacturing, logistics, marketing, etc.) in order to exploit location-specific advantages. Finally, Porter (1986) also considered a fifth dimension, labelled 'segment scope': firms may venture across borders with a narrow rather than a broad product range. Ghoshal and Nohria (1993) built their typology of international strategies on two dimensions: 'local responsiveness' and 'global integration or coordination'. They identified four generic strategies: 'global' (low local responsiveness, high global integration), 'multinational' (high local responsiveness, low global integration), 'international' (low/medium local responsiveness, low/medium global integration), and 'transnational' (high local responsiveness, high global integration). Porter (1986) mapped international strategies using two dimensions that describe the 'whats': 'geographic scope' and 'segment scope', and two dimensions that describe the 'hows': 'international configuration' and 'international coordination' of activities. The two classifications were not explicitly related to each other; in other words the whats and the hows were not integrated in a single typology.

The second approach relies on cross-sectional empirical studies, and provides a more comprehensive understanding of actual configurations. Several studies have produced strategy types by clustering cases. The sets of variables (attributes) are defined a priori among the theoretical dimensions suggested by the literature (Roth and Morrison, 1990; Morrison and Roth, 1992; Carpano et al., 1994). These studies have produced mixed results. On the one hand they confirmed the importance of some dimensions, for instance the 'level of global integration'. On the other hand they produced insignificant results concerning other variables, for instance the 'geographic configuration of activities'. The authors themselves recognized that the geographic configuration of activities was more a legacy from the firm's history than an element of its recent strategy. In other words, cross-sectional studies fail to capture the complex dynamics of internationalization.

The third approach to a classification of international strategies considers internationalization as a process. The theoretical foundations of this perspective can be found in Perlmutter (1969), who identified three generic attitudes toward internationalization: the 'ethnocentric' organization (home-country oriented), the 'polycentric' organization (host-country oriented), and the 'geocentric' organization (world oriented). Decisions concerning country targets, competitive advantages and functional policies reflect one of these basic attitudes. According to Adler (1986) the internationalization process corresponds to different stages of international maturity (from ethnocentric to geocentric). Internationalization is viewed as a 'cognitive process' (Kobrin, 1994) rooted in 'managers' mind-sets' (Perlmutter, 1969). The interactive process approach often relies on case studies that can provide a complex understanding and a historical perspective.

In this chapter we adopt a simplified version of the third approach, and we rely on a single respondent for each case study. Depth was traded for diversity, so that the number of cases (over 100) is sufficient to construct a taxonomy. Moreover it should be noted that respondents often described the strategies of other competitors, and that the analysis of published data (annual reports, the business press, etc.) often complemented the interviews. Such an unstructured historical perspective helps in the understanding of some combinations of strategic dimensions and the dynamic processes of internationalization that are salient to managerial knowledge.

In the first section we elicit the relevant concepts in managers' narratives about their firm as it is involved in the dynamics of international competition. These concepts can be grouped into three categories: international strategies, competitive advantage, and internationalization processes. Based upon this conceptual framework, in the second section we describe four types of 'worldwide player': 'quasi-global players', 'transnational restructurers', 'worldwide technology specialists' and 'global luxury niche players'. In the third section we describe four types of 'international challenger': 'continental leaders', 'opportunistic international challengers', 'geographic niche players' and 'country-centred players'.

Strategic concepts in top managers' espoused theories

The content analysis of interviews produced three higher order constructs: international strategies, competitive strategies and internationalization process (see Figure 6.1). Such broad constructs are useful in organizing a high number of variables (Miller, 1986).

Top managers explicitly discussed the links between the competitive strategy (or competitive advantage) of a firm and its international strategy. These relationships are neglected by the strategy literature which is focused on the global–local framework (Morrison and Roth, 1992). On the other hand a few authors provide some theoretical support for managers' views. A firm needs to develop a specific competitive advantage in its home country before it can expand successfully across borders (Hymer, 1976). The international development of a firm is also crucial in strengthening its core competitive advantages (Porter, 1986). Hence the two concepts – international strategy and the firm's competitive advantage – are inseparable. The process of internationalization is influenced by the firm's competitive advantage. First the transfer of competitive advantage to new territories creates barriers to imitation. Second, multinational positions can generate additional advantages that increase original strengths. Hence competitive advantage can drive the logic and the international development

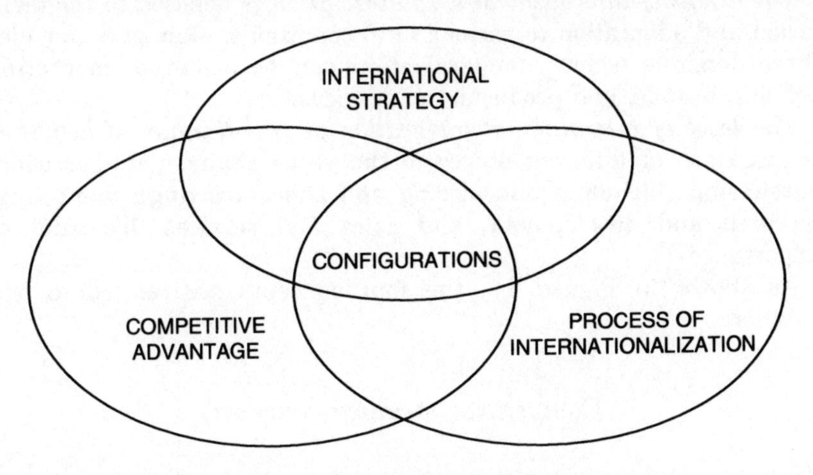

Figure 6.1 *Configurations of international strategies*

of a company. Finally a firm's strategic position and orientation at a given period results from an ongoing internationalization process.

Hence configurations (and their descriptions) include international strategy concepts, competitive strategy concepts, and concepts that characterize the internationalization process.

International strategy concepts

Within the 'international strategy' theme, concepts can be grouped into four main sub-themes: the scope of the firm (at the industry level), foreign investment policy, the extent of international standardization (vs. local responsiveness), and the level of international integration/coordination of activities.

The scope of the firm is defined by its geographic scope (the number of key countries in which the firm is involved) but also by its segment scope (the number of product-market segments in which the firm is involved). As suggested by Porter (1986), these two dimensions are related. In this study we are mainly concerned with the scope of the firm in a given industry; the synergies that diversified multinational companies may exploit across industries are overlooked.

The foreign investment policy is defined by the relative importance given to foreign direct investments as compared to exports and to total investments. Within the export solution managers differentiate between foreign sales subsidiaries and sales intermediaries. Within the foreign direct investment solution, managers differentiate between takeovers and greenfield affiliates, and joint ventures, licensing and franchising are considered as a third vector of international development.

The extent of international standardization is opposed to fragmentation and adaptation to various local conditions. Managers consider three domains where standardization can be achieved: marketing policies, brands, and products and services.

The level of international integration or coordination of activities is discussed at different stages of the value chain: manufacturing, purchasing (including outsourcing and subcontracting), marketing, research and development, and sales and services (by order of importance).

As shown in Figure 6.2, the four concepts are related to one another.

Competitive strategy concepts

Content analysis of practitioners' narratives elicits a large number of concepts used to characterize competitive strategies in relation to

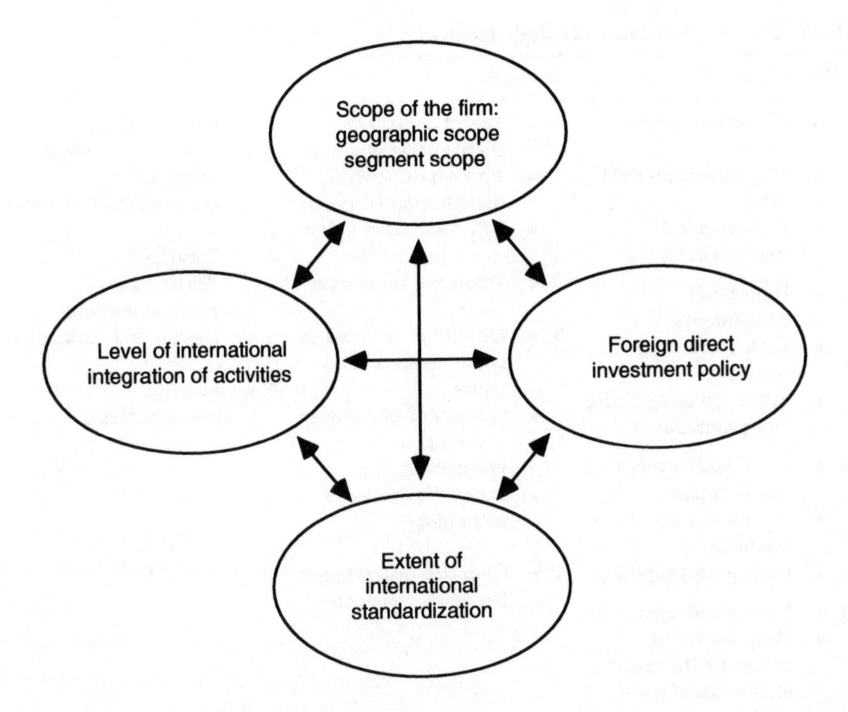

Figure 6.2 *International strategy concepts*

international strategies. Table 6.1 lists these concepts according to their importance in managerial discourses.

A posteriori, the concepts of competitive strategy can be classified into four groups: definition of the business, resource allocation, differentiation, and low cost. However, the original first order concepts were retained to describe configurations of international strategies.

Internationalization process concepts

Content analysis of practitioners' narratives elicits three broad categories of concept. Managers discuss the logic (or rationale) behind their decisions to develop internationally. They also emphasize the successive stages of the international expansion of their business in terms of targeted countries, development modes, and the most significant changes of direction. Third, they discuss the changing organization of their international operations, in terms of headquarters–subsidiaries relationships, decision processes and nationalities represented at the upper echelons (i.e. particular aspects of the ethnocentric-polycentric-geocentric framework). These concepts complete the description of holistic configurations of international strategies.

Table 6.1 *Competitive strategy concepts*

Often cited	Medium	Seldom cited
1 • Breadth of product range • Changes in product range • Technological specialization	1 • Direct control of distribution channels • Partnerships with distribution channels • Efficient outsourcing	1 • Private labels • Upstream vertical integration • Supply of full systems
2 • High R&D investments • High marketing expenses • Intensive advertising and promotion	2 • Intensive sales force	
3 • High quality products • Brand image • Unique (innovative) products • High priced products	3 • Quality of services to customers and end-users • Quality of manpower • Training of manpower • Innovative process technology	3 • Services to distributors • Fashion creation • Design and packaging
4 • Low priced products • Manufacturing efficiency through economies of scale • Cost control	4 • Capacity utilization • Economies of scope	4 • Flexible manufacturing

1 Definition of the business
2 Resource allocation
3 Differentiation
4 Low cost

The overall analysis of interviews with managers reveals eight configurations of international strategies. The first four configurations describe firms with a worldwide geographic scope:

- quasi global players,
- transnational restructurers,
- worldwide technology specialists,
- global luxury niche players.

The last four configurations describe firms with a more focused geographic scope and a position as international challengers:

- continental leaders,
- opportunistic international challengers,
- geographic niche players,
- country-centred players.

The following sections review the characteristics of each type of international strategy in relation to competitive advantages and processes of internationalization.

Worldwide players

'Worldwide' players expand across continents. Not all worldwide players necessarily adopt a 'global' strategy. The distinction between 'worldwide' and 'global' should be clear. A worldwide strategy (or scope) means that a firm is involved (in a significant way) in the most important markets of the world. A global strategy adds two characteristics to a worldwide scope: high standardization, and high cross-border integration (see Figure 6.2). Worldwide players from the same industry are not necessarily involved in frontal competition in all the key markets. For instance the frontal competition between Mars and Nestlé was limited to a segment, countlines, in some markets: the United Kingdom, France and Eastern Europe. There was frontal competition between Mars and Hershey in North America. As far as chocolate *tablettes* were concerned there was frontal competition between Nestlé and Jacobs Suchard in Europe. On the other hand there was frontal competition in most key markets between Nike, Reebok and Adidas in the sport footwear business.

By 'key markets' managers often refer to the top ten countries in terms of market size.

> You want to know which are the areas of the world that you ought to be concentrating on. [. . .] If you look at the top ten you find that over 70 per cent of the total sales are in those top ten countries. [. . .] Then if you look at the top 30 you find 93 per cent of the world consumption. (Chocolate and sugar confectionery)

Generally key markets include OECD countries and a dozen emerging high growth markets.

'Worldwide players' have in common their geographic scope: they target key markets worldwide. However, they may differ as far as the other dimensions of international strategy are concerned: segment scope, foreign investment policy, standardization, and international integration of value chain activities.

Table 6.2 summarizes the characteristics of four types of worldwide player: quasi-global players, transnational restructurers, worldwide technological specialists and global luxury niche players.

Table 6.3 lists the firms that belong to each cluster in our study.

Quasi-global players

In our study several companies are classified in this category: Nike, Reebok, Adidas, Fila, Bata, Timberland in the footwear industry; Mars, Ferrero, and Chupa Chups in the confectionery industry.

Table 6.2 *Four types of worldwide player*

	Quasi-global players	Transnational restructurers	Worldwide technology specialists	Global luxury niche players
Geographic scope	All key countries	All key countries	All key countries	All key countries
Segment scope	Narrow But concerns mass market	Large Most business segments	Narrow Technology-intensive segments	Narrow High priced segments
Foreign investment policy	Selective manufacturing investments Intensive commercial investments	Intensive manufacturing and commercial investments	Mainly exports Marginal investments	Exports Some commercial investments
Standardization	Homogeneous	Heterogeneous	Homogeneous	Homogeneous with some marginal adaptations
International integration of value chain activities	Integrated at the global level	Integrated at the regional level Coordinated worldwide	Integrated at the global level	Highly integrated at the global level

Table 6.3 *Clusters of worldwide players*

	Quasi-global players	Transnational restructurers	Worldwide technology specialists	Global luxury niche players
Footwear	*Nike*, Reebok, Adidas, Fila, Bata, Timberland		*Nokia Footwear*, Kelme, Palladium	*Charles Jourdan*, Clergerie, Kélian, Pancaldi, Rossetti, Ferragamo, Moreschi . . .
Cables and wires		*Alcatel Cables*, BICC, Pirelli Cavi	*Kerpenwerke*, Kabelwerke, Axon	
Paint		*Akzo Nobel*, ICI	*Herberts*, Courtaulds	
Chocolate and sugar confectionery	*Mars*, Ferrero, Chupa Chups	*Nestlé*		*Godiva*, Caffarel, Coq Blanc . . .

The most typical case in each cell is italicized.

'Quasi-global players' have *a worldwide geographic scope* and a relatively *narrow segment scope*. They focus on one or two industry segments on a worldwide basis, and they operate in the mass market. For instance they focus on sport-leisure footwear, a single segment in the footwear industry that represented a US $15 billion market in 1995. Pioneers with this strategy aim at gaining market share in most key countries. For instance Nike had a 28.5 per cent share of the world market in sport footwear and Mars had a 30 per cent share of the world market in countlines in the mid-1990s. Such market segments include a variety of products and customer groups which require specific and expensive marketing strategies. Quasi-global players have *significant commercial and manufacturing investments* in several key countries: sales subsidiaries and production subsidiaries. Production units are concentrated in a few countries and are sometimes completed with outsourcing facilities. Their international *strategy is homogeneous* across key countries, marketing variations are marginal and global brands are developed through massive communication expenses. The activities of the value chain that are dispersed in different countries are *tightly coordinated* and often *integrated* across borders.

The firms in our study do not follow a pure 'global' strategy (as described in the literature) hence the term 'quasi-global'. For instance, they concentrate production, outsourcing or R&D but they generally have several production units in a continent. A significant part of their sales are made in a couple of countries. For instance in 1995 the USA and the United Kingdom represented about 50 per cent of the total sales of Mars, North America represented about 60 per cent of the total sales of Nike, and Germany and Italy represented about 50 per cent of the total sales of Ferrero. Moreover, tight international coordination leaves some room for local initiatives. Mars recognized that competition might be country-specific. In the USA they competed with Hershey, in the UK and in France they competed with Nestlé-Rowntree, whereas in Germany they competed with Ferrero's and Jacobs Suchard's countlines. Hence marketing decisions are decentralized and the generic global strategy is adapted to local conditions through tactical action plans. The *quasi*-global character of these strategies may result from the *mixed* nature of the industries that we studied. It is probable that pure global industries or segments are more open to pure global strategies. Interestingly, all the cases of quasi-global strategy reported here belong to consumer goods industries, although these industries have the reputation of being favourable to multinational strategies (Bartlett and Ghoshal, 1989). Previous research may have underestimated the effect of global communication.

Quasi-global players are characterized by a specific *process of internationalization* and a *competitive strategy* based on differentiation.

The development of a quasi-global player generally starts with an innovative strategy in its home country (or in its regional base). The innovation relies on a unique combination of resources that generates a strong competitive advantage, and also on a new definition of the business at the frontier of the industry. For instance Mars bars represented a new concept somewhere between the chocolate industry and the snack industry.

> Bar lines like Mars, Twix, Bounty, or Snickers [. . .] are consumed by different consumers, in different places, at different times than, say, a box of chocolates. [. . .] Strategically they compete with other snack foods. [. . .] It is a choice of a piece of confectionery or a packet of crisps, or an ice-cream.

In a similar way Nike mixed two worlds: city shoes and sport equipment.

> Sport footwear, now you can see everywhere at any moment of the day. It is truly a hybrid concept – from a sport shoe it became leisure footwear and a city street shoe. [. . .] Actually most of the time they are used as walking shoes.

Timberland footwear was technically innovative in the 1960s with their injected soles that kept water out. This firm came out with a new concept of top quality leisure footwear for all seasons, and expanded it across borders.

Ferrero combined chocolate with a surprise toy in their Kinder-Surprise eggs. They turned a seasonal (Easter) concept into a small present for children to enjoy at any time, any day of the year. Chupa Chups reinvented lollipops: 'a sweet with a stick', sophisticated flavours, unique shape and packaging.

Quasi-global players start with conceptual innovations that have a potential universal appeal: a simple need, a large consumer base, a unique character.

The uniqueness of the concept is strengthened by a strong brand image based on massive advertising and promotion. In 1994 Nike spent about 12 per cent of its sales turnover on advertising and promotion; so did Reebok and Adidas (about 10 per cent). Mars preserved its brands against competition from private labels. In Europe, private labels represented only 2 per cent of the countline market, whereas they represented 20 per cent of the market of chocolate *tablettes*. At the world level, the sponsoring of sports teams and events further strengthens brand image. In sports footwear Nike, Reebok and Adidas competed for exclusive contracts with sports stars (half of Nike's advertising and promotion budget – 6 per cent of sales – went on sponsoring). Global brand advertising goes with global events and the competition for sponsoring extends beyond industry boundaries: for instance in 1990 Mars signed an agreement with the International Olympic Committee to become the only food sponsor of the 1992 Winter and Summer Olympics. Ferrero sponsored the Bologna basketball team, known as 'Kinder Bologna', with a total annual budget of US $24 million in order to win the Euroleague. Adidas sponsored the Marseilles football team (among others) who aimed to win the Champions League again.

Followers tend to imitate the original innovation, and pioneers try to maintain differentiation through continuous improvements. In the mid-1990s Nike renewed about 40 per cent of its product range every year. So did Reebok and Adidas. Technical innovations sustained differentiation: 'Air-Max' (1987) replaced 'Air' (1979) from Nike, 'Pump' (Reebok, 1988) and 'Torsion' (Adidas, 1989) competed with 'Air-Max'.

Design is a significant weapon, even in sugar confectionery: Salvador Dali himself designed the brilliant Chupa Chups red and yellow wrapper in the 1960s. Various forms of 'techno-marketing' are used to preserve differentiation, for instance in 1970 Mars invented Klix and Mars Money System to facilitate the use of its automatic selling machines. Techno-marketing reduces the need to launch new products with radically new functions.

Quasi-global players focus on a small number of brands in order to rationalize mass marketing and reap economies of scale. Mars's global strategy was organized around four mega brands: Mars, M&Ms, Snickers and Twix, each of which had a particular functionality and a broad target. It also included two brands considered as 'strategic niches': Milky Way and Balisto for children. Ferrero's worldwide strategy was built on three main brands: Mon Chéri pralines, Ferrero Rocher boxed chocolates, and the Kinder umbrella brand. In the business of sugar confectionery most competitors had a broad product range. Chupa Chups was an exception, they reduced their product line to a very narrow set of products: the Chupa Chups Classic, the Melody Pop and a few derivatives such as sugar-free lollipops.

A narrow product range helps to achieve manufacturing efficiency. Quasi-global players drive costs down by all possible means: full utilization of assets, long production runs, scale economies and the search for low labour costs. In the footwear industry comparative advantages are significant and relocation is crucial to cost-competitiveness. Since its creation Nike has outsourced the bulk of its manufacturing to Asia. The only exceptions have been a manufacturing unit for the prototypes (research and development) and high-tech shoes for sport competition in the United States, a manufacturing unit in Ireland for technical products sold in the European Community, and a rubber production unit in Malaysia. At the beginning subcontractors were located in Japan, then they moved to Korea, then to Thailand and Hong Kong, and later on to China, Vietnam and Indonesia, in search of the lowest labour costs. Between 1988 and 1992 Nike opened 35 plants in Asia and closed 20 plants (*Capital*, 1997: 62–63). Plant migration was organized and plants were managed by the regular Nike subcontractors from Korea and Taiwan. In 1996, the Taiwanese group Pou Chen manufactured about 1.2 million pairs of Nike every month in Jakarta (Indonesia). Manufacturing efficiency was also achieved through automatization and specialization: a single plant may manufacture a single generic product for a whole continent or several continents. Manufacturing of the eight generic products of Mars was organized as follows: eight plants in the USA, one in Mexico, one in Brazil, six in Western Europe (one in England, two in France, one in the Netherlands, one in Germany, one in Austria), one in East Asia, one in Australia, and three under construction in Eastern Europe. Mars, Ferrero and Chupa Chups developed their own machinery and manufacturing systems, in order to achieve superior productivity. Most of the time quasi-global firms prefer organic development to takeovers: organic development allows access to leading-edge manufacturing technology.

> Nestlé [. . .] have acquired existing companies [Perugina, Rowntree]. . . . Our strategy is not to do that. Because a fundamental part of our belief is that we get efficiency from the way we run plants. We make very small margins on our plants: this is deliberate, this is to give the consumer good value for money. That is our basic philosophy. When we do that we work our assets to death, 24 hours a day, seven days a week, and we also make sure they are the most modern assets. So we believe there is a gain in building and engineering our own stuff.

Quasi-global players rely on another source of competitive advantage: the relationship with distributors. As far as consumer goods are concerned, merchandising is a key success factor. They offer massive support and turnkey merchandising to distributors.

Back to the *internationalization process* and the logic that drives this process: quasi-global players transfer their successful concept from their home country to a foreign base and then to other key countries. Mars transferred countlines from the US to the UK, and from there to the rest of Europe and the world. Ferrero transferred its countlines from Italy to Germany and then to other countries. This transfer is 'narcissistic' in the sense that it does not involve much adaptation to foreign local markets. Narcissistic transfer is appropriate when the concept is both unique (radical innovation) and simple enough to be universally accepted.

> When companies like Nike or Reebok arrived on the European market around 15 years ago, many industry analysts were saying that there was no

> way they could succeed in Europe, because they were going to run into a need to adapt their offer to European tastes. In fact, within a span of five years, with a strategy that comes from the American market, with American methods, with American tastes, these companies have been able to impose their marketing by adapting their products very little to the European market. In the area of sports or leisure which targets the young and especially young males, you realize that the values come from America. The values are very simple and very universal: American culture is based on sports and sports is accessible to everybody, it is the biggest common denominator. [. . .] It started with tennis and the identification everyone had with the major tennis players, then basketball took on greater importance, and this culture was transferred from one continent to another. The adolescents in our inner cities are much closer to the adolescents in the American inner cities. And because of this, and the marketing tools and power that these companies have, the market exploded.

The whole internationalization process of quasi-global players can be summarized as follows:

- a strong innovative concept that allows conquest of the home country;
- international transfer of the concept to one or two foreign countries, through organic growth;
- the systematic transfer to a set of key countries, and the setting up of a global brand, through organic growth, and with superior operating efficiency;
- sustaining differentiation (through additional innovations and techno-marketing) and improving overall efficiency (manufacturing, logistics).

In the third stage early imitators (for instance Reebok in sport-leisure footwear), and in the fourth stage late imitators (for instance Adidas) join the group of quasi-global players.

It took time for Adidas to decode Nike's formula. For many years Adidas communicated on a technical image and the 'Made in Germany' label. It chose to sponsor teams whereas the trend was toward individual sports heroes. When Adidas turned to sponsoring individuals, for some time they missed the coordination between sponsoring and advertising (*Capital*, 1997: 62–63). Adidas finally caught up with Nike and Reebok at the beginning of the 1990s when a new CEO came in (Robert Louis-Dreyfus). Manufacturing was relocated to Asia: in 1996 about 85 per cent of production was outsourced in that region (to the local subcontractors who also supply the American rivals). With the exception of football and tennis (considered European sports), design and research and development were relocated to Portland, USA, a few minutes' drive from Nike's headquarters.

Early or late imitators try to differentiate their products and services. Reebok first focused on women's footwear and communicated on 'solidarity' (as opposed to Nike's concept of competition). Adidas communicated on genuineness and nature, and tried fashion sponsoring with Madonna and Claudia Schiffer (*Fortune*, 1995; *Eurostaf*, 1996; *Capital*, 1997).

In the chocolate industry, Ferrero followed Mars and successfully launched its own innovative concepts of countlines: the Kinder-Surprise egg and the Rocher.

> Ferrero's international strategy is to gradually conquer new markets with products that already exist. If Rocher has been successful in Italy, Germany, France and England, it will eventually penetrate the United States and Latin America. . . . We have an international scope and subsidiaries already set up all over the world.

However, Ferrero's products were quite different from Mars's products:

> We made *lighter* pralines, because the Mediterranean taste prefers lighter products. Ferrero invented the Rocher, with lots of hazelnut, a light praline. This is a global alternative to heavy Mars chocolate bars.

In their early years innovative concepts require a significant market base to flourish: large size, high level of consumption, sophisticated customers. The United States was a good base for a leisure footwear business. The country represented 55 per cent of the world market for sports footwear, and each American household owned six pairs of sport shoes (compared to 1.9 pairs in Europe). Mars started in the United States where the consumption level of candies and snacks is high, and expanded in the United Kingdom where the level of per capita consumption is even higher. In 1996 Mars's sales amounted to US $13 per capita in North America and US $34 per capita in the UK.

Once the key markets of the OECD have been conquered, quasi-global players are still tempted by growth strategies. First they look for opportunities in emerging high growth markets (Asia-Pacific, Eastern Europe, Brazil) and expand their geographic scope. Some competitors exploit the rapid internationalization of distribution channels. Some companies diversify their product portfolio, for instance Adidas took over Salomon the world leader in winter sports equipment and a major competitor in the golf equipment business. The general trend is toward worldwide development, but this does not necessarily mean more global strategies (i.e. more standardization and more integration). Quasi-global players may have to react to aggressive regional competitors and to retail chains who develop low-priced private labels. In such situations some quasi-global players are driven toward more local responsiveness.

Transnational restructurers

In our study several companies are classified in this category: Alcatel Cables, BICC, Pirelli Cavi in the cable industry, Akzo Nobel and ICI in the paint industry, and Nestlé in the chocolate industry.

Transnational restructurers have a worldwide geographic scope (often larger than quasi-global players) and a broad segment scope. They are involved in most of the product-market segments of their industry. These companies have complex configurations, with multiple locations and frequent organizational changes that correspond to successive rationalization programmes. Decision power is distributed throughout their matrix structures, and moves from key country subsidiaries to worldwide business lines. Organizational units share profit and loss responsibilities, whereas a number of horizontal *ad hoc* project groups contribute to interfunctional and international coordination.

Transnational restructurers expand their geographic scope in several segments, they aim at a worldwide leadership position, and achieve part of their high growth through a number of domestic or international mergers and acquisitions.

As a consequence, their assets are relatively dispersed across a number of countries, and they sometimes suffer from a duplication of resources and overcapacity. Transnational restructurers are forced to rationalize their assets, close down some plants, restructure their operations, simplify their complex portfolio of products and brands, in order to improve profitability. Through this process of 'take over and rationalize', these firms contribute to the restructuring of their industries.

The *internationalization process* of transnational restructurers is characterized by the extension of core competences in relation to international expansion. In this respect it is radically different from the process that drives quasi-global players (i.e. international diffusion of core competences through organic growth, which preserves internal consistency). Transnational restructurers enrich their core competences and acquire new competences when taking over foreign companies. For instance when Nestlé took over Rowntree in 1988, it absorbed crucial marketing skills and assets in the countline business. To some extent transnational restructurers recall the strategic profile of 'analysers' according to Miles and Snow (1978). 'Analysers' are viewed as a unique combination of the 'prospector' and the 'defender' types; 'analysers' seek effectiveness through both efficiency and innovation (new products and markets). This dual strategy may result in increased size because the organizations must engage in both mass production and research and development. In this process decision-makers position their firm on a chessboard where each square is a segment in a country.

In this strategic configuration, the pioneers *anticipate* changes in structural forces – for instance deregulation, concentration of distributors, international expansion of customers, scale economies. Indeed such anticipation generally helps to accelerate the transformation of structural forces: transnational restructurers drive the international development of their industry.

The 'transnational' attribute of this type of company corresponds to the model described by Bartlett and Ghoshal (1989). Some activities in the value chain, or some product-market segments, are globally integrated, whereas other activities are organized so as to preserve local responsiveness. In the cable industry, Alcatel centralized research and development at the world level while the manufacturing of land telecom and power cables was dispersed and decentralized, but key account managers coordinated sales to international customers. Other activities such as fibre optics and submarine cables were managed globally. In the paint industry ICI managed the business of can coating in a global manner, whereas there was more local responsiveness in the business of decorative paint. The group tried to promote a global brand, Dulux, but local adaptations were still implemented; strategic coordination was achieved at the regional (i.e. continental) level. Such complexity combined with frequent restructuring makes it difficult to describe this configuration in terms of international strategy and competitive advantage.

In summary, transnational restructurers adopt the following *international strategy*:

- positions in all key markets (including emerging high growth markets);
- a broad segment scope;
- global integration of R&D, regional integration of manufacturing and marketing;
- a dispersed configuration of assets, and a combination of several modes of development – greenfield affiliates, mergers and acquisitions, agreements (licensing, joint ventures), and types of subsidiaries (production, sales) in order to occupy key positions on the chessboard (for instance ICI had 42 wholly owned plants and 30 units in joint venture or licensing agreements, Akzo Nobel industrial coatings had 13 plants in its home countries, 13 production subsidiaries and 10 more units under joint venture or other alliances);
- a transnational organization in which global integration and local responsiveness coexist and vary depending on the activity (function or product-market segment).

As far as *competitive strategy* is concerned, transnational restructurers have the following characteristics:

- high product quality and strong corporate image;
- significant services to customers with a complete range of products and sometimes full systems;
- product innovation based on R&D;
- economies of scope in R&D and sometimes in marketing when they use umbrella brands;
- manufacturing efficiency through rationalization, and in spite of product diversity.

Such strategies require high amounts of resources. For this reason only a small number of competitors may become transnational restructurers in a given industry. Moreover, different industries shape slightly different competitors' profiles.

In the mid-1980s, Nestlé decided that chocolate confectionery should be a priority business in its corporate portfolio. Confectionery represented a US $68 billion market worldwide (as compared to US $105 billion for soft drinks, US $38 billion for coffee, and US $30 billion for biscuits). First Nestlé took over Perugina in Italy. Then they realized that they needed to strengthen their position in the growing segment of countlines (at the time Nestlé's strengths were in chocolate *tablettes* – a continental European concept – and boxed assortments). Nestlé took over Rowntree (based in the UK) and its strong countline brands; it also took over the chocolate and confectionery division of RJR Nabisco in the United States. Several strong countline brands came to enrich Nestlé's portfolio: KitKat, After Eight, Smarties, and Lion. At the beginning of the 1990s Nestlé had a transnational scope (in terms of segments and geography):

> Nestlé [. . .] is present in all product categories of the chocolate industry, in *tablettes*, in countlines, as well as pralines. They have a significant portfolio of products and brands, and with that they can be present everywhere. [. . .] In North America and in Europe, Nestlé has substantial market share [11 per cent in the USA and 23 per cent in Europe as compared to respectively 36 per cent and 17 per cent for Mars].

After the takeovers Nestlé had more than 50 international brands (as compared to eight at Mars) and a number of multipurpose plants. Clearly they had to rationalize their assets in Western Europe and in North America.

> Our industrial operations changed and they are continuing to change a lot within the framework of a rationalization process. [. . .] There is an entire programme of restructuring and revamping our industrial equipment.

Restructuring appeared a necessity if the company was to be price competitive and resist the pressures exerted by powerful distributors. Margins depended on manufacturing efficiency, and manufacturing efficiency could be achieved in specialized plants that could produce about 100,000 tons a year. Productivity improvements were needed to fund the massive marketing and sponsoring expenses that had become the rule in the industry. Nestlé's portfolios of research and development projects, products, and brands were rationalized in order to reap economies of scale.

> It is normal to both favour the habits of a given continent and offer products that are adequate [to local taste], and then have a certain number of products that [. . .] are able to cross all the continents. I think that we can have both positions, some products that have a more local character, and then some products that have a more global character. [. . .] We can have a certain number of global brands: the advantage is the economic synergy, the technological synergy, and the transfer of know-how from one continent to another.

In the mid-1990s such a 'mixed' configuration was unique as compared to quasi-global players such as Mars or Ferrero. It was also different from the position of continental players (such as Jacobs Suchard, Lindt, Hershey or Lote). Compared to continental players, Nestlé could exploit economies of scale and scope (with global brands and technological synergies). Compared to Mars, Nestlé could exploit the benefits of variety: a better adaptation to local demand (for instance heavy and chewy bars and light crispy bars) and competition. Nestlé's economies of scope (between the four segments) could compensate for Mars's economies of scale (within a single segment: countlines).

Finally Nestlé also played on the other areas of the chessboard: they started a significant expansion plan towards emerging high growth markets, particularly in Eastern Europe, through acquisitions and alliances.

> Nestlé is concentrating its attention on countries where it feels that chocolate consumption is 'insufficient', for instance Southern Europe, Eastern Europe, China and South America.

Nestlé acquired a manufacturing unit in Hungary (joint venture), set up a plant in the Czech Republic, a joint venture in China and another one in Russia, in order to complete its worldwide coverage of key markets.

It is interesting to contrast the case of Nestlé with the case of Cadbury-Schweppes, which was atypical in our study. Cadbury achieved significant international expansion, often through acquisitions or joint venture. They first showed particular interest in the countries of the Commonwealth. Then they selected foreign markets which belonged to the top 30 but where foreign competition was not yet firmly established. They set up operations in Spain, Argentina, Egypt, Poland, China and Russia. But, unlike Nestlé, Cadbury managed its foreign operations as a portfolio of countries.

> Basically we deliberately have a stance which is decentralized – protection of local brands – and our idea is to layer on our global brands on top of their local brands.

In other words Cadbury was more like a 'multinational' organization (Bartlett and Ghoshal, 1989) than like a 'transnational'. They did little restructuring in their international federation.

In the cable industry Alcatel Cables, BICC and Pirelli Cavi had a broad segment scope and a broad geographic scope, partly as a result of successive acquisitions (with the exception of the Japanese market, which was dominated by domestic competitors: Sumitomo, Furukawa, Hitachi and Fujikura).

Alcatel first expanded its activities through domestic acquisition of several specialist firms (Gorse SA, Roesch, Filotex, Cableries de Lens). Then it expanded through international acquisitions in the United States and in Europe (AEG Kabel AG in Germany; Northern Telecom STC-UK, submarine telecom cables; IKO Kabel in Sweden, power cables, etc.). Altogether, in 1995, the group included 20 production subsidiaries worldwide and more than 100 sales subsidiaries. Due to specific local regulations, foreign subsidiaries had substantial autonomy (some of them had their own research and development resources), with the exception of the most global segments: submarine cables and fibre optics.

> In the cable industry, [until the mid-1990s] the policy was to follow the rules of the game. [That is to say] having a series of foreign subsidiaries in a number of key countries, and giving them autonomy in running their business. And this inevitably led to a feudal configuration.

BICC and Pirelli followed Alcatel's strategy. Pirelli Cavi took significant positions in France, Great Britain, Spain, the USA, Canada, Brazil, Argentina and Australia. Then Alcatel started international integration of its dispersed activities before its rivals. The Alcatel name and brand was given to all units and products. Research and development competence centres were set up in various subsidiaries, with the mission to serve the needs of the whole group. For instance in the segment of submarine telecom cables, four specialized factories (in Australia, France, England and the USA) were coordinated; in the same way the two factories in the segment of submarine power cables (in France) were coordinated so as to serve the world market.

The first wave of international restructuration of the cable industry lasted until 1993. At the time there was frontal competition between the three European leaders: Alcatel, BICC and Pirelli. At the end of this period, Alcatel and Pirelli both had more than two-thirds of their sales in Europe (the position of BICC was spread more across continents). The second wave of international restructuring started in 1993 with significant takeovers and joint ventures in emerging high growth markets, and significant cross-border rationalization of manufacturing and logistics.

In 1993–94 Pirelli closed down nine production sites and specialized the remaining 53 sites dispersed among 11 countries:

> The current strategy is to follow the trends towards globalization, the formation of trade areas, and the restructuration of manufacturing. We had overcapacity due to falling demand. So we changed our structure and created large geographic areas that coordinate our activities: Nafta, the European Union, etc. [. . .] We are getting our company ready to deal with the new structure of our markets.

BICC went even further in the specialization of its European production units (UK cables division; CEAT Cavi, Italy; CEL-CAT, Portugal; KWO Kabel, Germany; BICC Cables, Spain) and its North American operations. They sold the Canadian building wire business, and merged the Canadian and the US utility and industrial businesses into a single unit. In the business of special industrial applications BICC closed two plants (York and Pennsylvania) so as to improve the efficiency of the two remaining manufacturing units (Tennessee and Connecticut).

Alcatel also went through a process of rationalization of its European and North American operations.

> Now we have achieved European specialization. For instance the flexible industrial cable factory supplies the whole European market, and we will go more towards that sort of thing. We will not necessarily have only one unit, we could have two, for security reasons, but they will be perfectly interchangeable.

Alcatel strengthened its position as a system provider and led the new wave of takeovers in Eastern Europe and in Asia together with BICC and Sumitomo, whereas Pirelli did not follow.

Experts believe that the new wave of international acquisitions and alliances (Alcatel's joint ventures in China and in the East, BICC's joint ventures and investments in Asia, Indonesia, Malaysia, India, etc.) announces a future consolidation at the worldwide level in the twenty first century.

In the paint industry, the two world leaders Akzo Nobel and ICI were viewed as transnational restructurers. Both groups relied on mergers and acquisitions in order to achieve their ambitious goals. Both also had to restructure their operations and, in so doing, contributed to a restructuring of the paint industry.

> In 1987, ICI's worldwide coating interests were a loose federation whereby the European business located in headquarters in the UK had a lot of influence but no executive authority. [. . .] Then we acquired a big company in the US to put us into this market for the first time. We made the organizational change to bring all the operations under a single international business: ICI Paints Worldwide. At that time we formulated a long term plan which was designed to reduce the diversity of our business portfolio by concentrating on three core businesses: decorative, car refinish and packaging coatings.

ICI's segment scope was still relatively large but it did not cover the whole range of industry segments (the three businesses corresponded to 60 per cent of the total volume sold in the industry).

When Akzo and Nobel merged they formed the largest group in the paint industry and started a significant restructuration process. European activities were organized in four divisions: decorative paint, industrial coatings, automotive refinish and aeronautic finishes. Akzo Nobel adopted a transnational organization, with different levels of international integration depending on segment-specific competitive forces. Aeronautic finishes were organized on a global basis. Automotive refinishes adopted a global organization of R&D and a regional organization for the other activities of the value chain (with three regions: Western Europe, North America, and the rest of the world). Industrial coatings were organized in two regions: Europe and North America. Decorative paint was split into two regions: Northern Europe (also in charge of expansion in Eastern Europe) and Southern Europe (also in charge of expansion in the Asia-Pacific region).

ICI and Akzo Nobel were in frontal competition in the largest segment of the paint industry: decorative paint (which represented about 50 per cent of total sales), and in one of the most profitable segments: automotive refinishes. Both had significant positions in Europe and growth ambitions in the US (36 per cent of the world market). ICI, Akzo Nobel and several other major competitors (for instance Total, Alcro Beckers) had grown through mergers and acquisitions since the beginning of the 1980s. They acquired strong national brands, some of which gave them access to new technologies, and strengthened their core activities.

In the mid-1990s the leaders accelerated the integration of their international activities, and launched a new wave of acquisitions and alliances. The challenge of integration was particularly important in research and development activities and in procurement so as to provide better products (i.e. environmentally friendly and easy to use). ICI seemed to lead the integration process and to bet on globalization of the industry. They promoted a Pan-European brand, Dulux, they created worldwide business lines for car refinish and can coating, and continental business lines for decorative paint (North America, Europe, Asia-Pacific). In 1995 Dulux was marketed in 23 countries, including the USA.

> I think in three to five years we will also have the decorative business managed on a worldwide basis with a single executive profit accountable for all our decorative businesses all over the world.

Akzo Nobel had a slightly different view of the global integration of the decorative paint business:

> It is very expensive to create a European brand name. ICI has taken this very far and committed themselves to create a single brand name. The dilemma is that you have to acquire other companies in order to grow in the mature paint business. If you buy market share, you are paying for the distribution of a brand name, so why should you get rid of this brand? [. . .] We work in a different way in different countries, we accept these differences. [. . .] For instance Akzo does not market any paint under the Akzo brand in Spain. If they put Akzo on the shelves, instead of Bruguer or Procolour, the lady shopping for paint would not know it, she would not even be able to pronounce the name.

In order to amortize their high R&D investments, ICI and Akzo Nobel sold more and more licences abroad. For instance ICI sold its water-based car refinishes technology to Rock Paint (Japan) and set up a joint venture with Kansaï Paint (the most international of the Japanese paint companies). A dozen firms worked under Akzo Nobel licences in Asia, and joint ventures were set up in China and in Vietnam (decorative paint and industrial powder paint). In South America ICI took over Burge Paints (decorative) and Akzo Nobel set up two joint ventures in the automotive refinish business (Brazil and Mexico).

Clearly, in the late 1990s ICI and Akzo Nobel went on expanding their geographic scope. On the other hand they seemed to diverge as far as global integration was concerned. This divergence suggests two possible developments for 'transnational restructurers'. Some may adopt a quasi-global strategy, whereas others may assert the transnational character of their organization, with a global integration of upstream activities and local responsiveness in downstream activities.

Worldwide technology specialists

In our study a number of companies are classified in this category, among them for instance: Kerpenwerke (Germany), Kabelwerke Reinshagen (Germany), Axon (France) in the cable industry; Herberts-Hoechst (Germany), International Paint-Courtaulds (UK) in the paint industry; Palladium (France), Kelme (Spain) and Nokia Footwear (Finland) in the footwear industry.

This is a relatively heterogeneous group: it includes small firms (with a significant international activity) as well as subsidiaries or divisions of multinational companies. It includes high-tech companies such as Axon, Kerpenwerke or Herberts-Hoechst as well as firms involved in the manufacturing of consumer goods (e.g. footwear) which do not require leading edge technologies.

'Worldwide technology specialists' are mainly characterized by the ownership of specific technological know-how that gives them a significant worldwide competitive advantage in a particular segment of their industry. As compared to the first cluster (quasi-global players), they are more focused, they do not target a mass market and their competitive advantage relies on superior technological skills. Worldwide technology specialists generally target all the key countries, at least those concerned with their technology. As a result they have a broad geographic scope (however, international expansion of the smaller firms is sometimes restrained by limited resources). Worldwide technology specialists have a standardized strategy across borders and a high level of global integration of their activities. They prefer export but they may establish foreign production units when customers demand local services and quick delivery, when the low-tech part of their production can be usefully relocated, or when they have to respond to host government demands.

Their competitive strategy relies on technological differentiation, services to customers and reputation or brand image in a particular segment. Their internationalization process often starts with the recognition that the firm's technical skills are sources of differentiation from the mass market. As a result they focus their international expansion on their unique set of technical skills.

> It is our goal to get rid of the mass business, that is the standard product, where the margins have shrunk and where foreign competition has become very intense. We want to go more into the specialties. [. . .] We push hard in this direction, to create solutions for the customers, solutions based on technical know-how, for which the price is not the main criterion. (Cable)
>
> We decided to optimize our top industrial know-how of rubber technology. [. . .] That means that we are not going to manufacture leather shoes. We know how to make boots from rubber and that is our strength. [. . .] We decided this specialization 15 years ago; we concentrate on our

> expertise. [. . .] Otherwise it is too expensive to manufacture shoes in Finland.
>
> We are involved in paints that require a sophisticated technology, in research and development intensive activities. [. . .] Ten years ago we clearly focused on this line of business, that includes car finishes and refinishes and special industrial paint with powder technology.

Indeed their know-how represents a significant potential for international expansion in a number of key countries.

> We are in high-tech products, thus the market is worldwide. We belong to a technical culture that includes plastics, electronics and micro-mechanics. In our high-tech niche, we decided to create four subsidiaries in major countries: the USA, the UK, Germany and Japan. This was done over a five-year period. (Cables)

In the mid-1990s, in the paint industry, more precisely in the segments of car finishes and refinishes (which represented about 12 per cent of the world market of paints), Hoechst emerged as a worldwide technological specialist. Car finishes is a technology-intensive business that requires powerful actors to deal with powerful customers: car manufacturers. The challenge is so hard that the world leader, the American PPG, sold its assets in the business of decorative paint (Corona was sold to ICI) in order to focus resources on its two core activities: industrial specialities and car finishes. First, Hoechst established a dense network of manufacturing units across Europe. They anticipated the procurement rationalization policy implemented by car makers in the 1990s. Hoechst further expanded its operations through acquisitions in Europe and in North America and increased their differentiation with quick development of two new technologies, powder and water-based car finishes, that preserve the environment from pollution by solvents. These new technologies were quickly transferred through their international network, and were particularly successful in the USA. In the mid-1990s Hoechst's operations in the business of car finishes and industrial paint included 20 manufacturing units and 40 sales subsidiaries worldwide. Research activities were concentrated in a single technological centre in Wuppertal. Technological adaptations were achieved at the plant level in order to match the specific demands of customers (in this business a given car manufacturer, say Volkswagen, may have different technical specifications, depending on the model).

In general, however, worldwide technological specialists tend to concentrate production in a few sites. For instance Nokia footwear concentrated the manufacturing of rubber boots in Finland. As far as components and other footwear were concerned, they organized 'cooperations' in China, South Korea, Italy and Spain.

Kelme, specializing in football boots, manufactured its technical products for professional players in Spain, its home country, while its less sophisticated products were produced in Moldavia, Indonesia and Taiwan. In labour-intensive businesses, such policies allow more proximity to sophisticated demand, contribute to an image of quality, and facilitate access to technical know-how.

The French footwear manufacturer Palladium defined itself as a worldwide technical specialist:

> Our key factors of success rely on our technological know-how, our ability to manufacture sport shoes with a process of compression and vulcanization of high quality rubber. [. . .] With that we can compete in a global market niche. [. . .] We are ambitious but we are still restrained by limited financial resources.

Palladium located 80 per cent of manufacturing in Tunisia and 20 per cent in France for the finishing of products. More than 75 per cent of sales were made abroad, essentially in Europe. Further intercontinental expansion was delayed until the firm could leverage enough resources to set up operations in North America and in Asia.

Sometimes worldwide technological specialists represent ideal acquisition targets for multinational corporations which plan to extend their segment scope or to increase their market share in high added value activities. Otherwise worldwide technological specialists tend to exploit their technical competitive advantage, renew their technological leadership and increase their geographic scope to the whole set of key markets.

Global luxury niche players

In our study a number of companies are classified in this category. They all belong to the sector of consumer goods: Charles Jourdan (France), Clergerie (France), Stéphane Kélian (France), Pancaldi (Italy), Fratelli Rossetti (Italy), Salvatore Ferragamo (Italy), Moreschi (Italy) and several other luxury brands in the footwear industry, Godiva (Belgium and US), Caffarel (Italy), Coq Blanc (France), and several other upmarket brands in the chocolate confectionery industry.

Like the previous cluster, the firms in this category rely on a strong differentiation that gives them access to worldwide markets, but here differentiation is based on top product and service quality (more than on technological expertise) associated with a strong company name and image that signals luxury items. The competitive advantage of global luxury niche players often is embedded in location-specific advantages. More precisely, firms in this category benefit from the image of their home country, for instance the luxury image of Italian footwear, French food, etc. The luxury image helps to penetrate key markets worldwide. The firm's presence in the major cities of the world is also a symbol of global conquest and helps to strengthen the image of the company. Home country image and global brand go together.

> In brief, Paris is the capital city of fashion. [In luxury footwear a French brand gives you the opportunity and] the credibility to succeed abroad. [. . . Then] success in the United States is very important. Also Asia gives credibility to a brand. If you are successful in Asia, you can be sure that it will affect your position in Europe and in the USA.
>
> The Belgian image of *maître chocolatier* is renowned worldwide. [. . .] As we are talking about luxury products, the relevant [geographic] scope is the Triad: the USA, Japan, and Europe. We are strong in Europe and we are very well established in the US and in Japan. . . . We have secured the number one position worldwide as an international prestige brand. [. . .] You need to be in the top ten cities, in the best street, and then you can sell in duty-free shops and in famous department stores: that is where the real volumes and the margin are.

International players in this category generally have a very narrow focus on high-priced products with a prestigious brand name. At the top of the market pyramid, many of them target a specific segment, for instance *women's* luxury footwear, or *leisure* luxury footwear. In the chocolate industry, the luxury segment represented about 2 per cent of the market, it was the domain of local craftsmen and of firms like Godiva or Caffarel. The segment scope of a company like Lindt (for instance) was different: they had some upmarket products competing with Godiva, but their product range was much broader and their brand image was mixed (at least in continental Europe, where consumers could find the products in mass market distribution channels).

Global luxury niche players develop a consistent brand image and product range across borders, with very marginal local adaptations. Generally they have a homogeneous core product line that represents the bulk of their international activity, and adaptations are limited to technical details such as sizes, colours or packaging.

> This is a product that must have its own particular look, our style. If we were to manufacture a collection for each market, we would end up having no identity. We do not pretend to set a style, but we want to adopt an international style that suits an international elitist clientele. (Footwear)
>
> We are trying to come up with a unified look to our packaging, standard packaging. . . . This box, the logo for seasonal items. Now all the boxes are the same, in the Americas, in Europe, in Japan . . . the design is standardized. The chocolate is standardized everywhere but North America. North

> America is only different because of some regulations: no alcohol filling, longer shelf life because of the size of the country, this kind of thing. So we had to slightly modify the formula.

Global luxury niche players tend to concentrate production in their home country (in spite of the high percentage of sales in foreign markets). This is due to the importance of the country's image and the 'made in . . .' label.

> This is an issue of brand credibility. [In the footwear industry] there is a whole emotional component about sourcing in Asia, which is synonymous with cheap mass market. Hence, in spite of the high labour costs our company has four factories in Switzerland, two in France, and one in the UK.

Italian luxury footwear manufacturers benefited from a strong 'fashion' image and relatively competitive labour costs, hence most of the manufacturing was done in Italy. French luxury footwear manufacturers tried to keep the major part of manufacturing in their home country, but they also outsourced production (or sold licences) to neighbouring countries: Spain, Portugal and Italy. For instance Charles Jourdan manufactured its women's luxury shoes in France, but they also had a team in Spain to purchase heels, and subcontractors in Italy for the production of men's footwear (which was not the core business of the company). Fratelli Rossetti, from Italy, sold licences in Spain, Turkey, Mexico, Greece, and in Asia for local manufacturing and sales.

A similar pattern was observed in the case of luxury chocolate confectionery.

> Belgium supplies the whole world . . . except North America. We have a factory in America which supplies the United States and Canada, but the rest of the world is supplied from here. It is important, as in places like Japan they want the real thing, which means 'made in Belgium'.

The concentration of manufacturing in the home country also obeys other rules: the availability of skills, or logistical imperatives.

Global luxury niche players adopt a consistent *competitive strategy*:

- top quality high-priced products;
- focus on a product line, unity of style but variety of items within the product line;
- importance of design;
- downstream partial integration through a network of wholly owned or franchised retail shops (under the name of the firm or the brand).

Design is crucial in luxury markets, particularly of course in fashion clothes and footwear. Many Italian firms were set up by designers. Fiamma Ferragamo manages the design of Salvatore Ferragamo women's shoes, and, according to Jourdan, fashion is a matter of design.

> We must be in close contact with the designers, it is they who initiate fashion trends, and most of our marketing effort is to push new products. Our strategy is very similar to that of the Salvatore brothers, in terms of products, design, image and price. (Footwear)

Luxury chocolate brands use design to differentiate their boxes. Audiberti Caffarel differentiated its seasonal 'collections' of 'fancy items' with exclusive packaging design. This is also a way to give some unity to a variety of items (several hundreds).

Finally, global luxury niche players tend to control their retail outlets.

> My strategy is to increase the number of retail stores under our name, be it stores that we manage ourselves or franchises. [. . .] In the end I would like all our sales to go through our distribution network. (Footwear)

For instance Ferragamo has set up a network of 30 retail shops in the largest cities of Europe, the United States and Asia. Roberto Monsani designed Ferragamo's stores and used similar themes: warm wood, beige, grey and pink granite floors, beige and grey carpeting, and beige leather seating.

Luxury chocolate manufacturers also try to control the retailing of their products.

> So I wish to be elitist, which means I do not want to be everywhere at once. First I could not afford it and most importantly, in a word, my strategy is retail; it means controlling our own retail outlets.

Global luxury niche players face several challenges. In the business of luxury footwear, firms have to decide on the future expansion of their retail networks, which represents a significant investment. There are limits to the proliferation of this type of store. Some competitors may also be tempted by relocation strategies, particularly to low labour cost countries that are not too distant from consumption zones. In doing so, there is the risk of weakening the firm's image.

As far as upmarket chocolate confectionery is concerned, firms face the same issue of financing the expansion of their specialized retail network. The other issue is the limited size of this market segment. Once a firm has achieved a presence in the major cities of the world and in the duty-free business, there seem to be limited further growth opportunities.

International challengers

As expected, the 'mixed' character of the industries that we studied means that there is a variety of international strategies, between the pure global and pure domestic extremes. Within the broad group of international challengers the variety of international strategies can be reduced to four categories. The first two clusters of firms adopt an offensive strategy:

- firms that aim at leadership at the level of a continent;
- firms that adopt an opportunistic approach in their international expansion.

The last two clusters have a defensive strategy:

- firms that hold a sustainable position within a homogeneous set of countries;
- firms that aim primarily at sustaining their position in their home country and consider exports a complementary activity.

The main characteristics of each cluster are summarized in Table 6.4. Table 6.5 lists the firms that belong to each cluster in our study.

Continental leaders

Continental leaders focus their international development on a single continent and have a relatively large segment scope. Generally they place special emphasis on the product-market segments which are significant in their geographic zone. For instance Nippon Paint and Kansaï Paint had particular strengths in car finishes and refinishes, given the importance of Japanese car manufacturers particularly in Asia. Hershey had particular strengths in countlines which represented a very significant part of the North American consumption of confectionery.

Continental leaders organize manufacturing at the continental level, and they achieve a high level of integration and coordination across their region. The range of products and services is relatively standardized within the region but adapted to continental specificities (as compared to other continents). Their competitive strategies have the following characteristics:

Table 6.4 *Four types of international challenger*

	Continental leaders	Opportunistic international challengers	Geographic niche players	Country-centred players
Geographic scope	All key countries in a continent	Home country and a few foreign key countries	A set of countries forming a homogeneous competitive territory (including the home country)	Home country (marginal exports to a few countries)
Segment scope	Relatively large	A few segments	Relatively narrow	Narrow
Foreign investment policy	Intensive manufacturing and commercial investments	Some manufacturing and commercial investments	Intensive commercial investments	Exports
Standardization	Relatively homogeneous	Variable	Homogeneous	Homogeneous
International integration of value chain activities	Integrated at the continental level	Variable	Integrated within the geographic niche	Concentrated in the home country

Table 6.5 *Clusters of international challengers*

	Continental leaders	Opportunistic international challengers	Geographic niche players	Country-centred players[1]
Footwear	Mizuno	*Eram*, Noël	*Lloyd*	
Cables and wires	Draka, Sumitomo	*ABB*, Ericsson (Nokia)	*Silisol*, Acebsa, GGC, Triveneta Cavi	
Paint	*Beckers*, Dyrup, Nippon Paint, Kansaï	*Total*, Tollens	*Maestria*, Lacker Union, Paint STO, Fepyr, Barpimo, Max Meyer, Boero, Salchi	San Marinese, Zolpan, V33
Chocolate and confectionery	*Hershey*, KJS, Cantalou	*Natra*, Katjes	*Fazer*, Cloetta Candelia, Ludwig, Hachez, Thornton, ICAM, Valor	Nutrexpa

The most typical case in each cell is italicized.

[1] The small number of firms in this category is the result of the sample selection criteria.

- product innovation (high rate of new product introduction);
- manufacturing efficiency;
- importance of services.

The dominant logic of these firms is to achieve and sustain leadership on a relatively large geographic area. As compared to worldwide players, they offer product lines which are particularly adapted to continental conditions, with a relatively high variety and significant innovations. As compared to local competitors, they achieve superior manufacturing efficiency and favourable cost structures. The importance given to services is a way to win customer loyalty and a response to the concentration of distributors.

In our study several companies are classified in this category: Kraft Jacobs Suchard, Hershey (US) and Cantalou (France) in the chocolate confectionery industry; Beckers (Sweden), Nippon Paint and Kansaï Paint (Japan) in the paint industry; Mizuno (Japan) in the footwear industry; Draka (the Netherlands) and Sumitomo (Japan) in the cable industry.

Continental leaders often make inroads in other continents, but these overseas activities remain marginal and are often followed by withdrawals. For instance Mizuno, the Japanese leader in sport-leisure footwear, tried to expand in the United States and in Europe, with upmarket products and sponsoring. Starting in 1990 they set up a few sales subsidiaries abroad but, in the mid-1990s, more than 90 per cent of Mizuno's sales were still coming from Japan and the rich Asian countries.

Hershey, the North American leader in the confectionery industry, was tempted by the European market: they took over some firms (in Germany, Belgium and Italy) and they sold licences in Japan. However, they seemed to concentrate on the American continent, where they invested a lot in mass production processes and kept on launching new products. With this strategy they increased their market share in North America, at the expense of Mars. In 1994 Hershey had a 34.5 per cent market share in the USA.

Jacobs Suchard, one of the European leaders in the chocolate industry, took over Brach in the United States but then changed its direction, sold its US assets and strengthened its European position by taking over Marabou, the Scandinavian leader.

> We clearly have the willingness to be a major actor in Europe in chocolate. This being said, strategies can be a little different from one country to another, with strong brands at any rate. Today we are the leader in *tablettes*, although Nestlé is leader of the overall chocolate industry.

Jacobs Suchard rationalized its portfolio of brands and created a few 'Eurobrands' and umbrella brands, for instance Milka, the leading brand in the segment of *tablettes*, and Milka Lila Pause, a chocolate bar adapted to the European taste and competing with Mars bars. After a number of mergers and acquisitions, Jacobs Suchard improved manufacturing efficiency, through specialization of its plants at the European level.

In the cable industry the Dutch group Draka took over a number of small cable businesses throughout Europe and started to form a European federation with activities in several segments of the industry.

Smaller firms can also aim at continental leadership, at least in a segment of an industry. The case of Cantalou is a good illustration of this strategy in the chocolate confectionery activity. Cantalou was a family business based in Perpignan (France). In order to survive the rapid concentration of the industry, they focused on manufacturing chocolate confectionery under private labels with the objective of becoming the number one in Europe in this activity. Cantalou's 1995 sales amounted to 2.8 billion French francs, 50 per cent of which was outside its home market (in Spain, Germany, the United Kingdom, Italy and Portugal). Cantalou acquired several small businesses in Europe in order to access foreign markets and master a diverse set of technologies. Cantalou had one factory in the UK, two factories in Germany, three in Spain and nine in France, and the plants were specialized in order to achieve superior productivity. Product development teams perfected 'me too' products, similar to those of leading brands; for instance, the British plant manufactured countlines which were similar to KitKat. Costs were kept down and quality was carefully managed in order to meet the standards and price levels expected by distributors. Indeed the international expansion of food retail chains and the success of private labels represented significant opportunities for such a strategy. Cantalou competed with a German firm and an Italian firm for European leadership in this particular market segment.

In the paint industry, the Danish group Dyrup became the European leader in the segment of wood treatment products, and the Swedish group Beckers was successfully competing with worldwide players such as ICI and Akzo Nobel. Becker was involved in several segments: consumer paint (Alcro Beckers), industrial coating (Becker), industrial wood coating (Acroma), and colours for artists (world leader with its brand ColArt). Becker's strengths were in coil coating, with a dominant market share of 24 per cent in Europe, particularly in the North, and manufacturing units in Sweden, France, Italy, Germany and the United Kingdom. Outside Europe the group had sold several licences and demonstrated its superior coil-coating technology. In the segment of decorative paint Alcro Beckers was number one in Scandinavia, and had significant positions and projects in the Baltic countries, Estonia, Lithuania, Poland, in Germany and in Russia. The growth of Beckers in Southern Europe was focused on upmarket segments. The strategic intent of the group was to be among the three Pan-European leaders before getting involved in other continents.

Continental leaders have several perspectives for their future international strategies. First they may prefer to consolidate their continental positions. Second, some of them may be tempted to exploit a significant technological advantage on a worldwide scale (and join the group of 'worldwide technology specialists'). This can be done by focusing on the high-tech activity and selling the rest, or through a dual strategy with a worldwide product line, and some regional product lines. Third, continental leaders who have secured regional domination may be tempted by a significant intercontinental move and join the group of 'transnational restructurers'. In this case they may get involved in intercontinental mergers.

Opportunistic international challengers

In our study several firms can be classified in this (relatively heterogeneous) category: Total (France) and Tollens (France) in the paint industry; ABB-cable (Sweden and Switzerland), Nokia-cable (Finland in 1995), Ericsson-cable (Sweden); Natra (Spain) and Katjes (Germany) in the chocolate confectionery industry; Eram (France) and Noël (France) in the footwear industry. These firms generally are among the industry leaders in their home country or in a particular segment of their industry. As far as international development is concerned they tend to focus on a few segments (e.g. high voltage cables at ABB) and to seize market opportunities (e.g. opportunities for international acquisitions at Total).

In our study many of these cases were divisions of larger corporations, for instance Total Paint, Tollens (within the Lafarge group), ABB, Nokia and Ericsson. Moreover the businesses (here paint or cables) are at the periphery of the 'core business' of these groups. This status may explain the selective and opportunistic behaviour of their strategists. The paint businesses within the Total group illustrate this point. The core business of the Total group was the oil industry, from which it diversified into the chemical industry, including chemical specialities such as paint. Diversification was achieved through several acquisitions. The first and most significant acquisitions were in France where Total quickly gained a dominant market share and prestigious brands such as Avi (consumer paint) and La Seigneurie (decorative paint for professionals). Then a major acquisition gave Total the fourth position in the British market. Other opportunities were seized in Portugal, in Hungary, in China and in Vietnam. As a result Total became a European challenger of ICI and Akzo Nobel (who were categorized as 'transnational restructurers'). However, it was hard to define the geographic scope of the company and the synergies that could be expected from such dispersed assets in the mid-1990s. Should Total manage its paint activities as a portfolio of country-centred businesses? Should it first focus on Europe and join the group of continental leaders? Should it invest massively in several continents and join the group of 'transnational restructurers'?

This is the kind of issue that opportunistic international challengers face. Some of them may even withdraw from the business. For instance the main challenge for Nokia was to lead the growth of mobile phones (which basically is wireless transmission). Considering the resources necessary to compete with worldwide players such as Alcatel Cables and BICC in the cable industry, it was not surprising that Nokia withdrew from the cable business in the late 1990s.

In the terms used by Miles and Snow (1978), opportunistic international challengers seem to adopt a 'reactor' strategic profile. Opportunism may stem from the perception of an unstable environment that requires an adaptive strategy. This seemed to be the case in the footwear industry for a firm like Eram. Indeed the mass market in the footwear industry was a turbulent business. At the production end the competition from low labour cost countries, for instance in Asia, was particularly tough. At the distribution end the power of specialized discounters was increasing dramatically. Eram, a French company with a large range of activities, manufactured and distributed many different products: mass market relatively low-priced fashion shoes for young people under the Eram brand, upmarket women's footwear under the Divergence brand, upper-middle-market footwear under the France Arno brand, upmarket sport-leisure footwear under the TBS brand. The manufacturing units were located in France (nine), in Portugal (one), and in Spain (one). Distribution was via 1,400 retail outlets. With this structure Eram was the French leader in the footwear industry in 1995. The group also sold some of its brands in Belgium and Germany and exported through sales agents to several other foreign countries in Northern Europe, in the Middle East and in Russia. Their sport-leisure footwear, TBS, was managed as an independent business and the export targets included a few countries of the Asia-Pacific region. However, international sales hardly exceeded 25 per cent of total sales. Eram was confronted with increasing international competition in foreign markets and with the increasing power of distributors in European markets. Should they maintain their international strategy in the late 1990s? Should they focus on a small number of countries and join the category of geographic niche players?

In summary, opportunistic international challengers seem to have growth ambitions and indeed their geographic scope can be quite large and extend beyond a single continent. However, given the dispersion of their international sales, they seldom gain a dominant market share in a foreign country. Several of these companies seem to be in a transitory stage, waiting for corporate priorities to be decided or environmental uncertainties to clear up. In this context, managers prefer to react to environmental constraints and opportunities.

Geographic niche players

In our study many firms are classified in this category: Cloetta (Sweden), Fazer (Finland), Candelia (Sweden), Ludwig (Germany), Hachez (Germany), Thornton (UK), ICAM (Italy), and Valor (Spain) in the chocolate and sugar confectionery industry; Silisol (France), Acebsa (Spain), Grupo General Cable (Spain), Triveneta Cavi (Italy) in the cable industry; Lloyd (Germany) in the footwear industry; Maestria (France), Lacker Union (Germany), Paint STO (Germany), Fepyr (Spain), Barpimo (Spain), Max Meyer (Italy), Boero (Italy), Salchi (Italy) in the paint industry.

These firms defend their (strong) position in their home country and extend it to a larger geographic zone that includes neighbouring countries or a set of countries that form a homogeneous or protected competitive territory. The competitive territory may correspond to an area of cultural and economic influence (e.g. old colonies, trade blocs), a set of countries where customers have similar behaviour, or an area that corresponds to the geographic scope of customers (cf. Chapter 2 on the formation of competitive territories). In these firms top managers perceive the dual nature of international competition. They recognize the relevance of worldwide strategies, but they observe that global competitors leave room for those who prefer to respond to local demands and conditions. Contrary to 'country-centred' players (see next section), 'geographic niche players' broaden their geographic scope to a wider homogeneous competitive territory in order to grow, to reach a critical size and sustain their position in the long term.

The competitive territory is exploited with a consistent product range and high commercial investment, including sales subsidiaries, in order to provide superior customer services. Geographic niche players define their competitive advantage as regional responsiveness, which is seen as the area of weakness of worldwide players.

The case of Fazer (chocolate and sugar confectionery, Finland) is a good illustration of this international strategy.

> We have no chance to become a worldwide, or even a Europe-wide player, because we are a mid-sized company confronted with international giants. For this reason we know we must be strong in Scandinavia, and in the countries around the Baltic Sea, and Russia of course. In these countries you can develop a system with production and marketing units. To this we add a specific international niche: the world duty-free market. In this

> geographic area we have cut down the number of our brands. Today, in Scandinavia we concentrate on around ten products. In other countries around the Baltic Sea we concentrate on two or three products. As a result we are strong in this area. In Scandinavia we are number two in chocolate after Marabou [recently acquired by Kraft Jacobs Suchard] and we are number one in sugar confectionery. [. . .] In Estonia we are number one, in Latvia we are very close to number one, in Russia in the Saint Petersburg area we are number one in our segment. [. . .] Ten years ago we were a domestic company . . . if we had not changed the strategy we would not be in the business any more.

Geographic niche players may differ from each other in the way they define their competitive territory and in the type of competitive advantage they develop. In many cases they rely on differentiation: products that meet regional demands, strong brand image, quality of products and services, efficient and flexible manufacturing, etc. A number of firms also rely on competitive costs. Mid-sized regional competitors often benefit from lower transport costs (as compared to distant worldwide players) and lower overheads. They do not necessarily suffer from a smaller scale (as far as manufacturing and marketing are concerned): it depends on their relative market share in their competitive territory.

The competitive territory is often defined as a homogeneous region with geographic proximity. Many firms choose to expand their operations into a set of neighbouring countries. For instance Acebsa (from Spain) exported 50 per cent of its enamelled wires to neighbouring countries in the European Union. Their competitive territory was bound by significant transport costs that limited the scope of exports.

Boero (from Italy), specializing in pleasure boat coating, defined its competitive territory as the neighbouring countries with a significant stock of boats: France, Switzerland, Spain, Greece and Turkey. Salchi and Milesi (from Italy) specializing in varnishes, exploited their technical know-how in France, Spain and Germany. In more distant markets, the USA, Japan, Korea and Taiwan, they preferred to sell licences. Barpimo (from Spain) expanded its activities to Latin America with a plant in Chile and a joint venture in Mexico, and to Latin Europe: Italy and France. STO (from Germany), specializing in paints for buildings (particularly façade insulation), targeted neighbouring countries: France, Switzerland, Austria and Scandinavia.

Several geographic niche players define their competitive territory according to the geographic scope of the customers they target. For instance Silisol (from France), specializing in high temperature power cables, followed the international expansion of their French customers in the home appliance industry. Silisol's foreign activities were developed in the other European countries with significant home appliance businesses: Germany, Italy, Spain and Northern Europe.

> Since the French home appliance industry exports finished products to Europe, we had no major problems in getting our components and know-how accepted in other European countries. [. . .] We just had to go through local certification processes.

The procurement policies of customers determine the international opportunities for the suppliers of components:

> Bosch, Siemens and Electrolux are well organized for their sourcing. They have commodity managers and matrix organizations in which purchasing is integrated. This type of procurement process is favourable for the suppliers, like us, who follow their customers across borders.

In the chocolate industry ICAM (from Italy), specializing in the manufacturing of confectionery products under private labels, targeted European countries where mass distribution was significant or rapidly growing: Germany, Spain and Portugal. They did not expand in France, where Cantalou (the continental leader in this segment) had a quasi-monopoly position.

A few geographic niche players define their competitive territory according to their focused product range. They select the countries in which consumers' preferences match the characteristics of their products. For instance Valor (from Spain) and Thornton (from the UK) both focused on luxury chocolate gifts.

> We [Valor] have a focused differentiation strategy. We produce high quality plain chocolate, in Spain we are the leader of *chocolate a la taza* [a bitter chocolate drink], a business in which no multinational company is involved. [. . .] Our product range is that of expensive gifts [. . .], and we sell through chocolate shops. [. . .] We target a few foreign countries: Portugal, Argentina and Japan, and we carefully select distributors who have access to a network of chocolate shops.

From its British base, Thornton targeted a few foreign countries which have a tradition and a significant demand for luxury chocolates: France and Belgium (where they controlled their retail outlets) and the rich countries of the Asia-Pacific region (where they sold through a franchise network).

A few strong international brands such as Church or John Loebb dominated the market of high-priced men's footwear. Lloyd (from Germany) chose a price range (about DM 200) below that of the most renowned brands, and relocated its production to Malta (whereas Church still manufactures shoes in the UK). The German market was Lloyd's priority, but they successfully expanded their competitive territory to Northern Europe: Austria, the Netherlands, Denmark and Sweden, where men care about comfort, solidity and classic elegance.

Geographic niche players often capture a high market share in the competitive territory they select. When they rely on differentiation – based on technological skills or regional responsiveness – they can compete successfully with worldwide or continental players. Actually they represent very attractive acquisition targets (particularly for transnational restructurers and continental players). Geographic niche players who are tempted by a more offensive international strategy are faced with a dilemma: gain market share within their niche or expand their geographic scope. The second solution often represents a major step and requires a significant amount of resources, with the risk of weakening the firm's competitive advantage. The appropriate response generally depends on the dynamics of structural forces in the industry.

Country-centred players

In our study a small number of firms are classified in this category, among others: Zolpan (France), V33 (France) and Colorificio San Marinese (Italy) in the paint industry, and Nutrexpa (Spain) in the chocolate confectionery industry. The small number of firms in this category is a result of the bias we introduced in the selection of the sample (the firms participating in the study should have a ratio of international sales to total sales higher than 20 per cent). Actually, in the four mixed industries studied, country-centred players, with marginal exports, may well form the majority of businesses.

'Country-centred players' focus on their home country and defend their position against foreign intrusion. Export activities are directed to one or a few neighbouring countries and/or a few more distant countries which offer opportunities. Exports are considered as a complement of the home market and remain marginal in the firm's corporate strategy. Foreign markets are reached through agents. In some cases these firms do not even search for agents in a deliberate and systematic manner.

> The majority of our foreign customers take the first step and import all sorts of things, from shoes to beer. . . . For instance last week I welcomed a man who has got ten orders ready, worth 100 million each [Italian lire] for Cuba. Among other activities, he was in charge of paint orders for painting I do not know how many hotels there. . . . (Paint)

The managers of these firms perceive international competition as essentially multidomestic. Thus, they believe there is room for domestic firms that focus on their home market and, eventually, 'skim' a few foreign markets.

Clearly we compete with multinational companies, but what matters to me is what they do in Spain. Of course what they do in Spain is related to what they do in other countries. But I am convinced, at the moment, and there is enough evidence to say that in the chocolate and candies market there are very strong national specificities, a fragmentation of tastes, attitudes and habits. . . . Do not come and tell me that the international strategies of Cadbury or Nestlé are global or Euroglobal! That is not true.

You think that the bigger and the more international a company, the more chances it has to succeed? I am not at all convinced of that. We realize it in our business, with firms which are much bigger than ours. We are still the leader in our home market [France]. It has been so for 20 years, and we also managed to be the leader with our most recent products. [. . .] We are not afraid of them. They are dangerous on the international level, they will bother us a lot in export, but they do not win in our home market. [. . .] The Danish group which dominates the European market and sells its original brand, Bondex, and acquired other brands, Xylophene and Xyladécor, now belongs to a British group. [. . .] Recently they lost market share in France, whereas we increased our share up to one third of the market. (Paint)

Country-centred players generally exploit the multidomestic character of some segments in their industry. Indeed they focus on one or a few product-market segments in which local responsiveness is a key success factor.

For instance V33 focused on lasures, which represented less than 2 per cent of total paint consumption in France. They actively supported their image of technical specialists and their presence in a complex distribution network. Zolpan focused on decorative paint sold to professionals, which was one of the most multidomestic activities in the paint industry (cf. Chapter 1). They also relied on their access to, and presence in the distribution network.

Access to local distribution networks appears to be a major element in the strategy of country-centred players. In this domain Zolpan provides a radical example: the company belonged to a group of wholesalers organized in a cooperative structure. This was a good way to secure Zolpan's number two position in the professional segment in France. As far as export activities were concerned, the firm benefited from the international expansion of some major customers such as Bouygues and Lyonnaise Dumez in the building sector.

At V33, relationships with retail chains such as Monsieur Bricolage, Castorama or Leroy Merlin were strengthened by the supply of lasures sold under private labels. Moreover V33 followed these 'do it yourself' retail chains in their international expansion in Italy, Spain and Germany.

In summary, the strategy of country-centred players is characterized by (1) a double focus – on the home country *and* on a multidomestic segment that calls for local responsiveness, (2) strong relationships with distribution networks, and (3) marginal export activities stimulated by market opportunities.

Country-centred players may envisage three main strategic developments. First they may strengthen their country-centred position: this is an interesting solution when the home market is large enough to provide growth opportunities (think of the USA, or Japan, or India . . .). This is a viable solution as long as the product-market segment requires some local responsiveness (i.e. specific needs) or as long as the country is protected from foreign competition. Second, they can become attractive acquisition targets for transnational restructurers, continental players or opportunistic international challengers. Third, they may turn to a more ambitious international strategy and try to join the group of geographic niche players. The last scenario represents a major step: it involves high resources and risks (relative to the size of the company), and most importantly a change in managers' mentality.

Concluding comments

This study used a configurational approach to analyse international strategies along a number of dimensions: geographic scope, segment scope, foreign investment policy, standardization, international integration/coordination of value chain activities, competitive advantages and internationalization process. It reveals eight configurations that give a simplified and holistic understanding of the sets of competitive actions that are at the core of the international dynamics of competition in mixed industries. The selection of mixed industries may explain the absence of extreme configurations: the *pure* global strategy and the *pure* multinational strategy. On the other hand the sample selection revealed a diverse set of international strategy formulas, generally more complex than what is suggested by the economic and strategic management literature. One may also question the empirical existence of *pure* extreme strategies. Indeed we found a significant group of *quasi*-global players. 'Quasi' expresses a nuance, the fact that these companies do not fully meet all the criteria of universalism (their market presence is not evenly distributed around the globe, and they concede some marginal adaptations to local conditions). But are there any firms in any industry that fulfil all the conditions, even in typically global businesses such as electronic components, computers or civil aeronautics? The surprising absence of pure multinational strategies may also be explained by the need to achieve at least a minimum level of international coordination, to reap the benefits of international positions. In our sample, Cadbury was a case close to a multinational strategy; however it did add a few international brands to the local brands of the companies it acquired, and transferred some skills across borders.

The findings also suggest a number of comments that may be helpful to practitioners and/or stimulate further research.

Some international strategies seem to be related to nationally bound administrative heritages (cf. Bartlett and Ghoshal, 1989) and competitive advantages (Porter, 1990). For instance French and Italian firms are well represented in the 'global luxury niche' category, in line with the tradition and the competitive advantage of these nations. North American firms are well represented in the 'quasi-global' category. The large size of the US mass market is favourable to the emergence of standardized innovative concepts, before they are transferred to foreign countries. American skills in the global diffusion of a brand can be explained by American universalism and by their cultural influence (music, movies, sports) on young people worldwide. Scandinavian firms are well represented in the 'geographic niche' category. In many cases their competitive territory is composed of the countries around the Baltic Sea (including Russia) which share geographical and cultural characteristics.

European firms in general (as compared to their US and Japanese counterparts) are well represented in the 'transnational restructurer' category. The recent political and economic history of Europe is marked by a major step from fragmented markets to a unified (but still diverse) market. Clearly this context has been favourable to international acquisitions, restructuring, and transnational organization.

An administrative heritage is both an asset and a liability. Managers involved in international strategies should rely on their firms' administrative heritage in order to select the product-market segments and the geographic areas for their international expansion. They should also correct their administrative biases when they face new market conditions. However, the above comments should not blur the main finding from this empirical study: the great variety of international strategies. Such variety generates complexity but also significant degrees of strategic freedom for firms with growth ambitions. Finally, the analysis of internationalization processes confirms that strategic choices interact with structural forces in the transformation of competitive systems.

From practice to theory: a summary

Managers think that the international strategy of the firm, its competitive advantage and its internationalization process are three inseparable concepts. A firm's international strategy can be analysed along four dimensions: the scope of the firm (further divided into geographic scope and segment scope), the foreign investment policy, the extent of international standardization, and the level of international integration or coordination of activities. The description of configurations should be integrative and include international strategy elements, competitive strategy elements and internationalization process elements.

The study reveals eight configurations of international strategies. The first four configurations describe firms with a worldwide geographic scope: 'quasi-global players', 'transnational restructurers', 'worldwide technology specialists', and 'global luxury niche players'. The last four configurations describe firms with a more focused geographic scope and positions as international challengers: 'continental leaders', 'opportunistic international challengers', 'geographic niche players', and 'country-centred players'.

Each configuration is characterized by a specific set of international strategy dimensions, type of competitive advantage and type of internationalization process. For instance 'quasi-global players' are defined as having the following *international strategy* characteristics: they target all key countries with a relatively narrow segment scope, their foreign commercial and manufacturing investments are significant, their strategy is homogeneous across key countries (marketing variations are marginal and global brands are promoted with heavy advertising and sponsoring expenses), the activities of the value chain are dispersed in different countries and tightly coordinated and integrated across borders. Quasi-global players base their *competitive advantage* on differentiation, more precisely on conceptual innovations that have a potential universal appeal: a simple need, a large consumer base, a unique character. The *internationalization process* of quasi-global players can be summarized as follows: (1) a strong innovative concept that allows the conquest of the home country, (2) international transfer of the concept to one or two foreign countries, and organic growth, (3) systematic transfer to a set of key countries, setting up a global brand, and organic growth, (4) sustaining differentiation and improving overall efficiency.

Analysing the process of internationalization gives a useful dynamic perspective for practitioners and for theory-building. For instance the trajectory (or migration path) of continental leaders reveals specific strategic alternatives once this position has been reached: (1) consolidating continental positions, or (2) adopting a dual strategy with one worldwide business line (based on technological advantage) and other businesses geographically bound to one region, or (3) becoming a 'transnational restructurer' through intercontinental mergers and acquisitions.

The taxonomy proposed in this chapter is both parsimonious and comprehensive. It is parsimonious in that it relies on a set of seven main strategic dimensions that suffice to discriminate between a large number of cases (geographic scope, segment scope, foreign investment policy, extent of international standardization, extent of international integration, competitive advantage, and internationalization process). It is comprehensive because the seven empirically derived dimensions integrate several frameworks from previous research (Doz, 1980; Porter, 1986; Bartlett and Ghoshal, 1989; Hymer, 1976; Perlmutter, 1969). The eight configurations found empirically can be useful points of reference for managers and consultants who want to assess the consistency of a firm's international strategy. This is not to say that there is no chance of success outside of these types; it only suggests that executives should be aware of deviations from these types. The eight configurations can also be useful points of reference for further theoretical developments. We suggest that these strategic configurations exist in most mixed industries, that the first four can be found in global industries, and that the last four can be found in multidomestic industries.

Bibliography

Several references to the strategy literature are mentioned in the text. The most useful contributions are summarized here.

Porter (1986) gives two complementary frameworks. The first describes the scope of the firm according to two variables 'geographic scope' and 'segment scope' that define four types of international strategy:

- 'Global cost leadership or differentiation' (global scope and many segments);
- 'Global segmentation' (global scope and few segments);
- 'Protected markets' (country-centred and many segments);
- 'National responsiveness' (country-centred and few segments).

The second framework combines 'the international configuration of value chain activities' (dispersed vs. concentrated) and the level of international coordination (high vs. low), and defines four international strategies:

- 'Simple global strategy' (geographically concentrated, and high coordination);
- 'High foreign investment' (dispersed) with extensive coordination among subsidiaries;
- 'Export based strategy with decentralized marketing' (concentrated, and low coordination);
- 'Country-centred strategy by multinationals' (dispersed and low coordination).

The two matrices are not integrated into a comprehensive framework.

Other dimensions can usefully complement Porter's frameworks:

- the extent of international 'standardization' vs. 'fragmentation' (Fayerweather, 1969; Doz, 1980);
- the level of 'global integration' vs. 'local responsiveness' as defined by Ghoshal and Nohria (1993).

Based on this literature Morrison and Roth (1992) proposed a taxonomy of global strategies. Adler (1986) took a different perspective and defined several stages in the *process* of internationalization.

A useful theoretical discussion on configurations and typologies can be found in the *Academy of Management Journal*, 'Special research forum: configurational approaches to organization' (36 (6), 1993), and in the *Academy of Management Review* (Doty and Glick, 1994).

Conclusion

The collective knowledge of practitioners was analysed so as to produce a framework for understanding the dynamics of international competition and contribute to theory development and practice.

A posteriori, the framework based on practitioners' collective knowledge shows two main qualities: it is comprehensive and integrative. It encompasses several aspects of the dynamics of an organizational field: the level of analysis (product-market segments: Chapter 1), the structure of competition (regional competitive territories: Chapter 2), the forces driving the dynamics (structural forces: Chapters 3 and 4, and actors' behaviours: Chapter 5), and a taxonomy of firms' strategies (Chapter 6). Moreover, its empirical-practical origin should facilitate its application in business life.

Applications

Analysing the dynamics of international competition is an ongoing activity in firms with international ambitions or in firms threatened by foreign competition. The composite framework based on collective experience can be used as a rudimentary expert system, to aid practitioners in a systematic review of international parameters.

First, a top management team concerned with a strategic review of their firm's international strategy should consider the broad picture and assess the forces that drive the international dynamics of their industry. For this purpose the general framework presented in Figure I.2 (p. 12) can be useful: it includes a 'reasonable' number of variables (18) within a comprehensive set (a systemic view of structures and behaviours). This analysis should be done at the level of each product-market segment (as the dynamics of international competition may be specific to a product-market segment, cf. Chapter 1). As standard classifications often are misleading, a preliminary industry segmentation exercise should be conducted by industry experts (for instance the members of the top management team themselves and, if possible, experts from diverse origins).

Second, the top management team should identify the fracture lines and the competitive territories in each product-market segment. The framework presented in Figure 2.1 (p. 53) can be useful to map competitive territories. Literally one can use a map of the world and draw lines between territories; the addition of lines (one for each of the seven factors that shape regions) will reveal fractures between regions. Then the respective positions (market shares) of national, regional and international players can be located on the map. Such an overall picture of the terrain and the actors may surface strategic threats and opportunities, from the perspective of the focal firm.

Third, the management team should assess the current international strategy of their company, given (1) the dynamics of competition, (2) the regional structure of competition, (3) the firm's resources compared to its competitors. The eight strategic configurations presented in Tables 6.2 and 6.4 (pp. 170, 192) can be used as references for this assessment.

Fourth, the decision-makers could usefully explore opportunities for international strategic innovation, opportunities to relocate some value chain activities, opportunities for international mergers, acquisitions and alliances, and the positions of national players who may block the entry in some key countries (as shown in Chapter 5).

Fifth, top management can formulate the international strategy of the firm with the framework presented in Chapter 6: (1) geographic scope, (2) segment scope, (3) foreign investment policy, (4) extent of international standardization, (5) level of international integration (concentration, centralization or coordination), (6) competitive advantage, (7) process of internationalization. This strategy may be qualified as innovative (if it is unique in the industry); it may correspond to one of the eight configurations described in Chapter 6 (Tables 6.2 and 6.4). The lack of correspondence with any typical configuration should not be viewed necessarily as a problem, but as a signal of abnormality.

These frameworks for analysis and strategy formulation draw attention to a comprehensive set of potentially relevant dimensions. Of course decision-makers still have to exercise their judgement to find out the most important factors in their case. They also have to exercise their judgement and intuition to construct their strategy, whether by adapting it to deterministic forces or by choosing a new way and changing the rules of competition.

In this book we have not reported the many individual cognitive maps and the differences (complementarities and contradictions) between them (except for differences related to diverse segments which were discussed in Chapter 1). However, in this study, our experience of the two levels of knowledge, individual and collective, clearly suggests that everyone knows something and that no one knows everything. In other words decision-makers would be advised to enrich their own cognitive map through interactions with other credible and reliable persons.

Variety and comprehensiveness

The framework based on the collective knowledge of experts-managers is comprehensive in the sense that it captures the great variety of internationalization scenarios. This conceptual quality is also known as differentiation.

The study of four industries showed the high diversity of dynamic configurations of forces. Managers identified six forces which are common to the four industries studied: four common structural forces – technological intensity, international customers, new high growth markets, differences in business cultures – and two common competitive actions – innovative international strategies, and national players who defend their positions. Ten structural forces are specific to some industries: comparative advantages, economies of scale in procurement and manufacturing, short life cycle, advertising-sponsoring intensity, sales-distribution intensity and diversity, differences in customers' tastes and preferences, government intervention, transportation costs, associated services, and chauvinism. Two categories of competitive actions are specific to some industries: relocation strategies, and international mergers-acquisitions-alliances.

The number of specific forces shows the high variety of internationalization scenarios.

In the chocolate and sugar confectionery industry the following configuration of forces shapes international competition: *high marketing intensity* (both advertising and sales), differences in business cultures, *differences in consumption patterns between countries*, international customers (retail chains), new high growth markets, defensive positions of national champions, *mergers and acquisitions*, and innovative international strategies.

In the footwear industry the following configuration of forces shapes international competition: *comparative advantages (labour cost)*, technological intensity, international customers (retail chains), new high growth markets, differences in business cultures, *relocation strategies*, and innovative international strategies.

In the paint industry the following configuration of forces shapes international competition: *technological intensity*, international customers, new high growth markets, *marketing intensity*, differences in business cultures, *differences in consumption patterns between countries*, defensive positions of national players, *mergers-acquisitions and alliances*, and innovative international strategies.

In the cable and wire industry the following configuration of forces shapes international competition: *technological intensity*, international customers, new high growth markets, comparative advantages (labour cost), differences in business cultures, *government intervention*, relocation strategies, *mergers-acquisitions and alliances*, and innovative international strategies.

In order to capture such a high variety, a multidimensional model of international competition is needed. The composite framework presented in Chapters 2 to 5 provides a basis for theory development: six common variables and 12 specific variables which fit in the generic global–local dialectics.

Industry averages hide a high variety of configurations across product-market segments. For instance in the paint industry, car finishes (global segment) is characterized by high technological intensity and powerful international customers, whereas decorative paint for professionals (multidomestic segment) is characterized by a relatively low technological intensity, local customers, high barriers to access local distribution networks, and different traditions across countries. Technological intensity drives international development in the segment of wood-treatment products whereas it is less important in the segment of decorative paint; transportation costs limit the geographical scope of decorative paint whereas they are negligible in the case of wood-treatment products which have a higher added value. To some extent, within industry heterogeneity was anticipated (Finger, 1975; Atamer, 1991) and the interview protocol was designed to gather information at the level of market segments. However, the emphasis managers placed on this characteristic was not expected. There is a significant between-industry variance in the forces driving or restraining international development, but there is also a significant variance within each industry. Moreover the study confirms that standard product-market classifications can be misleading, and suggests that their relevance among industry experts (for instance executives) be checked in order to define the units of analysis.

The composite framework based on the collective knowledge of managers is comprehensive in the sense that it captures the variety of competitive territories. The study shows that between the pure global and local extremes that define the scope of international markets, the bulk of competition is taking place within regions of the world separated by fracture lines. Regions can hardly be defined a priori: their identification requires some experience and knowledge of the industry. Managers pointed out seven forces which underlie the formation of regions and delineate fracture lines. We believe that this facet of the framework can be useful for further theory-building. Indeed researchers (and consultants) should reduce their theoretical bias towards the global and local extremes. They should posit that international competition is not necessarily homogeneous, and that globalization is not a continuous function. Then they should try to build a theory that explains the formation and transformation of competitive territories. In brief, geography (physical, economical and political) should matter more to international business.

High variety can be found primarily in mixed industries. We suggest that similar attenuated characteristics exist in global or multidomestic industries. Managers have to build a matrix in their mind with product-market segments in lines and geographical zones in columns. They also have to revise the matrix every now and then, since the segmentation is changing.

Comprehensiveness should not be achieved at the expense of parsimony: a framework should help practitioners and scholars not to drown themselves in diversity and multicausality. The managers who participated in this study were concerned with necessary simplifications in decision-making, they selected *key* variables in order to reach a balance of parsimony and comprehensiveness.

An integrative theory

A theory is viewed as integrative when it connects its elements, when it does not overlook any significant factor, and when it combines several partial theories into a broader framework. The collective knowledge of practitioners displays these qualities.

Connectedness is expressed in most of the citations. For instance several concepts and relationships are contained in a simple citation such as this:

> Decorative paint is a heavy product, the cost of transportation is high compared to total cost. This is a major constraint, and since manufacturing decorative paint is not very capital intensive, we can set up production sites abroad. Having a single production site that would supply the whole of Europe is not the best solution. Pan-European companies have dispersed plants, but they concentrate purchasing of raw materials and packaging.

This statement relates organizational design and manufacturing strategies with several structural forces: capital intensity and transportation costs (in relation to a physical characteristic of the product). It reveals the possible tension between the dispersion of manufacturing sites and the full utilization of expensive assets.

Connectedness is also expressed in the multiplicity of parameters which are related to a particular strategic move, for instance in the case of relocation strategies (Chapter 5). Also, configurations of international strategies (Chapter 6) are defined as sets of interrelated variables characterized by some mutual consistency over time.

Connectedness is also expressed in complex scenarios that combine structural forces and competitive actions in a dialectical tension between global integration and local responsiveness. For instance the discussion on international acquisitions (Chapter 5) shows that *when* several forces driving local responsiveness are high (particularly the intensity and diversity of distribution and the differences in consumer behaviour) *and when* there are opportunities for economies of scale in manufacturing and advertising (at least for a few potentially universal products) *and when* national players have strong positions in several key markets, a few competitors get involved in massive international acquisitions, adopt dual strategies (some global products and many local products) and rationalize their assets across borders, until they achieve the economies of scale and scope that they were aiming for.

As noted by Porter (1991: 98): 'all the interactions among the many variables in the frameworks cannot be rigorously drawn'; however, identifying some salient relationships is very useful both for practitioners and for theory-builders.

By putting the emphasis on some variables (and not on others) managers questioned existing economic and strategic theories, and as such contributed to theory development. For instance by splitting the concept of 'marketing intensity' into two concepts, 'advertising/sponsoring intensity' vs. 'distribution/sales intensity and diversity', managers cleared up the ambiguity concerning the effect of marketing intensity on the international dynamics of industries. Contrary to Kobrin (1991) and in line with Levitt (1983) they asserted that advertising intensity drives global integration; in line with Prahalad and Doz (1987) they asserted that distribution/sales intensity and diversity drive local responsiveness. The study also revealed the importance of demand factors that drive the international development of firms and industries: 'the geographic scope and negotiation power of clients' and 'the emergence of new high growth markets'. Mainstream economic theories and strategic theories have not paid enough attention to these forces, both supply factors and demand factors should be considered in an integrative theory of internationalization.

Finally managers emphasized the effect of innovative international strategies on global integration. When they celebrate competitive actions and first movers, they rejuvenate theories of economic innovation and growth (Schumpeter, 1934; Penrose, 1959). They offer more arguments to the authors who claim that strategic management is about doing things differently and changing industry recipes (Baden Fuller and Stopford, 1992; Hamel and Prahalad, 1994).

Overall the framework based on the collective knowledge of managers reconciles deterministic and voluntaristic theories of change in organization fields. Historical narratives and future scenarios integrate structural factors and actors' behaviour (Astley and Van de Ven, 1983; Hrebiniak and Joyce, 1985). The structural perspective borrows elements of theory from industry organization economics, resource dependence theory and contingency theory. The competitive action perspective also has multiple theoretical facets. In the Schumpeterian tradition, managers emphasize the individual action of an innovative business:

> The revolution came in 1979 from the USA. When Nike and Reebok arrived on the European market 15 years ago people did not believe they would succeed. Actually they did impose their marketing and their American concept became universal.

They *also* recognize the effect of the collective reaction of numerous other businesses and the relevance of neo-institutional theory (Di Maggio and Powell, 1983) that accounts for imitation processes:

> The cable industry became more international because some leaders decided to go international. They drove the industry behind them. Alcatel goes to India and to China, and now everyone is going to China.

In line with evolutionary theory (Nelson and Winter, 1982) however, the imitation of best practices is difficult because of the specific history, capabilities and routines of each firm: 'It took time for Adidas to decode Nike's formula', and for Nestlé to 'adopt a global strategy in the business of countlines'. Moreover, some firms re-engineer their capabilities and come out with variants of innovative strategies, for instance Fila in the footwear industry and Ferrero in the confectionery industry.

Finally managers recognize that some sub-populations of firms cannot follow industry transformations and fail, in line with population ecology (Hannan and Freeman, 1977):

> Here in Spain Cadbury bought Hueso, Jacobs Suchard bought El Almendro which makes *turrones*. [. . .] Twenty years ago regional Spanish brands dominated the market, for instance in the region of Valencia there were about 50 factories in Torrente and about 30 factories in Villajoyosa. They all closed down and now you can find a few national brands and the multinationals.

In other words, one should accept that the understanding of a complex phenomenon requires a framework that integrates several theories (in this case the theory of economic innovation, neo-institutional theory, evolutionary theory, and population ecology). In order to explain the dynamics of international competition, integrative theories (such as Vernon's, 1966) deserve more attention in future research.

The value of the collective knowledge of practitioners

After celebrating the virtues of practitioners' knowledge, one must admit the limits. First we recognize the limits and biases of individual accounts (of both the respondent and the analyst). The large variance in the quality of arguments among the whole sample demonstrates that great managers are not always great thinkers, but some of them are. This is precisely why a consultation with *several* experts was organized. At the level of the collective knowledge base the managerial population is probably biased toward a voluntaristic perspective. Managers are trained to be assertive, consequently they may have the illusion of controlling their destiny and the environment. Hence their emphasis on competitive actions and innovative international strategies.

Managers may have been wrong, they may have forgotten or ignored crucial elements of the complex dynamics of international business. The present study cannot be prescriptive, there has been no scientific demonstration of the accuracy and validity of a model. However, analysis of the collective knowledge base of experts questioned existing theories and produced a framework that 'makes sense' of managerial experience (Weick, 1995).

A manager's espoused theory about the dynamics of international competition has the qualities and the shortcomings of its 'contextual' nature (Tsoukas, 1994). Contextual knowledge is synthetic (it takes a pattern as the object of study), historic and dynamic; yet it is dispersive (it lacks an underlying structure) and does not allow generalized statements about empirical regularities (Tsoukas, 1994). That is where researchers help. By selecting experts, analysing their explicit knowledge and integrating their views into a consistent whole, researchers can produce 'organic' knowledge from contextual elements.

According to Pepper (1942: 283, quoted by Tsoukas, 1994) organic knowledge is characterized by seven features:

> (1) *Fragments* of experience which appear with (2) *nexuses* or connections or implications, which spontaneously lead as a result of the aggravation of (3) *contradictions*, gaps, opposition, or counteractions to resolution in (4) an *organic whole*, which is found to have been (5) *implicit* in the fragments, and to (6) transcend the previous contradictions by means of a coherent totality, which (7) *economizes*, saves, preserves all the original fragments of experience without any loss.

This is what we tried to achieve in this book: develop an organic theory from a collective knowledge base forged in action.

Appendix 1: The Global Integration/Local Responsiveness Framework

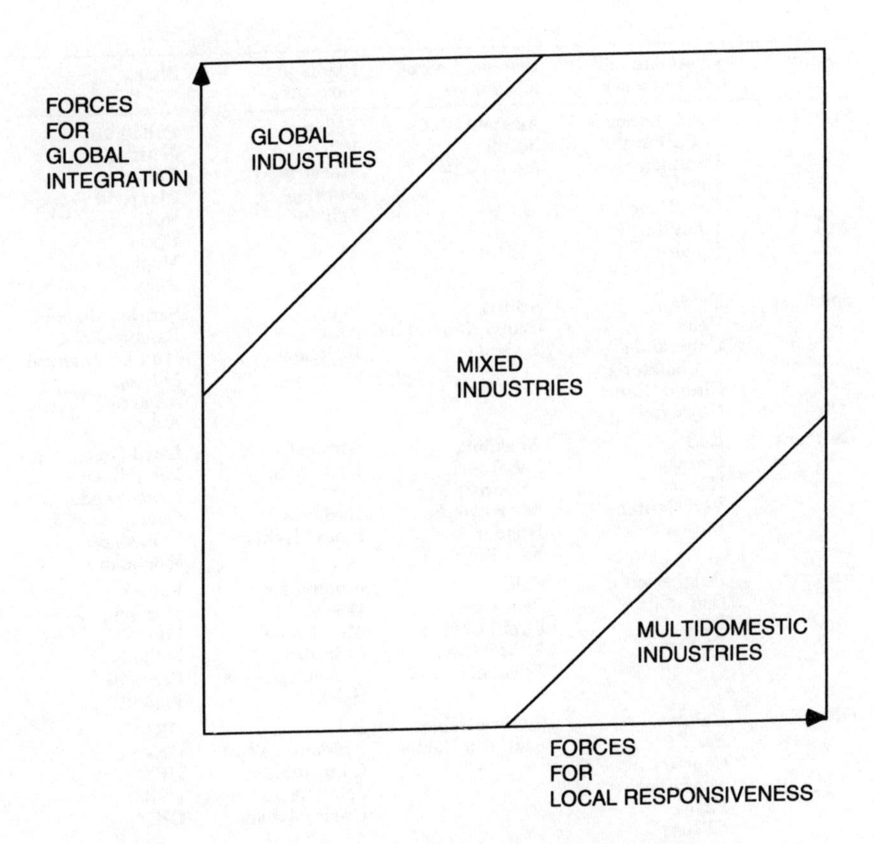

Adapted from Bartiett (1986: 370) and from Prahalad and Doz (1987)

Appendix 2: List of Firms in the Sample, by Industry and by Country

Country	Chocolate and confectionery	Insulated wires and cables	Paints and varnishes	Shoes
France	Kraft Jacobs Suchard[1] Cantalou Nestlé[2] Coq Blanc Lamy Lutti Danone	Alcatel Cable Silisol Axon Cable	Tollens V33 Maestria Euridep Zolpan	Palladium Jourdan Kelian Clergerie Noël Eram Mephisto Bally
Spain	Natra Valor General de Confeteria Chupa Chups Nutrexpa	Acebsa Grupo General de Cable	Fepyr Akzo Barpimo	Sancho Abarca Panama Jack Ivan Continental Lotusse Segarra Kelme
Germany	KJS[1] Ludwig Hachez Van Houten Katjes	Waskönig Kabelwerke Reinshagen Kerpenwerke Wagner Kwo Kabel	Glasurit Lackunion STO Herberts Spies Hecker	Lloyd Gmbh Peter Kaiser Erich Rohde Gabor Shoes & Fashion Wortmann
Italy	Bulgheroni Caffarel Icam Ferrero	FMC Ceat Cavi Pirelli Cavi Alcatel Cavi Triveneta Cavi	Junghanns Boero Max Meyer Colorificio Sanmarinese Salchi	Pollini Moreschi Fila Melania Pancaldi Rossetti
UK	Daintee Bendicks Cadbury Thornton Payne Glisten	Sunhra Cables Southern Cables	ICI Saddolin (Akzo) Courtaulds Johnston Creda Moben	UK1* UK2* UK3* UK4* UK5*
Sweden	Candelia Fazer Cloetta	Iko Kabel Erisson Cables Nokia Cables[3] ABB Cables	Alcro Beckers Becker Industrifarg Akzo Nobel	Ymer Arbesko Nokia Footwear[3] Ecco
Netherlands	Gerkens Cocoa	–	Veveo Paints Hasco Paints	Avang Durea
Belgium	Godiva[1] Mars[1]			

[1] US origin.
[2] Swiss origin.
[3] Finnish origin.
* The researcher promised the firm anonymity.

Appendix 3: Positions of Interviewees*

- Positions of respondents

Position	Number
Managing director	19
Export sales director	19
Chairman	15
Commercial director	8
Chief executive officer	5
Sales and marketing director	5
Director of strategy	4
Marketing development director	3
Vice-president	3
Joint managing director	3
Director of division	3
Miscellaneous (marketing coordinator, industrial director, director of international marketing, secretary-general)	6
Missing data	5

- Number of years in this position in the company

Years	Number
1 and below	14
2.	8
3.	6
4.	13
5.	8
6.	10
7.	5
8.	5
9.	2
10.	5
More than 10 years	17
Missing data	5

NB: All respondents had been in a senior management position in the same company and/or in the same industry for more than two years.

* On a total of 98 who agreed to be identified.

Appendix 4: Interviews

All of the interviews were unstructured. They included five broad themes:

Define the geographical scope of the [. . .] industry.
Describe the international development of the [. . .] industry in the past ten years.
Anticipate the international development of the [. . .] industry in the next ten years.
Describe the international strategies of competitors in the [. . .] industry.
Describe the international strategy of your firm in the [. . .] industry.

Interviews were tape-recorded and the content of transcripts was analysed. First order concepts were retained verbatim, and further grouped into second order categories.

Appendix 5: Content Analysis

Content analysis was used to surface concepts and links between concepts (Holsti, 1969). The analysis of the data involved five steps.

Phase one: Surfacing first order concepts and links

Interview transcripts were analysed according to the four broad theoretical dimensions defined ex ante: structural forces driving international development, structural forces restraining international development, competitive actions driving international development, competitive actions restraining international development.

The first order concepts and links were identified in terms of the exact wording used by the informants (citations). For example:

> The large are getting bigger, there will be more mergers because there are still many cable companies in the world . . .

is a first order concept further labelled 'mergers and acquisitions led by large firms'.

This first order concept is explicitly linked with another first order concept (scale economies in manufacturing):

> But first, conditions should be created to take advantage of scale economies in manufacturing . . .

There were three main sorts of links between concepts: similarity (vs. difference), cause–effect relationships, and tensions. For instance there is a tension between scale economies in manufacturing (above) and the diversity of national technical norms:

> Today the potential of scale economies is still limited because of all these variants and norms.

Phase two: Weighing concepts

Each concept was weighed according to four criteria: explicit mention of its importance by the manager, spontaneity, priority, and relative length of the discussion on the theme.

Phase three: Clustering first order concepts into second order concepts

First order concepts were clustered into second order concepts according to the similarity of meaning. Clustering produced the 18 second order concepts (or categories) presented in Figure I.2 (p. 12), for instance: 'international mergers, acquisitions and alliances', 'economies of scale in procurement and manufacturing'.

The definition of second order concepts was made with the whole set of first order concepts identified in the 117 transcripts.

Phase four: Drawing cognitive maps

A cognitive map is a schematic representation of the first order concepts and links between concepts discussed by one expert and organized according to the second order categories found in phase three (see for example Calori et al., 1994).

Phase five: Surfacing commonalities and specificities among the four industries

Many first order concepts and several second order concepts are specific to one or some industries. For instance the 'relocation of manufacturing' (second order concept) is very important in the footwear industry, less important in the cable industry, and insignificant in the other two industries. On the other hand the effect of 'international customers' on global integration is common to the four industries.

Appendix 6: Selecting Industries

Service activities were excluded from the range of this study, given their specificities (Segal-Horn and Faulkner, 1999). Chocolate and sugar confectionery and footwear are consumer goods, cables are industrial goods and paint is composed of industrial goods and consumer goods. In order to classify industries into categories, according to their international scope, Laurencin (1988) selected two ratios: the imports/domestic consumption ratio and the exports/domestic production ratio. 'Local' industries were defined by the two ratios being lower than 10 per cent, 'global' industries were defined by the two ratios being higher than 50 per cent, 'mixed' industries were defined by import and export ratios both higher than 10 per cent and lower than 50 per cent. Research on global industries generally considers a ratio of 50 per cent international intra-industry trade as a threshold above which an industry is viewed as global (Morrison, 1990; Yip, 1992).

We adopted the criteria proposed by Laurencin and computed import and export ratios for 151 industries recorded in the Eurostat database in 1992. Ratios were calculated for five large European countries: Germany, France, Italy, the United Kingdom and Spain, at the three-digit level of NACE codification (four-digit level statistics are not available).

Seventy-eight industries fulfilled the selection criteria. Further selection was made according to the recommendations of the European Commission (DG. XII), which funded the research: each industry should include more than one competitor with an international scope in each of the countries studied (Germany, France, the UK, Italy, Spain, Sweden). The following table summarizes the import (i) and export (e) ratios in the four selected industries, the five main countries, and the means (1992).

Table A.1 *Import and export ratios in the four industries studied (percentages)*

Industries		Germany	France	Italy	UK	Spain	Average
Paint	i	24	22	17	16	13	18.4
	e	49	18	17	24	13	24.2
Footwear	i	74	52	1	57	26	42.0
	e	41	31	80	27	60	47.8
Cables and wires	i	32	20	9	31	29	24.2
	e	27	20	20	22	44	26.6
Chocolate and sugar	i	14	23	24	14	13	17.6
confectionery	e	15	18	30	13	17	18.6

Appendix 7: Breakdown of Interviews*

Per country of origin of the firm: France (20), Germany (19), Spain (14), Sweden (12), UK (13), Italy (9), United States (4), The Netherlands (4), Finland (2), Switzerland (1)

Per industry and main product-market segments

Chocolate & sugar confectionery	28
Chocolate *tablettes*	5
Countlines	2
Chewing gum	2
Luxury	3
Miscellaneous	16
Paint	23
Decorative	9
Wood treatment	4
Car finish and refinish	3
Industrial coatings	3
Miscellaneous	4
Footwear	30
Mass market (street)	7
Sport-leisure	5
Upmarket	4
Women's luxury	4
Safety	2
Children's	2
Miscellaneous	6
Cables	17
Low and medium voltage power	5
Telecommunication	3
High voltage power	2
Miscellaneous	7

Per type of firm

Major competitors	37
Smaller competitors	61

* On a total of 98 who agreed to be identified.

Within each industry/country cell (for instance paint/France or cable/Germany) incumbent companies were selected according to several successive criteria. First the ratio of international sales turnover to total sales turnover had to be higher than 20 per cent, in order to ensure that the respondent would have significant experience of international markets. Then diversity was the main selection criterion: diversity in terms of product categories (defined by professional associations) and diversity in terms of firms' size: both market share leaders and smaller competitors had to be represented.

In some categories the original list had to be reduced arbitrarily, for instance a selection was made among the numerous small Italian firms with significant exports in the women's footwear business. Within each firm, the manager in charge of the international strategy and/or the international operations of the firm was identified (in *Kompass* or *Dun and Bradstreet Europe*), and confirmation was obtained by a telephone call. About 75 per cent of managers contacted for the study agreed to participate; a few new contacts were made to complete the group of respondents in some categories. A comparison between respondents and non-respondents was made on the French, Spanish and Swedish sub-samples. This showed that participation was not related to country, industry, product category, size or percentage of international sales turnover. On the one hand, the process adopted in forming the group of experts and the sampling biases did not allow representativeness of the whole population. On the other hand, diversity within the group of experts (in terms of countries, product categories and firms' size) provided a comprehensive and rich understanding of the international dynamics in the four industries.

The interviews were completed between June 1994 and June 1995.

References

Academy of Management Journal (1993). 'Special Research Forum: Configurational Approaches to Organization', 36 (6).

Adler, N.J. (1986). *International Dimensions of Organizational Behavior*, Kent Publishing Company, Boston, MA.

Anand, J. and B. Kogut (1997). 'Technological capabilities of countries, firm rivalry and foreign direct investment', *Journal of International Business Studies*, 28 (3), pp. 445–465.

Aoki, A. and D.S. Tachiki (1992). 'Overseas Japanese business operations: the emerging role of regional headquarters', *RIM Pacific Business and Industries*, 1, pp. 29–39.

Astley, W.G. and A.H. Van de Ven (1983). 'Central perspectives and debates in organization theory', *Administrative Science Quarterly*, 28, pp. 245–273.

Atamer, T. (1991). 'The Single Market: its impact on six industries', *Long Range Planning*, 24 (6), pp. 40–52.

Baden-Fuller, C. and J. Stopford (1992). *Rejuvenating the Mature Business*, Routledge, London.

Barney, J.B. (1991). 'Firm's resources and sustained competitive advantage', *Journal of Management*, 17, pp. 99–120.

Bartlett, C.A. (1986). 'Building and managing the transnational: the new organizational challenge', in M.E. Porter (ed.), *Competition in Global Industries*, Harvard Business School Press, Boston, MA, pp. 367–401.

Bartlett, C.A. and S. Ghoshal (1989). *Managing across Borders: The Transnational Solution*, Harvard Business School Press, Boston, MA.

Bartlett, C.A. and S. Ghoshal (1992). *Transnational Management: Text, Cases and Readings in Cross-Border Management*, Irwin, Chicago.

Bartlett, C.A., Y.L. Doz and G. Hedlund (eds) (1990). *Managing the Global Firm*, Routledge, London.

Bello, D. and L.D. Dahringer (1985). 'The influence of country and product on retailer practices', *International Marketing Review*, Summer, pp. 45–52.

Bettis, R.A. and C.K. Prahalad (1995). 'Dominant logic: retrospective and extension', *Strategic Management Journal*, 16, pp. 5–14.

Birkinshaw, J., A.J. Morrison and J. Hulland (1995). 'Structural and competitive determinants of global integration strategy', *Strategic Management Journal*, 16, pp. 637–655.

Bleeke, J., D. Ernst, J. Isono and D. Weinberg (1990). 'The new shape of cross-border mergers and acquisitions', *McKinsey Quarterly*, Spring, pp. 91–105.

Bourgeois, L.J. (1984). 'Strategic management and determinism', *Academy of Management Review*, 9, pp. 586–596.

Bower, J.L. (1970). *Managing the Resource Allocation Process*. Harvard Business Press, Boston, MA.

Buckley, P.J. and M.C. Casson (1976). *The Future of the Multinational Enterprise*, Macmillan, London.
Buckley, P.J. and M.C. Casson (1981). 'The optimal timing of a foreign investment', *Economic Journal*, 91, pp. 75–87.
Burgelman, R.A. (1994). 'Fading memories: a process theory of strategic business exit in dynamic environments', *Administrative Science Quarterly*, 39, pp. 239–262.
Calori, R., G. Johnson and P. Sarnin (1994). 'CEOs' cognitive maps and the scope of the organization', *Strategic Management Journal*, 15, pp. 437–457.
Capital (1997). 'Le match Nike – Reebok – Adidas', 66, pp. 62–63.
Carpano, C., J.J. Chrisman and K. Roth (1994). 'International strategy and environment: an assessment of the performance relationship', *Journal of International Business Studies*, third quarter, pp. 639–656.
Caves, R. (1971). 'International corporations: the industrial economics of foreign investment', *Economica*, February, pp. 1–27.
Caves, R. (1981). *Multinational Enterprise and Economic Analysis*. Cambridge University Press, Cambridge.
Chamberlin, E.H. (1933). *The Theory of Monopolistic Competition: A Reorientation of the Theory of Value*, Harvard University Press, Cambridge, MA.
Chandler, A.D. (1962). *Strategy and Structure: Chapters in the History of the American Enterprise*, MIT Press, Cambridge, MA.
Child, J. (1972). 'Organizational structure, environment and performance: the role of strategic choice', *Sociology*, 6, pp. 1–22.
Child, J. (1997). 'Strategic choice in the analysis of action, structure, organizations and environment: retrospect and prospect', *Organization Studies*, 18 (1), pp. 43–76.
Cooper, J.C. (1993). 'Logistics strategies for global business', *International Journal of Physical Distribution and Logistics Management*, 23 (4), pp. 12–23.
Czinkota, M.R. and I.A. Ronkainen (1997). 'International business and trade in the next decade: report from a Delphi study', *Journal of International Business Studies*, 28 (4), pp. 827–844.
Dahl, R.A. (1963). *Modern Political Analysis*, Prentice-Hall, Englewood Cliffs, NJ.
Daniels, J.D. (1997). 'Bridging national and global marketing strategies through regional operations', *International Marketing Review*, Autumn, pp. 29–44.
Di Maggio, P.J. and W.W. Powell (1983). 'The iron cage revisited: institutional isomorphism and collective rationality in organizational fields', *American Sociological Review*, 48, pp. 147–160.
Doty, D.H. and W.H. Glick (1994). 'Typologies as a unique form of theory building: toward improved understanding and modelling', *Academy of Management Review*, 19 (2), pp. 230–251.
Doz, Y. (1980). 'Strategic management in multinational companies', *Sloan Management Review*, 21 (4), pp. 27–46.
Dunning, J.H. (1981). *International Production and the Multinational Enterprise*, George Allen & Unwin, London.
Dunning, J.H. (1988). *Explaining International Production*, George Allen & Unwin, London.

Dunning, J.H. (1993). *The Globalization of Business*, Routledge, London.

Dunning, J.H. (1998). 'Location and the multinational enterprise: a neglected factor', *Journal of International Business Studies*, 29 (1), pp. 45–66.

Egelhoff, W.G. and S.R. Gates (1994). 'The changing role of the foreign subsidiary in Europe', paper presented at the Strategic Management Society Conference, September, Paris.

Eisenhardt, K.M. (1989). 'Building theories from case study research', *Academy of Management Review*, 14 (4), pp. 532–550.

Eurostaf (1996). 'Le Marché mondial des articles de sport', Eurostaf, Paris.

Fayerweather, J. (1969). *International Business Management*, McGraw Hill, New York.

Finger, G.M. (1975). 'Trade overlap and intra-industry trade', *Economic Inquiry*, December, pp. 581–589.

Fortune (1995). 'Nike vs. Reebok, a battle for hearts, minds and feet', 18 September.

Ghoshal, S. (1987). 'Global strategy: an organizing framework', *Strategic Management Journal*, 8, pp. 425–440.

Ghoshal, S. and N. Nohria (1993). 'Horses for courses: organizational forms for multinational corporations', *Sloan Management Review*, 34 (2), pp. 23–35.

Grant, R.M. (1988). 'On "dominant logic", relatedness and the link between diversity and performance', *Strategic Management Journal*, 9, pp. 639–642.

Guisinger, S. and T.L. Brewer (1998). 'Introduction to the symposium', *Journal of International Business Studies*, 29 (1), pp. 1–3.

Hamel, G. and C.K. Prahalad (1994). *Competing for the Future*, Harvard Business School Press, Boston, MA.

Hannan, M. and J. Freeman (1977). 'The population ecology of organizations', *American Journal of Sociology*, 82, pp. 929–964.

Hannan, M.T. and J.H. Freeman (1984). 'Structural inertia and organizational change', *American Sociological Review*, 49, pp. 149–164.

Haspeslagh, P. and D. Jemison (1991). *Managing Acquisitions*, Free Press, New York.

Hecksher, E.L. (1919). 'The effect of foreign trade on the distribution of income', in *Readings in the Theory of International Trade*, (Blakiston series of republished articles on economics, 1950) George Allen & Unwin, London, pp. 272–300.

Hedlund, G. and D. Rolander (1990). 'Action in heterarchies: new approaches to managing the MNC', in C.A. Bartlett, Y. Doz and G. Hedlund (eds), *Managing the Global Firm*, Routledge, London, pp. 15–46.

Holsti, O.R. (1969). *Content Analysis for the Social Sciences and Humanities*, Addison Wesley, Reading, MA.

Hrebiniak, L.G. and W.F. Joyce (1985). 'Organizational adaptation: strategic choice and environmental determinism', *Administrative Science Quarterly*, 30, pp. 336–349.

Huff, A.S. (ed.) (1990). *Mapping Strategic Thought*, John Wiley, Chichester.

Hymer, S. (1960). *The International Operations of National Firms: A Study of Direct Foreign Investment*, MIT Press, Cambridge, MA.

Hymer, S. (1976). *The International Operations of National Firms*, MIT Press, Cambridge, MA.

Hymer, S. and R. Rowthorn (1970). 'Multinational corporations and international oligopoly: the non-American challenge', in C.P. Kindleberger (ed.), *The International Corporation: A Symposium*, MIT Press, Cambridge, MA, pp. 112–138.

James, W. (1950). *The Principles of Psychology*, Vols. I and II, Dover Publications, New York.

Johansen, J. and F. Widershein-Paul (1975). 'The internationalization process of the firm – four Swedish cases', *Journal of Management Studies*, 12 (3), pp. 305–322.

Kaynar, E. and S.T. Cavusgil (1983). 'Consumer attitudes towards products of foreign origin', *International Journal of Advertising*, 2, pp. 147–157.

Kindleberger, C.P. (1969). *American Business Abroad. Six Lectures on Direct Investment*, Yale University Press, New Haven, CT.

Knickerbocker, F.T. (1973). *Oligopolistic Reaction and the Multinational Enterprise*, Harvard University Press, Cambridge, MA.

Kobrin, S.J. (1991). 'An empirical analysis of the determinants of global integration', *Strategic Management Journal*, 12, pp. 17–31.

Kobrin, S.J. (1994). 'Is there a relationship between a geocentric mind-set and multinational strategy?', *Journal of International Business Studies*, third quarter, pp. 493–511.

Kogut, B. (1985a). 'Designing global strategies: comparative and competitive value-added chains', *Sloan Management Review*, Summer, pp. 15–28.

Kogut, B. (1985b). 'Designing global strategies: profiting from operational flexibility', *Sloan Management Review*, Fall, pp. 27–38.

Kogut, B. (1989). 'A note on global strategies', *Strategic Management Journal*, 10 (4), pp. 383–389.

Kojima, K. (1978). *Direct Foreign Investment: a Model of Multinational Business Operations*, Croom Helm, London.

Lall, S. (1980). 'Monopolistic advantages and foreign involvement by US manufacturing industry', in S. Lall (ed.), *The Multinational Corporations. Nine Essays*, Macmillan, London, Chapter 1.

Laurencin, J.P. (1988). 'L'Impact sectoriel et régional du Grand Marché: le cas de l'industrie française', *Revue d'Economie Industrielle*, 49, pp. 67–95.

Lawrence, P.R. and J.W. Lorsch (1967). *Organization and Environment*, Harvard University Press, Boston, MA.

Lenz, R.T. and J.L. Engledow (1986). 'Environmental analysis: the applicability of current theory', *Strategic Management Journal*, 7, pp. 329–346.

Leonard Barton, D. (1992). 'Core capabilities and core rigidities: a paradox in managing new product development', *Strategic Management Journal*, 13S, pp. 111–125.

Levitt, T. (1983). 'The globalization of markets', *Harvard Business Review*, May–June, pp. 92–102.

Lewin, K. (1951). *Field Theory in Social Science*, Harper & Brothers, New York.

Linder, S.D. (1961). *An Essay on Trade and Transformation*, John Wiley, New York.

Lubatkin, M., W.S. Schulze, A. Mainkar and R.W. Cotterill (forthcoming). 'Towards a post-structural view of competition: three cases of horizontal merger', *Strategic Management Journal*.

Makhija, M.V., K. Kim and S.D. Williamson (1997). 'Measuring globalization of industries using a national industry approach: empirical evidence across five countries and over time', *Journal of International Business Studies*, 28 (4), pp. 679–710.

Malnight, T.W. (1996). 'The transition from decentralized to network-based MNC structures: an evolutionary perspective', *Journal of International Business Studies*, 27 (1), pp. 43–66.

March, J. (1991). 'Exploration and exploitation in organizational learning', *Organizational Science*, 2, pp. 71–87.

Melander, A. (1997). 'Industrial wisdom and strategic change: the Swedish pulp and paper industry 1945–1990', JIBS Dissertation Series, 001.

Melin, L. (1987). 'The field-of-force metaphor: a study in industrial change', *International Studies of Management and Organization*, 17 (1), pp. 24–33.

Melin, L. (1989). 'The field-of-force metaphor', in T. Cavusgil (ed.), *Advances in International Marketing*, 3, JAI Press, Greenwich, CT, pp. 161–179.

Mey, H. (1972). *Field-Theory: A Study of its Application in the Social Sciences*, Routledge & Kegan Paul, London.

Miles, M.B. and A.M. Huberman (1984). *Qualitative Data Analysis: A Sourcebook of New Methods*, Sage Publications, London.

Miles, R. and C. Snow (1978). *Organizational Strategy, Structure and Process*, McGraw Hill, New York.

Miller, D. (1986). 'Configurations of strategy and structure: towards a synthesis', *Strategic Management Journal*, 7, pp. 233–249.

Mintzberg, H. (1994). *The Rise and Fall of Strategic Planning*. Free Press, New York.

Morrison, A.J. (1990). *Strategies in Global Industries: How US Businesses Compete*, Quorum Books, New York.

Morrison, A.J. and K. Roth (1992). 'A taxonomy of business level strategies in global industries', *Strategic Management Journal*, 13, pp. 399–418.

Morrison, A.J., D. Ricks and K. Roth (1991). 'Globalization versus regionalization: which way for the multinational?', *Organizational Dynamics*, 19, pp. 17–29.

Mundell, R.A. (1957). 'International trade and factor mobility', *American Economic Review*, 47 (3), pp. 321–335.

Nelson, R.R. and S.G. Winter (1982). *An Evolutionary Theory of Economic Change*, Harvard University Press, Cambridge, MA.

Ohlin, B. (1933). 'Interregional and international trade', *Harvard Economic Studies*, Harvard University Press, Cambridge, MA.

Oliver, C. (1991). 'Strategic responses to institutional processes', *Academy of Management Review*, 16 (1), pp. 145–179.

Ostry, S. (1998). 'Technology, productivity and the multinational enterprise', *Journal of International Business Studies*, 29 (1), pp. 85–99.

Penrose, E.T. (1959). *The Theory of the Growth of the Firm*, John Wiley, New York.

Pepper, S. (1942). *World Hypotheses*, University of California Press, Berkeley, CA.

Perlmutter, H.V. (1969). 'The tortuous evolution of the multinational corporation', *Columbia Journal of World Business*, Jan.–Feb., pp. 9–18.

Perroux, F. (1973). *Pouvoir et économie*, Bordas, Paris.

Pfeffer, J. and G.R. Salancik (1978). *The External Control of Organizations: A Resource Dependence Perspective*, Harper & Row, New York.

Porac Joc, H.T. and C. Baden-Fuller (1989). 'Competitive groups as cognitive communities: the case of Scottish knitwear industry', *Journal of Management Studies*, 26, pp. 397–416.

Porter, M.E. (1980). *Competitive Strategy*, The Free Press, New York.

Porter, M.E. (1986). 'Competition in global industries: a conceptual framework', in M.E. Porter (ed.), *Competition in Global Industries*, Harvard Business School Press, Boston, MA, Chapter 1.

Porter, M.E. (1990). *The Competitive Advantage of Nations*, Macmillan, London.

Porter, M.E. (1991). 'Towards a dynamic theory of strategy', *Strategic Management Journal*, 12 (special issue), pp. 95–117.

Prahalad, C.K. and Y.L. Doz (1987). *The Multinational Mission: Balancing Local Demands and Global Vision*, The Free Press, New York.

Prahalad, C.K. and G. Hamel (1994). 'Strategy as a field of study: why search for a new paradigm?', *Strategic Management Journal*, 15 (special issue), pp. 5–16.

Roth, K. and A.J. Morrison (1990). 'An empirical analysis of the integration-responsiveness framework in global industries', *Journal of International Business Studies*, fourth quarter, pp. 541–564.

Rugman, A.M. (1979). *International Diversification and the Multinational Enterprise*, Lexington Books, Lexington, MA.

Rugman, A.M. (1981). *Inside the Multinationals: The Economics of Internal Markets*, Croom Helm, London.

Rugman, A.M. (1985). 'Multinationals and global competitive strategy', *International Studies of Management and Organization*, 15 (2), pp. 8–18.

Rugman, A.M. and A. Verbeke (1998). 'Multinational enterprises and public policy', *Journal of International Business Studies*, 29 (1), pp. 115–136.

Rumelt, R.P., D. Schendel and D. Teece (1991). 'Strategic management and economics', *Strategic Management Journal*, 12 (special issue), pp. 5–29.

Sabel, C.F. (1989). 'Flexible specialization and the re-emergence of regional economies', in P. Hirst and J. Zeitlin (eds), *Reversing Industrial Decline*, St Martin's Press, New York, pp. 17–70.

Samuelson, P.A. (1948). 'International trade and the equalization of factor prices', *The Economic Journal*, June.

Scherer, F.M. and D. Ross (1990). *Industrial Market Structure and Economic Performance*, Houghton Mifflin, Boston, MA.

Schmalensee, R.L. (1989). 'Inter-industry studies of structure and performance', in R.L. Schmalensee and R. Wallis (eds), *Handbook of Industrial Economics*, North Holland, New York, pp. 951–1009.

Schumpeter, J.A. (1934). *The Theory of Economic Development*, Harvard University Press, Cambridge, MA.

Schumpeter, J.A. (1954). *History of Economic Analysis*, Oxford University Press, New York.

Segal-Horn, S. and D. Faulkner (1999). *The Dynamics of International Strategy*, International Thomson Business Press, London.

Simon, H.A. (1957). *Models of Man*, John Wiley, New York.

Simon, H.A. (1993). *Is International Management Different from Management?*, Working Paper 94.1, Carnegie Bosch Institute, Pittsburgh, PA.

Smircich, L. and C. Stubbart (1985). 'Strategic management in an enacted world', *Academy of Management Review*, 10 (4), pp. 724–736.

Spender, J.C. (1989). *Industry Recipes: The Nature and Sources of Managerial Judgement*, Basil Blackwell, Oxford.
Spender, J.C. (1996). 'Making knowledge the basis of a dynamic theory of the firm', *Strategic Management Journal*, 17 (special issue), pp. 45–62.
Teece, D.J. (1976). *The Multinational Corporation and the Resource Cost of International Technology Transfer*, Ballinger, Cambridge, MA.
Teece, D.J. (1985). 'Transaction cost economics and the multinational enterprise: an assessment', *Journal of Economic Behavior and Organization*, 7, pp. 21–45.
Teece, D.J. (1986). 'Profiting from technological innovation', *Research Policy*, 15 (6), pp. 252–373.
Thurow, L. (1993). *Head to Head: the Coming Economic Battle among Japan, Europe and America*, Nicholas Brealey, London.
Tsoukas, H. (1994). 'Refining common sense: types of knowledge in management studies', *Journal of Management Studies*, 31 (6), pp. 761–780.
Tsoukas, H. and S. Cummings (1997). 'Marginalization and recovery: the emergence of Aristotelian themes in Organization Studies', *Organization Studies*, 18 (4), pp. 655–683.
Van de Ven, A.H. and M.S. Poole (1988). 'Paradoxical requirements for a theory of organizational change', in R.E. Quinn and K.S. Cameron (eds), *Paradox and Transformation: Toward a Theory of Change in Organization and Management*, Ballinger, Cambridge, MA, pp. 19–63.
Van de Ven, A.H., H.L. Angle and M.S. Poole (eds) (1989). *Research on the Management of Innovation: The Minnesota Studies*, Harper & Row, New York.
Vernon, R. (1966). 'International investment and international trade in the product cycle', *Quarterly Journal of Economics*, 80, pp. 190–207.
Wack, P. (1985). 'Scenarios: uncharted waters ahead', *Harvard Business Review*, 63 (5), pp. 73–89.
Warren, R. (1967). 'The interorganizational field as a focus for investigation', *Administrative Science Quarterly*, 12, pp. 397–419.
Webster's New World Dictionary (1994). 3rd college edition, Macmillan, New York.
Weick, K.E. (1979). *The Social Psychology of Organizing*, Addison Wesley, Reading, MA.
Weick, K.E. (1995). *Sensemaking in Organizations*, Sage Publications, Thousand Oaks, CA.
Wells, L.T. (1998). 'Multinationals and the developing countries', *Journal of International Business Studies*, 29 (1), pp. 101–113.
Wernerfelt, B. (1984). 'A resource-based view of the firm', *Strategic Management Journal*, 5, pp. 171–180.
Yip, G. (1992). *Total Global Strategy*, Prentice-Hall, Englewood Cliffs, NJ.

Index